Savarkar

Praise for the book

'A lively, well-researched, and balanced account of a hugely controversial figure. Full of rich, moral ambiguity, it will fascinate and provoke even if you don't agree.' **Gurcharan Das**

'Vinayak Damodar Savarkar was controversial, while he was alive, and remains so, even after his death. Strong in his convictions (the manner of his death is an example), he inspired, but perhaps did not always endear. His political differences also explain why he did not always get his due. Vaibhav Purandare has written a wonderful biography, based on a considerable amount of research. Veer Savarkar truly comes alive, a product of his life and times, not easily compartmentalized into black or white. For those prone to clichés and stereotyping, an extremely balanced book.' **Bibek Debroy**

'Superbly written and deeply researched, this book is neither hagiographic nor does it suffer from unbalanced criticism. Vaibhav Purandare's portrayal of Savarkar's life and politics shows us a revolutionary freedom fighter who, sadly, became the ideologue of divisive Hindutva, with the needle of suspicion forever pointing at him for his involvement in the plot to kill Mahatma Gandhi.' **Sudheendra Kulkarni**

Savarkar

The True Story of the Father of Hindutva

Vaibhav Purandare

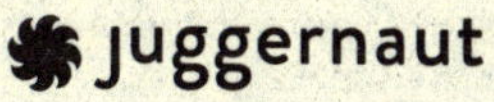

JUGGERNAUT BOOKS
KS House, 118 Shahpur Jat, New Delhi 110049, India

First published by Juggernaut Books 2019

10 9 8 7 6 5 4 3 2 1

P-ISBN: 9789353454425
E-ISBN: 9789353450557

Typeset in Adobe Caslon Pro by R. Ajith Kumar, Noida

Printed and bound in India by Thomson Press India Ltd.

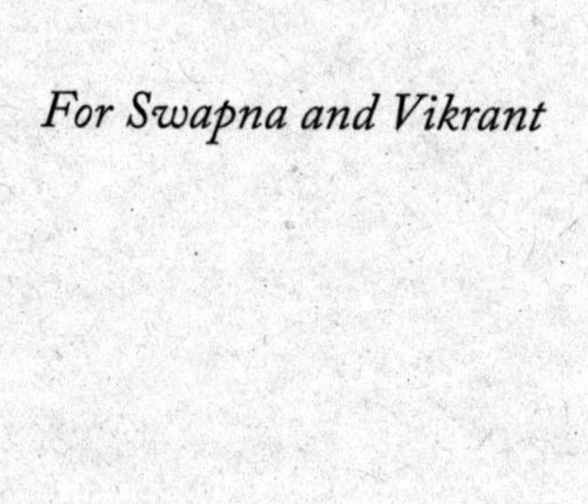

For Swapna and Vikrant

Contents

Author's Note

In December 2018, Prime Minister Narendra Modi of the ruling Bharatiya Janata Party (BJP) visited Cellular Jail on the Andaman and Nicobar Islands, where scores of India's freedom fighters were once incarcerated for long periods by the British government. This was a place of pilgrimage for him, Modi said: after all, Vinayak Damodar Savarkar, ardent nationalist and revolutionary, had spent a whole decade in a damp cell there. As a product of the Hindu nationalist movement, Modi's sense of nationhood is underpinned by Savarkar's theory of Hindutva or Hinduness, and so is his idea of sinewy national self-assertion and a foreign policy based not on an abstract dream on the distant horizon but on realism and realpolitik. Thus, once inside Savarkar's cell, Modi took on the posture of a pilgrim. He sat cross-legged on the floor, eyes shut in a prayerful, meditative way, in front of a photograph of Savarkar that has been kept there – the devotee invoking silently, inside the sanctum sanctorum, the image of his presiding deity.

At around the same time, Rahul Gandhi, the scion of free India's longest-ruling dynasty, the Nehru–Gandhis, was mounting a sharp attack on Savarkar, labelling him as someone who wrote letters of abject apology to a foreign ruler simply to be able to get out of prison; the Rahul-skippered Congress even described Savarkar as a 'traitor'. Rahul contrasted Savarkar's approach with that of Mahatma Gandhi and of India's first prime minister, Jawaharlal Nehru, who, he said, had never given in to British bullying despite all the hardships they faced in so many jails.

When Savarkar died in 1966, he was on the fringes of Indian politics and was an ignominious figure, having been arrested and named as an accused in the plot to assassinate Gandhi. His infamy in the Gandhi murder case and his relative political obscurity would remain undisturbed in the future, it was believed.

Savarkar's political resurrection in the new millennium and the robust revival of his story and myth are, therefore, remarkable. The resurrection actually began in the mid-1980s, when Hindu nationalism, for long dismissed as a marginal and spent force, suddenly burst on the Indian scene with the BJP and its leader L.K. Advani championing the cause of religious identity. After the Indian experience of BJP governments led by A.B. Vajpayee, which nudged India into the new century on the back of nuclear tests and an intense India–Pakistan armed conflict, and especially since Modi's emergence amid communal violence in Gujarat in 2002 and his subsequent rise to the prime minister's post, Savarkar's Hindutva has unleashed the kind of political energies it was never really expected to.

With his brand of nationalism gaining so much ground and at least momentarily eclipsing the Nehruvian social and political template that once appeared impossible to supplant in a pluralistic society, the historical figure of Savarkar now looms large in the Indian political landscape. In fact, his prominence in the realm of public debate today is far more striking than it had been at several points in his own chequered life. Not since 1966, when Dhananjay Keer's biography of Savarkar was published in the year of Savarkar's death, has there been a full-length biography of the man in English. A fresh look at his life, especially given his prominence in India today, is in order.

A man of extremes, Savarkar also evokes extreme reactions. The most fervent commentary on Savarkar is centred principally on four points: his status as freedom fighter owing to mercy petitions he wrote to the Raj from Port Blair, his advocacy of Hindutva, his opposition to the Quit India movement and his alleged role in Gandhi's assassination. We will come to each of these turn by turn.

Savarkar was given two terms of life imprisonment by the British Raj, and they were meant to run consecutively and not concurrently. Life imprisonment then meant twenty-five years, so he was to spend fifty years in jail in all. He was dispatched to the Andamans and was incarcerated there for ten years, from 1911 to 1921. During this time he wrote at least seven petitions asking for mercy and requesting an early release.

To cry 'cowardice' and 'surrender', to call him a 'traitor', or to say he was 'begging for mercy from the British while Gandhi was sleeping on the dirt floor of a jail' is unwarranted and puerile. While he was in prison, Savarkar was tortured in the most abominable, medieval ways. He was put into solitary confinement for long stretches of time. He was deprived of food and water and made to do hard labour; he would faint from exhaustion but still wasn't given reprieve from work. He was chained to a wall, hands extended above his head, for hours at a stretch on consecutive days. During these spells, he was not even allowed to go to the bathroom to relieve himself and had to stand in his own filth chained to the wall. Is it really fair to judge what a person says or does under such conditions of inhuman torture?

Savarkar, by the way, was not the only one to submit such mercy petitions. His fellow prisoner and revolutionary Barindra Kumar Ghose, Aurobindo Ghose's brother, did so, as did Satyendranath Bose and many other celebrated Indian rebels, not merely in the notorious Cellular Jail of Kaala Paani but in comparatively milder prisons on the Indian mainland as well. In the late 1920s, for instance, many of the widely revered revolutionaries convicted in the Kakori conspiracy case involving an attack on a train carrying government funds, including the protagonists of the attack Ramprasad Bismil and Sachindranath Sanyal, wrote mercy pleas. Thankfully we do not brand them as traitors. Savarkar certainly does not deserve singling out on this count.

While Savarkar was seen as a fringe player towards the end of his life, he started out as a fearless and pioneering anti-colonial crusader. He called for complete independence from the British Raj at least twenty years before the Congress did so in its resolution of 1929. Savarkar called for Purna Swaraj at a time when India's most enthusiastic nationalists were submitting mild representations to the Raj, at most pushing for greater representation on the central and provincial law-making councils or for 'home rule', which meant self-government or responsible government under the overarching umbrella of a sunset-defying Empire. This does not make the one greater and the other less great, for the Congress, under Gandhi, was the biggest mass organizer of the liberation movement. But Savarkar was among the earliest to push the boundaries and propel the national movement towards its chief goal.

Indeed, Savarkar was a central figure in Indian politics, certainly a pivotal one in the first half of his political life. When Gandhi visited London during the years that Savarkar lived there (1906–11), he interacted with Gandhi, then and later, as an equal. He had similar interactions and correspondences with Subhas Chandra Bose and Babasaheb Ambedkar in subsequent years, other hints to his status. In the early 1940s, Muhammad Ali Jinnah was secretly planning to engineer a meeting with Savarkar when the issue of Pakistan had become hugely contentious. (Whatever their political differences, none of these luminaries seem to have viewed Savarkar as a 'traitor'.)

Savarkar and the numerous cases against him were at the heart of much correspondence between top British officials, from the level of the Secretary of State, the official in charge of Indian affairs in London, to the Viceroy, the Raj's hands-on head on Indian soil. Savarkar triggered a significant amount of discussion among British politicians, journalists and opinion-makers before and after his arrest in the English capital in 1910 and attempted escape in Marseilles the same year, and he created an international furore and diplomatic tensions between France and Britain as his case for political refuge on French territory came up for adjudication before an international tribunal in The Hague in 1911. Among the Englishmen who demanded his instant release from British captivity at the time was none other than the then home secretary Winston Churchill.

On the point of his ideology of Hindutva: Savarkar underwent a dramatic transformation, roughly halfway through his life, from being an advocate of Hindu–Muslim unity to being the chief theorist and champion of Hindutva when he wrote his tract on the contentious subject in 1921. So massive and fundamental was this ideological metamorphosis that it is impossible to get a complete picture of Savarkar's life story and his complex personality without seeing what triggered it and what implications the change carried for him and for the larger Hindu community and India as a whole in the longer term – implications which are real and acutely felt in this day and age. For Savarkar this change was both profoundly personal and intensely political in nature – personal because of certain experiences he had had in Cellular Jail, and political because it emerged in the aftermath of the Gandhi-backed Khilafat movement and in an era of inflamed Hindu–Muslim tensions.

There has been much argument on what constitutes the core of Hindutva or Hindu nationalism. Yet, whatever its many variations – soft, hardline, or the push for acknowledgement that Hindu culture and civilization must be seen as the seedbed for the structure of the nation state – Savarkar's version of Hindutva started out as essentially exclusivist by removing from the ambit of Indian nationhood Muslims and other communities. With time, he became more and more hardline and extremist, asking for the elimination of Urdu words from Marathi and Hindi in the 1920s and 1930s and, a few years before his death in the 1960s, calling for violent reprisals against Muslims, including sexual violence against Muslim women. It is impossible to defend these extremist positions of Savarkar's.

The Quit India movement is a far more complicated issue,

however, but Savarkar's opposition to it does not make him a British collaborator. There was significant opposition to the movement from Indians across the political spectrum such as the deprived classes hero B.R. Ambedkar, the Indian Liberals, the All India Students' Conference, the communists and the Muslim League leader Muhammad Ali Jinnah. Some of the opposition was over whether the time was opportune for such a mass agitation, given that the Japanese were on the verge of showing up on India's borders, and over whether it would work as a tactical and strategic gambit. Even Nehru was in favour of cooperating with the British in the war effort, and although he finally gave in to the Mahatma, his political guru, despite his deep internal conflict, the many kisan sabhas across the country set up with Nehru's blessings vigorously opposed Gandhi's call.

This period of history is, in fact, thanks largely to our school and university textbooks, wrongly understood to be one where Indians stood as a monolithic force against the British. There were key questions to be decided at that time. What would a post-British India look like? What accommodation and arrangement would there be between various Indian communities and religious groups? What of the separate electorates and reserved seats that the British had granted on the basis of religion? What of voting rights, which were not equal in British India – only taxpayers and the landed were allowed to vote, and the principle of separate electorates implied that one Hindu vote had less power than one Muslim vote.

Right through the freedom movement, Indians were preoccupied with these questions, and whether it was Savarkar, Ambedkar, the Indian Liberals, Jinnah or several others, Gandhi and Nehru included, they felt, from time to time, that they had concerns to address or policies to prioritize which were either as critical as their responses to British rule or, at some huge inflection points, more important for the moment than dealing with the British. For Savarkar the war was an opportunity to strengthen Hindu society militarily – should military strength be needed to be deployed in a post-British India to assert Hindu dominance – and for working out an arrangement for representative politics and democracy between India's various communities. He simply chose to focus on that, at that fraught moment, and not on evicting the British. Whether one agrees with Savarkar's priorities is a separate issue. But it is a pointlessly Congress-centric view to say that those who were not taking part in the Quit India movement were all British collaborators.

Perhaps the prickliest issue of all is the one related to Mahatma Gandhi's assassination. Savarkar was arrested and arraigned in the case and later acquitted. That acquittal stands, and even the government of the time did not challenge it; yet in the public realm, the circumstantial evidence that was marshalled and offered during the trial shows why the finger of suspicion was pointed at him and why the jury is still out on the subject. The evidence against Savarkar includes his open endorsement of Nathuram Godse's aggressive anti-minority agenda and his purported meetings with Godse and some of the other conspirators just days before the killing. Savarkar's sharp alignment with such a group alone was enough to take much lustre off his original standing in the imagination of his contemporaries as an outstanding revolutionary hero. Sardar Vallabhbhai Patel, India's deputy prime minister and home minister, put it bluntly and correctly: Savarkar couldn't escape the moral burden of the assassination even if he was not criminally culpable.

~

Savarkar's life was dramatic, and the drama got more and more intense as his life went on – particularly because of the fundamental transformations, some of which we have glimpsed in this introductory note, that Savarkar underwent. This book looks in depth at the contradictory phases of Savarkar's life. It aims to pack in detail and at the same time make easily accessible the man's complete story – the various parts of the puzzle which, if seen separately and in isolation, cannot inform us adequately about his controversial and ever-changing personality.

To tell Savarkar's story accurately and comprehensively, it is imperative to make a deep dive into the fundamental Marathi sources. Most of Savarkar's writings and speeches are in Marathi and comprise eight volumes published by the Swatantryaveer Savarkar Smarak in Mumbai. Some works have been translated into English, but the translations are either inadequate and awkward or archaic and dense. For this book I have exhaustively gone through all his Marathi writings in the original – a few thousand pages filled with essays, a series of autobiographical works, his books on Indian history, letters, public statements, and fiction too, in the form of novels, novellas, poems and plays. Speeches too are a part of the eight volumes, but there are some available in audio format as well, listening to which helped me understand the subject of this biography better as a public communicator thanks to tone, tenor, voice and intensity that plain text simply cannot capture.

Trawling through Marathi newspaper archives enabled me to reference a whole range of opinions on Savarkar by his contemporaries, opinions altogether unnoticed till date because they remained untranslated and thus inaccessible to English readers or totally obscured in the mists of time. These include views expressed by the likes of Lokmanya Tilak in his paper *Kesari*, the brilliant editor of *Kaal*, S.M. Paranjpe, the famous historian V.K. Rajwade, Savarkar's fellow revolutionary-turned-Gandhian P.M. or 'Senapati' Bapat and, fascinatingly, the campaigning editor and agent provocateur P.K. Atre with whom Savarkar had controversial verbal combats on a series of topics ranging from Hindutva and Mahatma Gandhi to the Indian response to the British Raj and after.

Many people who knew Savarkar well, among them his doctors, friends, critics and followers, have also written meticulous accounts of their experiences and conversations with him in Marathi, which again have remained inaccessible to English readers. I have gone through all these accounts and brought to light anecdotes which have so far remained unknown, after cross-checking these with other dependable sources from the period. Savarkar's friend S.L. Karandikar, editor of *Trikaal*, for instance, had a series of conversations with him from 1937 to 1939, among the most contentious years of his life as he assumed leadership of the Hindu Mahasabha while war clouds were on the horizon; Karandikar's biography of Savarkar in Marathi, published in 1943, has gripping material which lay unexplored; likewise the book *Shodh Savarkarancha* by the noted Marathi historian Y.D. Phadke, who grew up as an admirer of Savarkar and later turned into a trenchant critic. Nathuram Godse's brother Gopal Godse's account of the Gandhi assassination is well known to English readers, but his other memoir, related to one full year he spent with Savarkar in the Red Fort prison when the latter was held as an accused in Gandhi's killing, is hardly known, but has been useful in throwing light on the episode.

I have consulted in the original some entirely ignored Hindi sources too, such as the works of the legendary writer Yashpal, who was a part of the revolutionary movement in north India in the late 1920s and early 1930s.

Documents of the British Raj, all in English, from India and the UK – police and court records, confidential reports issued about Savarkar by crime and intelligence department sleuths to their bosses, official correspondence from the level of secretaries to the Viceroys, India Office papers and UK parliamentary debates – have been studied, as have reports of the Cardew and other commissions set up by the British to examine conditions in the penal colony in the Andamans at the time Savarkar and his brother Babarao were there. For this period the impressions of Savarkar that his fellow prisoners such as Barindra Kumar Ghose and Ullaskar Dutt and prison officials developed, and which have long been overlooked by historians, have been recorded, as are the views – again mostly overlooked in the context of the Savarkar story – of both top Liberal and Conservative British leaders such as the Labour Party founder Keir Hardie, the first big British Marxist and Social Democratic Federation leader H.M. Hyndman, the fearless UK parliamentarian Josiah Wedgwood, the well-known Secretary of State for India Lord Morley, the one-time Bombay governor Lord Sydenham, Viceroy Lord Linlithgow and the unabashed imperialist Winston Churchill. A host of French publications of the time have been looked at as well, along with a number of British newspapers of different political orientations, for the record of Savarkar's years in London, furious debates on The Hague case, and for his later radically altered ideological stance.

Papers such as the *Bombay Chronicle*, which followed the lives of Indian nationalists closely and both praised and criticized Savarkar, were of inestimable value, as was the material about him – both in his avatar as a revolutionary and as chief architect of Hindutva – written by contemporary national leaders such as Gandhi, Nehru, Bose, Patel, Jinnah and Ambedkar, and even well-wishers of India such as Gandhi's friend C.F. Andrews and Savarkar's friends the English littérateurs David Garnett and the fiery socialist Guy Aldred. Their exchanges in themselves show the many trajectories and currents of the Indian freedom movement and Savarkar's positions at various critical points.

Finally, I have mined the audio archive of Cambridge University's Centre of South Asian Studies, where many audio interviews of Indians who witnessed the freedom struggle, Partition and the first two decades of independent India lie untapped. These tapes have also brought to the fore material never before used to tell Savarkar's story.

~

It is important to know Savarkar's story to be able to make sense of India today, and possibly the India of tomorrow. Savarkar would have certainly approved of 'ghar wapsi', the Hindu right's campaign to reconvert people back into the Hindu fold.

He would also have likely approved of the BJP government's displays of muscular nationalism. He was all for displays of military strength against India's often-hostile neighbours such as Pakistan and China, and favoured timely and proper reprisals against their acts of aggression. But while Savarkar's common ground with the ruling BJP and the Rashtriya Swayamsevak Sangh (RSS) is well known, some other ideas of his actually fly in the face of conservative political opinion but would find a resounding echo in liberal chambers. For instance, his firm opposition to cow worship and the Hindu penchant of making too much of it. Or the fact that he provocatively said, 'The epitaph for the RSS volunteer will be that he was born, he joined the RSS and he died without accomplishing anything.'

Savarkar was a radical figure, at times hard to contain in a box. His life story is riveting and extraordinary, and in getting to know Savarkar we may better understand the multiple dimensions of the Indian freedom movement and the various strands of thinking, and action, that we witness in public life today.

1

The eye of the empire

June was the month in which the mood of young Indians in cold, dreary London normally appeared to lift a little. Summer came and with it, some amount of cheer. But 1909 was proving to be something of an exception, especially for a bunch of students that in the past few years had been known to frequent India House, a sprawling five-storey mansion in the northern suburb of Highgate. The British Secret Service was familiar with the 63 Cromwell Avenue structure as the rendezvous of firm believers in the theory of armed rebellion against the Raj, and its detectives had been tailing some of the regular visitors dutifully for some time. A handful of these twenty-something Indians, all members of the Free India Society formed in the heart of the Empire in 1907, were immensely perturbed, and not just because they suspected they were being shadowed.

They took a petition to the leader of the Free India Society, Vinayak Damodar Savarkar, a twenty-five-year-old law student in London. He routinely assigned them tasks to further their revolutionary cause, and directed and coordinated their covert activities. They wanted him to immediately sack one of the group's Punjabi Hindu members – Madan Lal Dhingra.

'He's cosying up to British officials.'

'He's ratting on us and passing on inside information.'

'Looks like he's gone over completely to the other side.'

Only four months younger than Savarkar, Dhingra had appeared for a while to be passionate about the idea of an armed revolution against the British and was an ardent follower of Savarkar. But in recent months his associates had developed doubts that he was playing a double game.

Little did they suspect that the very man they were complaining to was in fact scripting that game. Dhingra was just playing the part determined for him by Savarkar himself.

They certainly didn't want a betrayer in their midst. As it was, the previous year had brought somewhat mixed results for these freedom fighters of a revolutionary bent of mind. While an eighteen-year-old greenhorn from Midnapur, Khudiram Bose, had created a sensation by hurling a bomb at a carriage in Muzaffarpur in Bihar and killing two Englishwomen (his real target was Sessions Judge Douglas Kingsford, who had ordered the whipping of a fourteen-year-old Indian boy for minor offences), the system of colonial justice had swiftly fastened the handcuffs on his teenage wrists and decreed and carried out his hanging. His aide Prafulla Choki of Bogra had committed suicide before he could be arrested, and during the police probe into the bombing plot, guns and bombs had been seized from the garden house of the Ghose brothers Aurobindo and Barindra Kumar in the Calcutta suburb of Maniktala;

Aurobindo was a major catch as he had, after his education at King's College, Cambridge, turned into a radical revolutionary and was well known as editor of the English-language newspaper *Bande Mataram*. Thirty-seven Bengalis in all were arraigned in the case before the Alipur sessions court on charges of waging war against the King-Emperor and collecting men and arms to wage war. In a further blow to nationalist morale, Bal Gangadhar Tilak, the leader of the Extremists within the Indian National Congress – the section that wanted self-rule immediately as a right and not as a concession, though its votaries never openly advocated violence – and an inspiration for Aurobindo, had been booked for sedition and for inciting hatred between Indians and Europeans, accused by Justice D.D. Davar of the Bombay High Court of possessing 'a diseased and perverted mind that can think that bombs are legitimate instruments in political agitations', and sent at the age of fifty-two, for the second time in his life, to a prison in Mandalay, Burma, for six years. It would be impossible for the young men of the Free India Society in London to get any of their plans executed if the authorities managed to get crucial leads on what they were up to from Madan Lal Dhingra.

The heat had in any case been on from 1907. *The Times* of London and the *National Review* had raised a red flag that year about their headquarters, India House, which they called the Highgate 'house of mystery', forcing the property's owner and patron of its residents, Pandit Shyamji Krishnavarma, and his feisty Parsi aide, Bhikaiji Cama, to shift to Paris to evade action.[1] Krishnavarma had been maintaining the place as a hostel where Indian students could stay and interact with their compatriots elsewhere in the British capital, but his principal motive was to put together a young squad dedicated to the cause of freedom. Just when he thought things were finally coming together and more and more Indian students were showing an interest in attending weekend meetings at his address to discuss issues related to their homeland, he had had to pack his bags.

After his sudden departure, Savarkar had more than simply kept the band of revolutionaries together as Krishnavarma had kept up the flow of funds from Paris. He had solidified contacts with Irish and Turkish nationalists, obtained manuals on the use and procurement of arms and, having added some more members to his clandestine inner circle, the Free India Society, he had emerged as the undisputed leader of India House.

A Marathi-speaking Brahman from the Nasik region of the Bombay Presidency, Savarkar was then a law student at Gray's Inn, one of the four Inns of Court in London. He was thin, wiry, of medium height and had, as a correspondent for the *Sunday Chronicle* said, 'a clear olive complexion, clear, deep, penetrating eyes' and 'a width of jaw such as I have seen in few men'. His small, aquiline nose, his thick black hair, the neat western coat and trousers he always wore and his expression of seriousness even as a slender smile played on the lips gave him the overall appearance of a student both sincere and clear about the goals he had set for himself. In his portrait of the 'nimble-minded' Savarkar who had 'excellent' command over the English language, the *Chronicle* journalist said, 'If I mistake not Mr Savarkar will go far – I hope he will go far in the right direction.' This last bit was suggestive of 'anarchist' activities the British believed India House was involved in. The journalist wrote that 'the fact is Mr V D Savarkar believes in India for Indians, in the complete emancipation of India from British rule' and stated that he had asked the young leader about the likelihood of his entire group being tailed by Scotland Yard and the secret service operatives. Savarkar had told him, 'We do not mind detectives watching outside and following us, if the climate suits them!' The reporter observed, 'That last is a quite English touch. It shows how the British hand has moulded the intellect of young India. It has even breathed into it the British joke.'[2]

Yet the overwhelming sentiment among India House regulars was that they needed to be very watchful and vigilant if they didn't want a clampdown to derail, if not altogether dismantle, the plans they were putting in place. Now Dhingra emerged as a threat to those plans.

Besides, from their point of view, Dhingra's background aroused considerable doubt. His father, a well-known retired civil surgeon, counted among his friends a number of senior British officials, among them William Curzon Wyllie, the political secretary to the Secretary of State for India John Morley, and Colonel Dunlop Smith, an aide of the Viceroy, Lord Minto. Three of Madan Lal's older brothers too were doctors, two others were lawyers, and one was a student of law in London. As if to underline where the family's allegiances lay, one of the siblings had declared his resolve to set up a residential school for affluent Indian children in the country's north; one of the school's objectives, he had stated, would be to make its students 'God-fearing and loyal to the Crown'. Madan Lal, a quiet, brooding youth, had himself studied arts in municipal colleges in Amritsar and Lahore and done a few odd jobs in India before moving to London's University College to study mechanical engineering. His general drift and the switching of subjects indicated that he did not have the academic focus his brothers had demonstrated. He had gradually cut down on his visits to India House and, while maintaining contact with Savarkar, had consciously distanced himself from most of the inmates and visitors. He had even recently joined the National Indian Association and the Aristocratic Club, both reasonably famous places where British officials, serving and retired, spent their evenings discussing the Empire's proud possessions with educated, English-speaking Indians and assorted Indian royals.

Savarkar's associates were aware that, a few months earlier, Savarkar had publicly berated Madan Lal for disturbing a meeting of the Free India Society at India House by playing the gramophone in an adjacent passage. What they perhaps did not know, and what would have triggered far greater alarm, was that Madan Lal's father had, around that time, written a letter to Curzon Wyllie expressing concern over his son's India House connection and that Wyllie had, in turn, asked the youngster to meet him at the India Office, the government centre that dealt with all affairs related to the subcontinent. Any truck with Wyllie was an absolute no-no for an Indian imbued with the nationalist spirit. An India veteran of more than twenty years who had worked with the princes of Rajputana, Baroda and Hyderabad, Wyllie had recently been appointed by Morley on an advisory committee established 'for the purpose of counteracting and defeating the anarchist propaganda among Indian students' in London.[3]

But the movers of the resolution for Dhingra's removal were surprised to discover that Savarkar was against the idea of taking a stern line. Counselling restraint, he told them calmly that given the Punjabi student's long-time links to India House and to the Free India Society, any hasty denunciation would be unnecessary and unfair. He wanted to wait awhile and see how things unfolded; if any evidence emerged meanwhile of Dhingra having been in any way disloyal to the group and its cause, he would of course be expelled without a moment's delay. The matter was not discussed again for some days, for Savarkar was soon occupied by a crisis that affected him personally: his older brother Ganesh, or Babarao as he was called, was sentenced to transportation for life (which at that time meant a period of twenty-five years) to the penal colony on the Andaman and Nicobar Islands for his role in anti-British activities.

Just a few weeks after the motion to expel Dhingra was placed before Savarkar, on 1 July at about eight in the evening, Dhingra, a short, slender man with a curved nose, a small black moustache and gold-rimmed spectacles, set out in a cab from his lodgings at 108 Ledbury Road, Bayswater, for Jehangir Hall at the Imperial Institute in South Kensington. He had been invited for an evening of entertainment and conversation there by Miss Emma Josephine Beck, the honorary secretary of the National Indian Association founded in 1870 'for the purpose of establishing friendly relations between the peoples of Great Britain and India'.[4] Two hundred people, mostly members of the association and its patrons, were to attend. Curzon Wyllie, the body's honorary treasurer, would also be there. So would Fazalbhoy Currimbhoy Ebrahim, a Mumbai-based Khoja Muslim businessman and chairman of the then-powerful Bombay Mill Owners Association; Cowasji Jehangir, a Parsi merchant and, like Currimbhoy, a famous Mumbai figure; and Princess Sophia Duleep Singh, the exiled granddaughter of the 'Lion of Punjab' Ranjit Singh, who enjoyed a special status in Britain as Queen Victoria's beloved goddaughter.

Dhingra entered the resplendent hall wearing a pale blue turban, a buff lounge suit and a dark tie that contrasted agreeably with the white linen shirt beneath his waistcoat. The *Daily Mail* described the scene as one of Oriental splendour, with 'gorgeous Indian screens and radiant embroideries' forming the backdrop of a platform and a number of Indian women 'in brilliant robes' contributing to its beauty and 'picturesqueness'. A musical performance was on, and a 'young Hindu student' in particular seemed to have made an impression on the guests as he 'rendered an Urdu song in a remarkably sweet tenor voice'.[5]

Familiar with quite a few faces in the gathering, Dhingra blended in with consummate ease. Sometime after 10 p.m. he was seen engaged in a friendly chat with Miss Beck. She inquired about his educational pursuits, and he told her he had finished his course and would head straight home after his final exams in October. She asked if he was acquainted with any of the guests, and he said yes, he knew some of them. Curzon Wyllie came in a little late in the evening, accompanied by his wife, and at once struck up a conversation with the Indians, distinguished and common.

At 11 p.m., with just the last leg of the cultural show left, many of the guests started to make their way downstairs to the cloakrooms. One of them was Curzon Wyllie's wife. Wyllie himself was very slow in moving towards the stairs as more and more guests came up to him to exchange pleasantries or to have brief chats. When he was finally close to the landing, Dhingra walked up to him and began speaking in a slow, low and polite voice. Wyllie leaned forward to lend an attentive ear, but before he could figure out what was happening, Dhingra whipped out a pistol from his coat pocket and shot him in the face. Four near-precision shots. One bullet pierced the right eye, one went through the left, one struck Wyllie below the left ear and the fourth one over the left eyebrow. The first two bullets exited through the back of the head; the other two were later found lodged inside. 'Death must have been instantaneous,' the doctor who conducted the post-mortem concluded.[6]

A fifth shot too was fired as the Secretary of State's aide 'swung from side to side and fell', an eyewitness recounted at the inquest.[7] But it missed its target. As shrieks went around the corridor, Cawas Lalcaca, a Parsi physician from Mumbai who stood a few yards away, rushed in to try to rein in the assailant. He was shot in the side before he could reach Dhingra and fell a couple of yards next to where Wyllie lay. Two Britishers running in from opposite sides somehow got a grip on the Punjabi with difficulty, and in the struggle that ensued Dhingra momentarily freed the hand that held the pistol and, holding the muzzle to his own head, pulled the trigger. All he got was an innocuous click. He had exhausted all his bullets and was now securely held by the two men, one a luminary of the National Liberal Club, Douglas William Thorburn, and the other a colonial administrator, Lesley Probyn. In the struggle Probyn had fallen and suffered injuries to his nose and ribs. The police were called, and Thorburn, in a state of shock, asked Dhingra, 'What have you done? Why did you do it?' The youth 'looked at me quietly and did not say anything. He later on said, "Let me put my spectacles on,"' Thorburn recalled in his deposition in court during the trial. Another horrified Britisher, Captain Charles Rolleston of Hampstead, asked Dhingra why he had committed the crime. Dhingra only told him, 'in a slow, measured tone', that he would tell the police. Rolleston knew Hindustani too, so he posed the same question again in that language, 'but he would give no information'. Rolleston said at the inquest that Dhingra 'appeared to be in a dreamy, dazed condition', which made the Englishman suspect that 'he had taken a drug, probably bhang'. (Mary Harris, with whom Dhingra was a lodger, however, later testified that she did not think Dhingra took drugs.) Another witness, Dr John Buchanan, said, 'Dhingra seemed the calmest man in the crowd.'[8]

Wyllie's wife, who had rushed from the cloakroom on hearing the commotion upstairs, at first could not recognize the man struck lifeless as his face had been disfigured. Within seconds she was filled with horror and said, 'It is my husband, my husband! Why wasn't I with him!'[9]

In Dhingra's right-hand breast coat pocket the police officers, who rushed to the spot to make the arrest, found another automatic pistol, a Colt, which was 'loaded in all its chambers'. In another pocket was 'a new dagger in a leather case', bearing the name of Rodgers and Sons, of Sheffield.[10]

The killing sent shock waves throughout the Empire as it was the first fatal blow struck against a British official by an Indian on British soil (the earlier assassinations had all been in India) and evoked a degree of disbelief as it was common knowledge that Dhingra's family had healthy ties with the India Office mandarins in general and Curzon Wyllie in particular. It drew a blizzard of condemnation and spawned various theories on whether it was an isolated incident or part of an elaborate conspiracy. The British Prime Minister H.H. Asquith said his country was 'horrified at the detestable crime' which he saw as 'startling evidence of the character of a conspiracy' which, although 'confined to a small number of people', was 'desperate and determined in its methods'.[11] The Raj in India let it be known to a Reuters correspondent that it had 'constantly drawn the attention of the India Office to the serious danger of India House',[12] and the Conservative papers in Britain called for immediate action to 'suppress the India House agitation' and 'root out the conspirators' at this 'extremist club', where Dhingra had 'had his mind poisoned . . . to the point of committing murder'.[13] The spokesperson of students at this 'club', Savarkar, naturally came under sharp scrutiny, and a group of angry Englishmen marched to the London address of the Indian nationalist leader Bipin Chandra Pal, where Savarkar was then staying, and registered a vociferous protest. Pal sought to pacify them, saying that Savarkar was simply his lodger and that he had absolutely no other connection with the young man. Dhingra's anguished father sent a letter to Morley and to the two victims' families, in which he called his son 'cursed' and said he had killed a man 'we have been indebted to' in 'a fit of madness'.[14] The Moderate Indian nationalist Gopal Krishna Gokhale denounced the assailant at a public meeting in Pune, and another Moderate, Surendranath Banerjea, addressing a well-attended gathering of young Indians at the New Reform Club in London on 4 July, stated unequivocally that 'murder is murder . . . no matter what may be the determining motive', although he contested Asquith's assertion and said 'there was not a tittle of evidence to show that there is any conspiracy'.[15]

The next day – Dhingra's fourth in Brixton prison after his arrest from the murder scene – there was an even bigger public meeting of Indians, including Indian students, at the Caxton Hall in Westminster. So 'impressive' and 'most representative' was this gathering 'of all shades of Indian opinion', *The Times* of London reported, that 'the room originally hired was soon seen to be utterly inadequate', and when a shift was made to 'one of the largest rooms in the building', there too 'the seats rapidly filled, the gangways were blocked with late comers, and the audience overflowed to the ante-room and even to the corridor'.[16]

The meeting was presided over by the Aga Khan, the imam and spiritual leader of the Ismaili Muslims, and its convener was Mancherjee Bhownaggree, the second Indian (after Dadabhai Naoroji) to be elected to the British Parliament and, as a Conservative Party loyalist, a staunch supporter of British rule. The first two Indians appointed to the Secretary of State's India Council, K.C. Gupta and Syed Hussain Bilgrami, were also there, and so were Wyllie's friend Fazalbhoy Currimbhoy and Surendranath Banerjea. Savarkar, too, had decided to go. He reached Caxton Hall with three members of his inner circle. While two of them, Gyanchand Varma and V.V.S. Aiyar, sat in the front row along with him, the third, M.P.T. Acharya, occupied a seat right behind them in the second row.

Speaking first, the Aga Khan said Sir Curzon Wyllie's assassination had cast a 'foul stain' upon 'the fair name and fame of their beloved country', and the thought uppermost in the minds of Indians was what they could do 'to repair the ruin caused by that catastrophe' and how they could 'rehabilitate themselves among the fellow-subjects of the Empire in face of that dastardly act'.

The first resolution expressing sympathy with Lady Curzon Wyllie having been passed, Bhownaggree, who spoke after the Aga Khan, introduced a second, against Dhingra, and launched into a comprehensive condemnation of the incarcerated Punjabi. Syed Ameer Ali, the first Indian on the Privy Council's judicial panel and another solid Raj backer, was the third speaker, and while he too criticized Dhingra, his remarks seemed to many less harsh than Bhownaggree's. The moment Ali had finished speaking, Dhingra's London-based younger brother was brought on to the dais, led rather dramatically by the hand by Theodore Morrison, a member of the India Council, the Secretary of State's advisory body on Indian affairs. Equally dramatically, Morrison told the gathering that this youth who stood by his side deserved their sympathy. The boy had approached him earlier in the day to ask him 'how he should express his own horror' at his brother's crime, Morrison said. And Morrison's reply to him had simply been, 'Your proper course is to come and purge yourself of all sympathy with the crime before your own countrymen at the meeting to-night.' In what appeared to be a memorized short speech, Dhingra's brother called his sibling 'a blot on the family'. This apparently orchestrated act did not have quite the effect that was desired, and there were audible whispers in the auditorium, not all of them approving.

Perhaps realizing that the drama had backfired, Bhownaggree put to vote his second resolution damning Dhingra, even before the whispers had completely died down. As several hands went up quickly in assent, he declared the resolution unanimously carried. 'No, not all are in favour,' Savarkar said, in a voice that could be heard by most of those gathered. As he stood up to explain his position, whispers grew louder, and many guests wore surprised looks. But no one could get an opportunity to hear him any further. Bhownaggree jumped off the dais and spluttered, in outrage, 'Hold him, eject him.' The correspondent for *The Times* reported there were 'loud and indignant cries of "Put him out!"'[17] from many others too. The meeting descended into a complete mess. Chairs and abuses were tossed about by partisans on both sides. The women in the hall panicked and screamed, and many of them, apprehensive of another Dhingra-like shootout, hid beneath or behind still-undisturbed chairs and tables or simply ran out to safety.

In the ruckus Savarkar tried to continue speaking. But without any success. A barrister by the name of Palmer, described by newspapers that recorded the incident as a Eurasian, lunged forward and struck Savarkar in the eye. There are two versions of the nature of the assault. One is that Savarkar was hit with bare hands; the other has Palmer wielding an umbrella. Whichever is correct, the fact is the blow was a powerful one, and Palmer had drawn some blood. The sight appalled Surendranath Banerjea. He walked out in disgust, registering his protest at the use of physical force, and Savarkar's confidant M.P.T. Acharya, seeking instant reprisal, brought his stick down on Palmer's head. It hit his cheek, drawing blood. Before things could get any more ugly, the cops rushed in. According to the Indians, they escorted Savarkar and his friends out; according to *The Times*, though, 'Mr Savarkar was ignominiously expelled, in spite of the crowded state of the hall.'[18]

An indignant Palmer, advancing upon the platform, then proceeded to make a brief speech whose effect, London's premier newspaper said, 'was heightened by the sight of blood streaming from his face'. Palmer pointed out that the Indians in England 'were enjoying the hospitality of the noble British people, and at the present time constitutional privileges were being granted to India. So a man who could, in such circumstances, go to that meeting and object to condemnation of the dastardly crime of last Thursday was not worthy of any consideration at their hands.' To this the crowd that remained, mostly British, responded with 'loud cheers'.[19]

The commotion-creating Indian was described by the *Daily Despatch* thus: 'The pale youth who made so dramatic a protest . . . turns out to be Mr Vinayak Damodar Savarkar. He is a fervent nationalist . . . Like most of his nationalists he is a political theorist, and is deeply versed in all the literature of political liberty.'[20]

The Times carried a longish letter by Savarkar himself. He had returned to his lodgings, drafted it and dispatched it to the newspaper's office ahead of the deadline the very same evening. In it he set out to explain what he had done and why. The resolution moved had presumed, in his view, Dhingra's criminality. 'The man accused of the murder has made no confession,' he stressed. 'It seemed to me an encroachment upon and assumption of the authority of the Law Courts to declare a man who is still under trial to be a criminal . . . It seemed to be more just and appropriate to omit the words "crime" and "criminals" from the resolution. As the proceedings had advanced too far to effect this, I simply voted against the resolution as it stood and wanted to bring to the notice of the president the fact that the resolution could not be declared as passed unanimously.' After that 'the proper way' for the president would have been 'to count the votes against and for and declare the result', Savarkar wrote, 'but some excited spirits forgot themselves so much as to [say] "Eject him" etc, and even went so far as to threaten me with physical force'. Still, he said, he had 'stood perfectly calm, simply asserting my right and without giving the least provocation'. In a minute or two Palmer had reached the place where he was standing and attacked him 'while I was actually in the act of explaining the meaning of my opposition in clear terms, though they were drowned in the cry of the excited few'. He was writing this letter, he informed the paper's editor, 'to prevent any misunderstanding or misinterpretation' of his conduct at the meeting, and he was confident that the man who had hit him 'will soon be brought before the Courts'.[21]

In subsequent gatherings held to condemn the murder, the resolutions were far more carefully worded – from one of them, Dhingra's name was left out altogether. And though Palmer was never brought before any court, nor was Acharya for using a walking stick to deliver a thump on someone's cheek.

Sarojini Naidu's brother Virendra Chattopadhyaya or 'Chatto', studying at the Middle Temple at the time, sought to shore up the Indian argument further by dispatching his own letter to *The Times*. In it he said he had read V.D. Savarkar's letter in the paper 'with much satisfaction'. He had himself had every intention of proceeding to the protest meeting at Caxton Hall and had decided 'in the event of Mr M L Dhingra's criminality being assumed by the supporters of the resolution, to enter an emphatic protest'. He was unable to attend as he was 'detained by urgent business'. But, he added, 'I am glad that this [the voicing of the protest] was done by Mr Savarkar. Had I been present, I would have supported him at the risk of being ejected, and there would have been two dissentient voices raised against the resolution.' Chatto said he had no sympathy with the idea of political assassination and considered the method 'an absolutely suicidal one'. 'But I think we all have the right to express our opinions honestly, and if we take objection to the words of the resolution, I see no reason why force should be used to expel us,' he wrote.[22]

Savarkar sought simultaneously to influence the court of public opinion in India by focusing on the success of the revolutionaries. He had been writing regular dispatches from the British capital for *Kaal*, a Marathi newspaper published from Pune. Valentine Chirol, foreign editor of *The Times* of London, stated that Savarkar had in an article for the Marathi paper 'magnified the success of the [murder] plot by describing its chief victim as "the eyes of the Secretary of State through which he saw all Indian affairs"'.[23] In effect, Savarkar had plainly indicated that the Viceroy was the head of government in India, but the Secretary of State had a still more powerful and exalted status. He was the Viceroy's boss.

It soon emerged during the trial that Dhingra, for the few months he had mostly stayed away from India House, had been practising regularly at a rifle club on Tottenham Court Road. He had obtained a gun licence and bought a six-chamber Colt automatic magazine revolver before enrolling himself there. He justified the political assassination. 'I hold the English people responsible for the murder of eighty millions of Indian people in the last 50 years and they are also responsible for taking away 100 million pounds every year from India to this country,' he told the court. 'Just as the Germans have no right to occupy this country, so the English people have no right to occupy India; and it is perfectly justifiable on our part to kill the Englishman who is polluting our sacred land.'

But he had had no intention of killing the Parsi doctor Lalcaca, who had been on a holiday in England from Shanghai, where he had moved to from his native Mumbai several years ago. 'I did not know him. When he advanced to get hold of me I simply fired in self-defence,' Dhingra said.[24]

Dhingra emphasized that no English court had a right to pass sentence upon him and refused to have a counsel to defend him or to cross-examine any of the witnesses. Yet he definitely wanted to be hanged, 'for in that case the vengeance of my countrymen will be all the more keen'.

Before summing up the case to the jury, the chief justice asked Dhingra if he had any other statement to make. Dhingra said the police had confiscated a statement written on foolscap paper that he was carrying with him in his pocket at the time of his arrest. 'Whatever else' he had to say was in that document, he said.[25] Another copy of it had been found by the police when they searched Dhingra's rooms. 'I do not care what was in your pocket. With what you had written before, we have nothing to do,' the Chief Justice told him sternly. An American observer in the courtroom recorded that the jury took less than a minute to bring a verdict of guilty, and Dhingra was sentenced to be hanged on 17 August. The trial itself had been astoundingly speedy: it had concluded in twenty-one days after the arrest, and the hanging was scheduled on the forty-seventh day.[26]

Dhingra's confiscated declaration, not allowed to be part of the case records, was believed to have been buried forever. But a day before he was hanged, it mysteriously appeared in full in the pages of the *Daily News* of London. 'I admit, the other day I attempted to shed English blood as a humble revenge for the inhuman hangings and deportations [to the Andamans] of patriotic Indian youths. In this attempt I have consulted none but my own conscience. I have conspired with none but my own duty. I believe that a nation held in bondage with the help of foreign bayonets is in a perpetual state of war. Since open battle is rendered impossible to a disarmed race, I attacked by surprise; since guns were denied to me, I drew forth my pistol and fired,' it read. Invoking the names of Ram and Krishna, the Hindu deities venerated for leading truth to triumph over falsehood and evil, the statement referred to India as 'the Mother' and said any wrong done to her was 'an insult to God'.

The bewilderment of the official establishment was total. How had the contents of the statement leaked when the original, along with the copy taken from Dhingra's rooms, was securely in possession of the authorities? Obviously, there was one more copy floating around. Who had it?

Among the English friends Savarkar had cultivated in London was eighteen-year-old David Garnett, the sprightly son of the writer Edward Garnett and his wife Constance, who had a literary reputation of her own as Tolstoy's translator. David, himself a man of letters who later became a key member of the distinguished Bloomsbury circle that included Virginia Woolf and Lytton Strachey, knew Robert Lynd, an editor at the *Daily News*, fairly well. Savarkar had asked David if he could help him bring Dhingra's statement to light, and the teenager had lent a hand by promptly informing Lynd and sending the statement across to him.

The embarrassment for the law-enforcing agencies was made worse by the conclusion drawn by *The Times*: there was unmistakably a hidden hand behind Dhingra's actions. 'There is every reason to believe that Dhingra did not compose the statement but that it was composed by those who egged him on to commit murder,' the paper wrote. '[T]he statement found in Dhingra's room was the copy of a document, the original of which is in the hands of others. Moreover, the style of the composition of the statement is entirely unlike the style of Dhingra's statement before the magistrate.'[27]

'I guessed who the author of it was,' Garnett later wrote.

2

In the land of the Ramayana

In India's sacred geography Nasik is one of the most luminous spots. It is situated very close to one of the twelve places in the country where, according to the myths, Lord Shiva pierced into the soil his powerful column of light, the jyotirlinga. With Shiva around, the celestial river Ganga couldn't be too far, and sure enough, on a hill above the jyotirlinga of Tryambaka is the source of the Godavari, considered one of the seven Gangas in India. If in the Himalayas the Ganga is believed to have descended to earth on the sage Bhagirath's request, she is said to have brought her waters to the Brahmagiri hill in this north-western part of Maharashtra in response to the saint Gautam's prayers. To break her mighty fall, she first landed on Shiva's matted hair and from there on top of the Brahmagiri. And, as she came down the hill, she proceeded straight into the heart of Nasik. There she was diverted by devotees into numerous pools and tanks (called kunds) which in time acquired banks, their steps built of stone for pilgrims to carry out their bathing and other rituals.

Nasik's other, older name is Panchavati, the place in the Dandaka forest where the epic hero Ram, his wife Sita and brother Lakshman came to live in a hut during their exile. It is here that Surpanakha, the sister of Ravan, spotted Ram and, transfixed by his handsomeness, proposed marriage to him. When Ram rejected her, saying he was already married, the demoness lunged at Sita to kill her and endured serious humiliation, with Lakshman famously cutting off her nose and ears. Tearful and bleeding, she ran off to her brother, the ruler of Lanka, and asked him to avenge the insult. His act of retribution was the kidnapping of Sita. Nasik literally means the nose, the catalyst for the Ramayana's big turning point.

Vinayak Savarkar was born on 28 May 1883 in Bhagur, a nondescript village twenty kilometres from Nasik, which had the big town's shadow forever looming large over it.[1] His parents, Damodar and Radha, were delighted at his birth. Married around 1870, they had lost two children one after the other. They had since had two children, a boy, Ganesh or Babarao, who was born in 1879, and a girl, Maina, who came soon after him. But those were times when parents looked forward to having a second son, and Vinayak was seen as a genuine blessing. Five years after his birth, the couple had yet another son, Narayan.

The Savarkars were not originally from Bhagur. Hailing from the Konkanastha or Chitpavan Brahman community, they had their roots in the Konkan, the coastal strip of Maharashtra which runs all the way down to Goa and thence to Karnataka. Not too far north of Goa is the verdant belt of Guhagar of

Maharashtra, which became the centre of a controversy in the 1990s when the multinational firm Enron unveiled its plans to set up a power plant there (the project was scrapped after fierce opposition from locals). In the Guhagar belt was a village called Palshet, which was also known as Savar Wadi. One of the families of the village began to call themselves Savarkar[2] and, like many other Chitpavan families, came into prominence in the eighteenth century during the highly successful reign of the Peshwas, their fellow sub-castemen.

The Savarkars, Vinayak's ancestors, acquired Rahuri village near Nasik and Bhagur as an inam (land grant) in 1756 from the Peshwas, and their position in the Pune durbar appears to have risen subsequently – one Parshuram Savarkar was among two chosen representatives of the Marathas sent for pre-war negotiations with the British in 1817.[3]

Vinayak's father, Damodar, and his brother Mahadeo had taken good care of their inam, so the family, if not rich, was reasonably well off by Indian standards. Their house was spacious, if spartan, with four to five rooms, a mud floor and mud walls. Like most Indian families of the time, they preferred to sleep on the floor. The family owned fields and even boasted of a mango orchard.

The Savarkars had taken enthusiastically to the new system of education institutionalized by the British after Maratha rule collapsed in 1818. Damodar was the first boy from Bhagur to complete his matriculation in English; his primary schooling was in Marathi in his own village, and he attended secondary school in Nasik. He was keen that his children be educated in similar fashion, and Vinayak was enrolled in a primary school in the village at the age of six. The language of instruction was his native Marathi. Never top of his class, Vinayak nevertheless acquired a reputation among his teachers and classmates during his early school years for being adept at memorizing both prose and verse and for the uncommon habit of actively seeking out books beyond the syllabus. By the time he was in classes 3 and 4, he was reading pretty much everything he could lay his hands on; and on the shelf in his house he found a number of religious texts such as the Smritis, the Puranas and the two great epics, the Ramayana and the Mahabharata, and some historical accounts in the form of the Peshwa bakhars (records). His father was a conscientious reader of Marathi newspapers such as *Kesari* (edited by Tilak) and *Nasik Vaibhav* and, since they were usually lying about the house, the boy began to read them and quickly developed an interest in public affairs. His sister-in-law Yesubai later wrote in her reminiscences that he would also get hold of other newspapers, particularly those coming in from Pune and Mumbai that some neighbours subscribed to, and would return them to their owners once he had finished going through them.[4]

At the same time, Vinayak was known to give a lot of time to his friends, among the earliest of whom were Parshuram and Rajaram Shimpi.[5] They were of the tailor caste and the Savarkars the so-called claimants of both secular and spiritual authority (being both Brahman and the holders of the inam), yet neither family seems to have looked askance at the friendship or their frequent excursions into the fields that Vinayak's parents owned. The Shimpis had their own tamasha troupe, and Vinayak wrote some songs and lines for them, which were intended for public education. The Shimpi brothers, who were famous for singing lavnis as well as for dancing and playing the role of coquettish women draped in nine-yard saris, punctuated their own risqué performances with Vinayak's serious messages. Later, for quite a few decades in the twentieth century, this raucous art form would evoke disdain from a section of the urban middle classes in western India because of its explicitness, but Vinayak took immense pride in his association with his friends' troupe.

He was also known, at least within his family, for his pranks. One such prank infuriated his father so much that his older brother had to hide him for a while in the family safe. Another time, he ended up breaking his little sister's bangles, again inviting the patriarch's wrath.[6]

Even so, Damodar, a man of stern disposition, was very fond of the boy, and Vinayak seems to have suffered none of the neglect that middle children are sometimes subjected to. He was given charge of the puja room in the house, where daily prayers were offered to Goddess Durga. The boy's natural inclination towards poetry too made his father happy. Damodar loved dabbling in verse, and Vinayak not only read the *Navneet*, a famous collection of Marathi poems, while he was still in primary school, but he also started writing some poetry of his own at an early age. Much of it was about Goddess Durga, slayer of evil. Damodar, for his part, enthusiastically read to him Alexander Pope's translation of Homer's *Iliad*.

Of the several literary works at home, the one which undoubtedly held the greatest fascination for Vinayak was the *Nibandhamala*, a collection of contemporary essays by the eminent scholar and teacher Vishnu Krishna or Vishnushastri Chiplunkar. Written with the explicit purpose of restoring Indians' respect for their own cultural heritage in the face of widespread colonial propaganda that the natives were barbaric, backward and desperately in need of western civilizing influences, these essays had canonical status in the nationalist literature of the period.

Vinayak also discovered, in his father's collection, back issues of the periodical *Katha Saar*, which carried Marathi translations of episodes from the Mahabharata. Far more easily accessible to a schoolboy than the ancient Sanskrit text, these crisply told stories captured his imagination and helped him develop his own opinions about the epic. Whenever elders in the family or the village lavished praise on the great warrior Arjun, Vinayak would vigorously assert that the second of the five Pandavas, Bhim, was actually the superior combatant. 'The course of action that Bhim suggested at critical points was often the one that his brothers and even their mentor Krishna had to finally adopt after they had exhausted all other options. Arjun was vulnerable to temptation, Bhim wasn't. And Arjun needed to be counselled, in the sense that the Gita had to be told to him by Krishna, but not Bhim,' he would argue, drawing, as he recollected later, 'howls of laughter' from the listeners.[7]

Vinayak's mother, Radha, was quite indulgent of him. Polite to a fault, she showered care and affection on her children and was known never to lose her temper. She went about managing the household on her own while her husband was caught up with land-related matters. The only thing she always insisted on was that her children read the sacred texts regularly, which Vinayak did in any case.

In 1892, when Vinayak had just turned nine years old, his mother died of cholera. Describing the last few hours of her life, he recounted that she had cooked food for several guests invited home by his father that afternoon. While serving them she suddenly felt giddy and uneasy. So 'she lay down for some rest near the prayer room and never woke up again', the son wrote.[8] After his mother's passing, Vinayak increasingly took to seeking refuge in the family's prayer room.

Around the same time, famines became distressingly routine in the Deccan region, and the Savarkars, mostly dependent on land rents and a share of the cultivated harvest, suffered heavy financial losses. Vinayak later recalled his father as saying about his departed wife, 'She came into our house as Lakshmi, the goddess of wealth. With her death the goddess Lakshmi has deserted us too.'[9]

~

Vinayak had been devout since early childhood and could sometimes lose himself in prayer, but he had ceased to be an unquestioning believer after his mother's death. Back then his father was in desperate need of money as the famine had severely dented the family's funds. One evening in Bhagur, Vinayak noticed that his father had his eyes firmly fixed on the door of their house and the path outside. The son soon found out that he was awaiting a lawyer from Nasik to whom he had lent some money. When the lawyer didn't turn up at the expected hour and the delay grew longer, Damodar started pacing up and down the corridor frantically. Unable to take his father's anxiety any more, Vinayak stepped quietly into the puja room and sent up a fervent prayer of his own. But his hopes were dashed. Damodar never got the money back and was later forced to return empty-handed from a visit to the lawyer's residence in Nasik.[10]

If Savarkar developed a degree of scepticism about religion reasonably early in life, he also identified two clear objects of devotion: the pursuit of knowledge, for which he took passionately to reading and writing, and the motherland, which was under the bondage of the British.

He was only twelve years old when a poem of his was accepted and published by one of his favourite journals, the *Jagadecchu* of Pune. The precocious feat created a sensation in his village, and elders as well as friends who had openly sneered at his compositions earlier began to look at him with a certain regard. 'Thank God the editors didn't know it was a 12-year-old who had written the poem, else they wouldn't have published it,' Savarkar later wrote, stating that at many publications 'who wrote the poem was more important than how it was'.[11]

From Vishnushastri Chiplunkar's *Nibandhamala* Savarkar developed, along with an idea of outstanding literary merit, a conception of Indian nationhood. Chiplunkar wanted Indians to help themselves and not ask the British rulers for favours and patronage; the English, he said, 'are not gods, similarly we are not demons or animals'.[12] He praised the Peshwas for their expansion of Maratha rule and their fight against the Mughals and later the British, and also Indian religion, which he said was under attack from Christian missionaries. When Bal Gangadhar or Lokmanya Tilak upheld Chiplunkar's views and, after the outbreak of communal riots between Hindus and Muslims first in Junagadh and then in Mumbai in July–August 1893, openly espoused the Hindu cause, the defence of the country became conflated with the defence of Hindus. Savarkar was one such Indian to take up this idea.

Sometime in 1894–95, a period that witnessed widespread Hindu–Muslim violence in Yeola and Dhule in Nasik district, the eleven-year-old Savarkar gathered a group of ten to twelve schoolmates to 'avenge the attacks on Hindus' and sneaked, in the dead of night, into an abandoned mosque on Bhagur's outskirts. There was nobody there and, according to the account provided by Savarkar of the incident, he and his mates caused some damage. When a section of Muslim students from an Urdu school situated bang opposite Savarkar's school subsequently found out about the vandalism, the boys from the two communities had a fistfight, at the end of which a truce was declared, with the two parties agreeing that neither would report the incident to their teachers.[13]

Since the reminiscences in which Savarkar recalled this incident were written by him a few decades later, by which time he had come up with his own theory of nationalism, a few chroniclers have wondered if it was more invention than reality. Their theory is based on the fact that there is no other evidence of Savarkar's nationalism acquiring an anti-Muslim character in the first two decades of his life – or more. Savarkar's fierce critics, on the other hand, assert that the act of vandalism is proof that he harboured an inherently bigoted outlook. Savarkar is unlikely to have fictionalized this episode but that doesn't mean he was anti-Muslim at this stage of his life. For one he was but a boy. And the march on the mosque was more likely a classic example of what could happen to someone in the middle of a communal conflagration, when sentiments of a sectarian nature are running especially high. Such effects of group hysteria on otherwise reasonable individuals we have seen before Savarkar's time, and after.

A couple of years after the controversial matter of the Bhagur mosque came a serious expression of anti-British sentiment. When the plague struck Mumbai, Pune and other areas of the Deccan in the mid-1890s, the colonial authorities were widely accused of taking brutally repressive measures to contain the outbreak. Indians and the Indian nationalist press complained that officials had forced their way into people's homes, inflicted violence on those who resisted their invasive checks and in some cases targeted women. On 22 June 1897, two youths from Pimpri-Chinchwad near Pune, Damodar Hari Chapekar and his brother Balkrishna, shot dead the plague commissioner for the region, Walter Charles Rand, and another British officer, Charles Ayerst. They were caught and sentenced to death.

Not too long after the assassinations, Vinayak, then studying at the Nasik school, was back in his Bhagur house for a few days to rest and recover from a bout of smallpox. Late one night, his father awoke from slumber and saw the fourteen-year-old boy engaged in writing something on a piece of paper by a tiny lantern. On examining the sheet, Damodar was instantly filled with dread: Vinayak had been working on a poetic tribute to the Chapekar brothers. The father chose not to react in anger, possibly to conceal his apprehension, but told Vinayak in no uncertain terms to focus on writing lighter, more apolitical stuff instead. 'You must make something of your own life. The path of revolution is dangerous and self-destroying,' he cautioned the son.[14]

Damodar Savarkar obviously didn't want his son to come under the scanner of the authorities. He had dreams for the boy, and he wanted them fulfilled. He was aware that they were living through a delicate phase, in which any 'native' who said anything remotely positive about the Chapekars would appear on the police radar and could even be placed under surveillance.

Though Vinayak never pointed it out, there was a contradiction in the father's approach. Damodar was himself a follower of Lokmanya Tilak, who had posed a grave challenge to the leadership of the Moderates among the Indian nationalists with caustic attacks on the Empire. The Moderates, as their leading light Gopal Krishna Gokhale wrote, accepted the 'British connection, as ordained, in the inscrutable dispensation of Providence, for India's good';[15] Tilak and the Extremists saw it as neither ordained nor necessary. The Moderates were desirous of obtaining concessions from the British and committed to constitutional progress; the Extremists spoke of 'rights', not concessions, and were not content with making incremental improvements towards self-governance. The Moderates felt India would not be ready for self-rule until Indian society had carried out social and faith-based reforms; Tilak and his followers wanted for Indians the liberty to control their own lives right away. Gokhale's idea of self-government included the 'natives' of all religions, with Hindu–Muslim solidarity as a foundational principle; the Tilak school of thought did not see why self-governance should wait until certain reforms were effected and did not view 'natives' as one bloc but looked at securing Hindu interests separately as well. The Extremists were careful not to overstep the line and call for violence, for that could endanger their claim for leadership of the mainstream national movement, but it was a poorly kept secret that Tilak believed the Indians would have to sooner or later pick up arms to evict the British.

Besides, scattered all over the Savarkar residence in Bhagur were books filled with political writings, some of which advocated a strong nationalist stand, if not a revolutionary approach. Going a step further, Damodar had bought, particularly for Vinayak, the bakhar of the era of the Maratha hero Chhatrapati Shivaji. The timing of this purchase too was significant: the Englishman James Grant Duff had only recently been accused by nationalist Indians of demonizing Shivaji and his successors in a new history of the Marathas, and Marathi writers such as Chiplunkar were trying to bring about an awakening among the people by invoking the name of Shivaji and his spirit of revolt against unjust and foreign rule.

In the event, the poem on the Chapekar brothers brought no trouble; Vinayak kept it to himself at the time, much to his father's relief.

~

As the Savarkars' financial woes became acute due to the famine, Vinayak, after clearing class 5, was compelled to study on his own at home for the first and second years of secondary school. After that, however, he was dispatched to the Shivaji secondary school in Nasik, where the standards of education were believed to be far better than in the village. The Nasik school, approving of the academic progress the boy had made on his own at home, admitted him straight to class 8. Babarao had already been enrolled in the same school, and he began cooking for the younger sibling in a small room they shared between them in the temple town. Vinayak had joined the school only a few months before the annual exams, but he managed to clear all his papers and was promoted to the next class.

Some developments in the next few years appeared to bring

a significant amount of relief, and even a degree of happiness, for the household. Babarao got married while still pursuing his school education. So did his sister, Maina, and Vinayak's studies too were progressing well. But barely had a measure of stability been gained when Savarkar's father and uncle died within days of each other in 1899, taken down cruelly along with numerous others by an outbreak of plague in the Deccan. Vinayak was fifteen years old and orphaned.

While the father's body lay in their house, the British colonial administration slapped a notice on the door asking all members of the family to move out immediately. The disinfecting team, the notice peremptorily said, would be taking charge of the premises without any delay. Babarao had been staying there after his marriage, and the younger brother Narayan too was in the same house, while Vinayak would return during his school holidays and vacations and sometimes on the weekends.

But now the entire family was made to leave Bhagur in a great hurry, and they managed to take hardly any of their possessions along. They sought temporary shelter in a worn-down temple on the outskirts of the village. There, they discovered to their growing dismay that Narayan had also caught the plague.

Narayan was immediately admitted to the Plague Hospital in Nasik, and while Vinayak and his sister-in-law Yesubai mostly stayed put in a room the family briefly rented in the town, Babarao chose to spend all his time alongside his ailing brother at the hospital, sleeping in the corridors at night.

From the rented room Vinayak would carry meals and a fresh pair of clothes for his brothers every day, and Babarao made sure that he himself always picked them up at the hospital's gates so that Vinayak would not have to step in and risk catching the infection. One day, Babarao wasn't present at the hospital entrance at the appointed hour. After a while the knot in the teenaged Vinayak's stomach grew tighter. With all kinds of fears in his mind, he entered the hospital. Once inside, the worst was confirmed. Babarao, too, was now stricken with the plague. The family was in danger of being completely wiped out.

Fortunately, that threat passed, and the two brothers were back home in a couple of months, fully recovered. A much-relieved Vinayak was finally able to return to his studies in Nasik.

Life had changed momentously in the seven years since his mother had died. After the brothers were forced to move out of the Bhagur house in the wake of their father's death, all of their possessions had been taken away by a neighbour. The boys' only uncle had never married and had no children, and he had told his nephews that he had kept all of his savings – a few thousand rupees, which amounted to a great deal at the time – with a lawyer. But the uncle had never given them his name or address and so they could never claim their inheritance.

To make matters worse, the Savarkars' tenants who had been granted rights to till the inam lands refused to hand over their plots to the family or even to acknowledge their authority to collect revenue. The one family in the neighbourhood that could perhaps have been relied upon to offer some assistance, the Shimpis of the tamasha troupe, had abandoned their home in the village, rendered destitute by the plague.

The oldest of the Savarkar siblings, Babarao, was forced to take up odd jobs, and his wife, Yesubai, had to sell all the jewellery her parents had gifted her at her wedding. Babarao's visits to local moneylenders to borrow small amounts, not surprisingly, became somewhat regular.

On top of it all, Babarao fell into a seemingly ridiculous trap set for him by a fellow villager. On a visit to Bhagur to see if any dues owed to his late father by the native cultivators could be recovered, he was accosted by a local resident. We know this man only by his surname, Karanjkar; Savarkar does not mention his first name in his record of his childhood. The Savarkars, it seems, had helped the Karanjkars at various moments of crises. The villager, sounding gravely concerned, told Babarao that he wanted to help them in whatever way possible to repay the debt of gratitude that his family owed them. He told Babarao that he had reliable information that a fair amount of treasure, easily worth around ten thousand rupees, lay buried in a field near the banks of the river Darna that ran past the village. He promised to dig it up at night and hand the whole haul over to Babarao. But before that could be done, he told Babarao, the local goddess needed to be appeased with food and some rites. For that, he needed an amount in excess of Rs 200. Tempted by what appeared to be 'a solution to all problems', Babarao handed over a sum of Rs 300, which was all the money he had left with him. Not surprisingly, Karanjkar disappeared. When he resurfaced after a fortnight and was pinned down by a livid Babarao, he explained to him that he had been waylaid by a band of robbers and had lost everything. The robbers had threatened to kill him if he didn't part with the money, he said.[16]

Vinayak was not as naive – or blindly religious or superstitious – as his brother. According to his account, he had told Babarao, soon after he was informed of the cash given to the villager for digging up the purported treasure, that he had been royally conned and that he must consider the money 'as good as gone'.[17]

~

Vinayak's respect for Babarao did not waver – not even after the village con incident. One reason was that Babarao had ensured his family stayed afloat after they were orphaned through his commitment and effort. If Vinayak did not have to give up his studies despite the family's precarious situation, it was entirely on account of Babarao's resolve to keep things going.

Vinayak responded to all the support in his own way, making decent progress in the classroom and more than decent progress outside of it. He continued to write for papers: the *Nasik Vaibhav*, a prominent paper in the district, published an article on Hindu culture written by Savarkar on its editorial pages. Initially the paper's editor would not believe that the piece was written by a teenager, but after Savarkar's schoolteachers confirmed that he was indeed the author, it was cleared for publication. Savarkar also won the top prize at a debating society in Nasik, although here again, the jury had to be persuaded by his teachers that he had written the winning speech himself. Then, on a visit to Pune, Savarkar heard of a debate organized in that city, decided to take part and was adjudged the best speaker. The prize he received here was an annual subscription to the Marathi weekly *Kaal* (Time).[18] It was to make a critical contribution to the development of Savarkar's incipient political consciousness.

3

Turbulence at home

The British presence changed India dramatically in the nineteenth century. And a sixteen-year-old Vinayak Savarkar saw, as the century drew to a close after the last of the Chapekar brothers was hanged in 1899, that the ghosts of the past were hanging over the present.

Once the blinding cloud of dust thrown up by the great revolt of 1857 had settled, the rapacious East India Company was disbanded[1] by a special law enacted by the British parliament, and the British crown came to control the company's possessions in India. Its rule came to be known as the Raj, and its two big bosses were the Viceroy, the crown's representative based in India, and the Secretary of State who presided over the India Council in London in place of the earlier Company board of control. The three major presidencies of Bombay, Calcutta and Madras were ruled by governors, who came under the Viceroy, and the other provinces were ruled by lieutenant governors.[2]

To try to assuage the feelings of those Indians who might still have misgivings about what the British were doing on the subcontinent, Queen Victoria, thirty-eight years old in 1858, issued a proclamation that said 'it is Our earnest desire . . . to administer the government for the benefit of all Our subjects . . . In their prosperity will be Our strength, in their contentment Our security, and in their gratitude Our best reward.' She promised absolute non-interference in faith issues – a critical point for both Hindus and Muslims as Indian sipahis (white officials corrupted the word to 'sepoy') had sparked the revolt of 1857 when they rebelled believing they had been given new cartridges greased with either cow or pig fat. The proclamation continued, 'Our subjects, of whatever race or creed, be freely and impartially admitted to office in Our service.'[3]

But the reality was far removed from the statement's seeming generosity. The Code of Civil Procedure supplanted Hindu and Muslim religious codes except in matters of marriage and inheritance, and the Indian Penal Code placed curbs on individual rights. Nineteen sections of the criminal law were about severe penalties for disobeying public servants; ten sections related to 'offences against the state'; and any 'dishonour' to symbols of imperial authority – such as stamps – would result in stringent punishment. The Indian Civil Service (ICS), the most elite body of administrators, had been theoretically thrown open to Indians, but the first Indian was chosen for it ten years after the Queen's proclamation, and one of the earliest 'native' ICS members, Surendranath Banerjea, became a victim of brazen racial discrimination and was dismissed from service on spurious grounds. And although the spread of western education was rapid and several Indians entered the prestigious legal profession, a few even getting appointed as judges, an Indian judge could not try Europeans outside the cities and towns. Some of the worst outrages committed by Europeans took place in the rest of the country, where European judges were arbiters. One European tea planter who murdered his Indian labourer was allowed by the magistrate to walk free after he had paid a fine of two pounds; another planter complained that Indian workers, if assaulted, were 'capable . . . of dying to spite you'; and Robert Bulwer-Lytton or Lord Lytton, Viceroy for four years starting 1876, justified such senseless killings by saying, 'Asiatics are subject to internal disease which often renders fatal to life even a slight external shock.'[14]

Economically India was being squeezed dry, argued the Parsi businessman Dadabhai Naoroji in 1867. Himself an Anglophile, Naoroji said 50 per cent of the government's total earnings were being taken to Britain rather than being spent on India. This 'drain of wealth' came to more than 100 per cent of the total land revenue plus one-third of India's savings and was the chief cause of the country's impoverishment, he said. He and some other Indians developed the wealth drain theory further as the years went by, attributing recurring famines with their huge death tolls to this 'sad bleeding'.

The Indian Councils Act of 1861 had created two bodies: the Executive Council, a cabinet with five white officials heading various departments, and the Legislative Council, comprising members of the Executive Council and a maximum of twelve members, British or Indian, nominated. The Legislative Council was toothless and seats for Indians in the central legislature were a sorry example of tokenism. It could discuss nothing without obtaining the government's sanction and force no corrective budgetary, administrative or legal action on the Viceroy or his Executive Council as it was purely consultative in character; the Indians appointed on it were tasked mainly with alerting the body to local views so that the smallest signs of disaffection could be contained before they developed into a threat to the regime.

Public rallies were still to gain traction (there were no loudspeakers), so the only reliable means available for voicing opinion was the press, which Indians embraced wholeheartedly. That too was sought to be taken away, first in 1870 by a section in the penal code that allowed any editor who created 'disaffection' to be transported to the Andaman Islands for life, and later, following criticism from local publications over the administration's handling of the devastating famine of 1876–77, by empowering authorities to confiscate printing presses and other paraphernalia of 'seditious' vernacular papers.

In the year of Savarkar's birth, Courtney Ilbert, the law member of Viceroy Ripon's Executive Council, brought in a bill seeking to permit Indian magistrates to try Europeans in courts outside cities and towns. The British officialdom's response was righteous indignation. Apart from the European business community and the planters, all top judges of the Calcutta court, Bengal's lieutenant governor, senior lawyers, bureaucrats and the Anglo-Indian press called the measure unacceptable. One letter widely distributed said, 'The only people who have any right to India are the British. The SO-CALLED Indians have no right whatever.'[5] Cowed down completely, Ripon knocked the teeth off the bill and decided Europeans would have the right to be tried by an all-European jury.

All in all, the Indian population, already demoralized after 1857, looked hardly in a position to contest the Raj's hold on power for the foreseeable future. Significant numbers of the Indian elite who received the benefits of western education even began to see British dominance as a blessing.

One such member of the elite was Mahadev Govind Ranade. Like Savarkar, he was a Chitpavan whose family, with roots in the Konkan, had moved to the Nasik belt. Grateful for what European teachers had taught him at Mumbai's Elphinstone School and College, this outstanding student who in time became a legal luminary considered the Raj a 'providential dispensation', for it had provided Indians a window to the world of modern scientific knowledge and social, political and economic theory. European education sparked in him a desire to push for his own society's advancement, politically and in other ways. Social reform movements in the form of the Brahmo Samaj in Bengal and the Prarthana Samaj in Mumbai were already roiling Hindu society, and the Arya Samaj too was to emerge in the north soon. The Brahmo Samaj and the Prarthana Samaj had launched a war on superstitious practices while upholding the sanctity of pure, simple and sincere prayer and believed that Indians would help themselves if they embraced a number of things British. The Arya Samaj was reformist too, but with a difference: it sought an end to blind beliefs but rejected western thought.

Ranade, a member of the Prarthana Samaj, became the leading light in 1871 of India's first broadly representative national organization, the Poona Sarvajanik Sabha (PSS). If Bengal in the east, the first Indian territory where the Company established its dominance, was a trailblazer in social reform, the Maharashtrian Deccan in the west became the pioneer of the national movement.

There had been other semi-political indigenous organizations earlier, but they had chiefly represented the interests only of specific groups. Ranade's group went beyond the western-educated Brahmans that formed its core by making it mandatory for every new member to get a '*mukhtiarnama* [power of attorney] signed by at least fifty adults authorizing him to speak and act on their behalf in all public matters'.[6] And it showed the locals how they could organize themselves and make representations to the authorities. When the British prime minister W.E. Gladstone set up a parliamentary panel in 1871 to prepare a report on Indian finance, the PSS's countermeasure was to conduct its own parallel probe, submit its conclusions in the form of a study and ask the government for remedial action where necessary. Next, Ranade made a plea for 'responsible self-government', by which he meant representation for eleven Indians in the British parliament. All Indian matters must be decided with their approval, he stated, his petition supported by thousands of signatures the PSS had obtained. After a series of attacks by poor farmers on village moneylenders which came to be known as the Deccan Riots of 1875, he wrote to the authorities saying their system of land taxation was at the root of the problem. With the Deccan reeling under famine two years later even as a grand durbar was held in Delhi to celebrate the Queen's assumption of the title of Empress of India, the PSS again sent in its own representatives into famine-struck areas to carry out an independent inquiry, and Ranade handed in a report to the government disputing the official version of destruction and deaths. For the Queen he wrote another message: as Empress, she must grant 'responsible self-government' and constitute a Council of Representatives and a Chamber of Princes so both the people and princely rulers could have their say.

Ranade did not stint on praise for the administration when he felt it was due, yet the Raj came to look upon the PSS with increasing suspicion. It had an inherent distrust of Marathi-speaking Brahmans. It believed they had never really reconciled to the loss of Peshwa rule and were bent on instigating trouble the moment they smelled an opportunity. The role of these Brahmans in the 1857 revolt was the reason the Marathas, along with people from Oudh (the official name for Awadh at the time) and Bengal, had been excluded from the list of 'martial races' the Raj had prepared for recruitment into the army. And when another Chitpavan, Vasudev Balwant Phadke, conducted a series of raids on colonial assets in the Deccan with the help of locals and burnt some state-owned buildings in 1879, the British saw confirmation of the opinion of former governor Mountstuart Elphinstone that the Maratha Brahmans were an 'intriguing, lying, corrupt, licentious and unprincipled race'. The incumbent Bombay governor Richard Temple added his own echo to this stereotypical view when he hinted that the invisible hand behind Phadke's raids was that of the Ranade group.

Phadke died in British captivity in Aden only a few months before Savarkar's birth. By then the anxiety caused to the regime by the Chitpavans had grown bigger. Two brilliant men – Bal Gangadhar Tilak and Gopal Ganesh Agarkar – had joined hands with the iconic Chiplunkar to start a school for Indians in Pune and launched two newspapers, *Kesari* (Lion) in

Marathi and *Mahratta* in English. Through Savarkar's infancy and childhood, Tilak and his slowly expanding group – with the exception of the Moderate within them, Gopal Krishna Gokhale, who had joined them in 1886 – advocated a radical line for protection of Indian interests and left no doubt that their endeavours were not those of petitioners but those who demanded rights.

Both Tilak and Gokhale joined the Indian National Congress formed in 1885. It quickly overshadowed the PSS as it was more broadly representative of Indian opinion, and Tilak caused alarm throughout the Empire as he started, through his writings and speeches, pulling down, brick by brick, the wall that had kept the Indian educated elite and the unlettered masses apart. By the time the schoolboy Savarkar was reading about the Chapekars in the papers, Tilak had so comprehensively listed the offences racked up by the Raj and generated so much resonance – and Indian self-confidence and self-respect – with his public celebrations of the Shivaji and Ganesh festivals that a panicky administration booked him for sedition, holding his writings responsible for inciting the Pune killings, and sentenced him to eighteen months in prison.

Tilak, the biggest hero for the nationalist-minded Savarkar, would go on to define an epoch, but the subscription the teenager had won to the weekly *Kaal* made him look up to another intrepid journalist, Shivram Mahadev Paranjpe. His paper went where even the leonine *Kesari*, cagey about supporting political assassinations, did not: the Chapekars were not murderers but martyrs, it said. This was exactly the argument Savarkar was making in discussions with friends.

While doing the rounds of the Nasik hospital to deliver

lunch boxes for his plague-ridden brothers, he got acquainted with one of the hospital's officials, T. Mhaskar. Though Mhaskar was thirty and Savarkar all of sixteen, they got on really well as they had common interests; the friendship was cemented when Savarkar found out that Mhaskar wrote pieces for *Kaal* under a pseudonym and shared his political beliefs. Mhaskar introduced the boy to another similar-thinking state staffer, R.K. Pagey. Both Mhaskar and Pagey had limited their political activities, despite their proclivities, to participation in the Shivaji and Ganesh festivals. The precocious Savarkar suggested that was inadequate and came up with the idea of setting up a secret society.

Savarkar saw the Indian National Congress and its British leaders like Allan Octavian Hume (and later Henry Cotton) as lethally submissive to the Raj – mere plea-makers rather than aggressively demanding and claiming rights for Indians. Hume, he felt, wanted the Congress as a 'safety valve' for the regime so that Indians could get to voice their grievances and remain caught up in the dream of social and constitutional reform, bogged down by bureaucratic and procedural niceties, and nothing else. Tilak was of the view that militancy, not begging, was the need of the hour and force was the only language the imperialists understood, but he could not openly advocate violent methods as he was a mainstream leader who would have to stay overground in order to lead the masses, distinct from Gokhale and some others who appealed mainly to the elite. What Tilak couldn't say and do, a secret group must, Savarkar argued.

Mhaskar and Pagey agreed. So did Ram and Waman Datar, brothers in the family the Savarkars had come to live with in Nagarkar lane in Nasik, and their neighbours, the Vartak siblings Nana and Tryambak. The idea was crystallized during the friends' visit to a local theatre on the first day of the twentieth century. News arrived in the middle of the play that the militant Natu brothers, deemed close to the Chapekars, had been released from jail, and Savarkar and his pals requested the organizers to stop the performance for a few brief speeches hailing the Natus' release. A couple of elderly regional satraps who were present shot down the suggestion, prompting the group led by Savarkar to march out in protest. The same evening, the group formed its own clandestine organization called the Mitra Mela (Friends' Society) with the aim of overthrowing British rule.

The Datar and Vartak siblings were roughly the same age as Vinayak and Babarao. Soon, more boys from Nagarkar lane joined in. One of them was Aaba Darekar, the disabled son of a single mother who worked as a servant in the neighbourhood. Darekar couldn't write but loved composing poems; he would recite them, and some other boy would put them down in writing for the record. He was curious about Savarkar because, like him, the Bhagur boy was into poetry and had a way with words. A strong bond developed between the two, with Savarkar teaching the unschooled kid the Devanagari alphabet and lending him his dictionary for use. Darekar was, to an extent, in awe of Savarkar owing to the range of his vocabulary, and Vinayak admired his friend's prodigious natural talent.

Nagarkar lane was narrow and dark, and within it lay an even darker and more congested alley, called Tilamandeshwar. It had ten houses in all, not a single one of them remotely spacious or comfortable. The group's initial meetings were held here until they settled on a passage right at the end of the alley for their conversations as it was farthest from the main road and safest for being out of earshot. The group decided to meet on Saturday and Sunday evenings to have discussions, hold readings on key subjects and make speeches. Individual members were assigned stuff to read or talk about, topics for general discussion were chosen in advance so that no one came unprepared, and Vinayak, as founder-leader, usually made the speeches.

In one of his earliest speeches in that cramped space, Savarkar said petitions by Moderate nationalists would get Indians jobs but not sovereignty, and Tilak's methods (then called Extremist) would get them some rights but not the fundamental right to freedom that guarantees all other rights. Unlike the Moderates, who were all too happy with minor concessions made by the British to Indians over a period of time, Tilak was demanding immediate benefits and pushing for self-governance, but that he did not make a direct call to arms meant that the 'vast engine of oppression',[7] as Tilak called the Raj, could not be smashed at once by dealing it a single, devastating blow.

Savarkar was advocating more extreme methods than what Tilak professed publicly. 'If we have a poisonous tree, would it help to simply cut off some branches? Shouldn't the tree itself be uprooted?' he asked. Their secret society, however, was grateful to both nationalist factions, he insisted, for they had pushed the country in the direction of freedom.[8]

The Mitra Mela's first major activity was to organize the Shivaji festival in Nasik that year, in honour of the seventeenth-century Maratha hero who posed the biggest challenge to the Mughal Empire, crowned himself an independent Hindu sovereign and unleashed a political force that established itself as India's foremost in the eighteenth century. This was followed by the celebration of the Sarvajanik [public] Ganeshotsav. In an address during the Shivaji celebrations, Savarkar asserted that the Maratha hero represented what they wanted – complete independence; if they were looking for someone who desired 'rightful pensions' and other 'concessions', then their adulation of Shivaji would have to be replaced by adulation for the dissolute Bajirao II, who had heralded the end of Maratha rule. This kind of talk was both witty and unsettling, and it helped bring the group slowly to people's notice in the temple town. The Mitra Mela's public visage was that of a fervent celebrator of native festivals, and at its private core was a secret goal. Its founder coined for it the slogan 'Swatantrya-Lakshmi ki Jai', hailing the goddess of freedom and hoping for a swift end to chants of 'God Save the King'. Recited during festivals, Savarkar's ballads on Shivaji's lieutenants Tanaji Malusare and Baji Prabhu Deshpande, who laid down their lives for an independent kingdom, and Darekar's ballad on Shivaji's killing of Bijapur general Afzal Khan and Lord Ram's war on Ravan became a minor sensation in Nasik, and those who felt particularly stirred by the renderings and went up to Savarkar for a chat formed the catchment area for recruiting more members to the hush-hush group.

Then plague struck again and continued into 1901 as Savarkar entered his matriculation year of school. Initially he and his friends tended to some of the sick, helped carry a number of victims to the local crematorium and sometimes even helped with the last rites. They found themselves totally shaken when they had to cremate one of their own, the good-natured government functionary Mhaskar, who had always been jokingly described by Savarkar as 'plague-proof'. After Mhaskar's death his friend Pagey too died, and Savarkar was left with the queasy feeling that he was now the only one of the 'core group of three' to be still alive.

His doubts about the group's survival were dispelled during a temporary shift to his maternal uncle's place in Kothur outside of Nasik in the plague season. There, he succeeded in opening a local branch of the Mitra Mela by roping in a few youngsters. Those in Nasik too regathered once the epidemic ended and Savarkar returned. Quietly one night, they put up posters across town to protest against a function to be held in honour of King Edward, who had ascended the throne following Victoria's death. Savarkar scathingly referred to a resident pandit's Sanskrit poem lauding the new king as 'pearls thrown before swine'.[9]

From the age of twelve Savarkar had become a stickler for exercise. When in Bhagur he mainly did the suryanamaskar. In Nasik at the age of sixteen, though still reed thin, he began working out with dumb-bells and bars, did sit ups and learnt the malkhamb, the traditional Indian art of climbing a vertical teakwood pole. Swimming came naturally to most boys in the town, growing up as they did next to the mighty Godavari, and Vinayak loved plunging into its waters and climbing the hills in the region with his friends. There was much light banter and leg pulling during these excursions and, according to Savarkar, visitors to a temple in the vicinity of Nagarkar lane often had all sorts of things hurled at them by the boys from a small terrace. Not everything was hurled either: blobs of spit were released ever so gently, with a singular focus on finding the intended target.[10]

The Mitra Mela's unwritten constitution demanded a certain

level of fitness of its constituents in order to prepare them for prison terms and police harassment and torture. It also underscored the importance of education, so that the cause of India's liberation could get powerful arguers regardless of the careers they would take up. (Lists of members and dates of meetings and their resolutions maintained by Savarkar were later destroyed following a police crackdown.)

Savarkar had developed his own, fixed, pattern of studying. He would read non-course-related material through the year and pick up books on his syllabus a couple of months before the exams. He followed the same pattern in his matriculation year: he spent most of his time absorbed in the Marathi poet Moropant's works (accessed in the Nasik Civic Library), the histories of various nations, Marathi translations of sociologist-philosopher Herbert Spencer's writings (he read the English originals in London some years later) and James Mill and Jeremy Bentham's theory of utilitarianism.[11] In the meantime, despite his desire not to join the colonial bureaucracy, he cleared the public service exams ahead of his final exams so that if the family situation forced his hand, he could take up the job of mamlatdar, a revenue official in charge of a subdistrict. Besides, he wanted to study further in Pune and the job could help fund the fees. He had written to one of his idols, the *Kaal* editor Paranjpe in Pune, asking him if he would give him a job at his press or even as an office assistant so that he could avoid a government job, but there was no reply.

Before he could decide on a way forward, Savarkar's maternal uncle landed up in Nasik and told him he had fixed his marriage to the daughter of an acquaintance. Yamuna was the girl's name, the uncle said. Her father, R. Trimbak (or Bhaurao) Chiplunkar, was the dewan or chief treasury and administrative official in the princely state of Jawhar, in whose palatial home Vinayak and Babarao had stayed for a few days during their visit to Pune.

This was a time-honoured tradition of fixing marriages, without consulting either boy or girl. Yet Vinayak offered a certain amount of resistance, saying he needed to concentrate on his exams. After some pushing, however, he relented, on the condition that his prospective father-in-law would help fund his college education. Bhaurao Chiplunkar was happy to do that. And so, at the age of nineteen, Vinayak married Yamuna in Nasik, wrote and cleared his matriculation exams in Mumbai and obtained admission to Fergusson College in Pune. Vinayak's father-in-law kept the funds flowing till he got his bachelor's degree. Chiplunkar too did not blindly toe the Raj's line: he opposed the move to send Jawhar's orphaned ten-year-old prince Yeshwantrao Mukne to England for education and later berated the prince's little daughter Asharaje's Anglo-Indian nanny for bandaging her knees badly.[12] For his part, the son-in-law Vinayak, while in Pune, lived frugally and dispatched to the Chiplunkars regular and detailed accounts of his expenses though no one had asked for it.

When the college accepted him, Vinayak's mind was filled with conflicting emotions. He was thrilled, as Pune was the intellectual capital of western India, throbbing with activity of the nationalist variety. Nasik had hoary traditions no doubt, but Savarkar was acutely aware that it had, centuries ago, slipped in terms of significance and was in danger of becoming a town in decay. In contrast, Pune was attracting students not only from the neighbouring districts but from northern and central India, so he could tap into a broader base for his secret society.

And yet, he was overcome with sadness at the thought of imminent separation from his new bride, his brothers and especially his sister-in-law, Yesubai. She had been a pillar of support in a turbulent period for the family. After his mother's death, the image of Goddess Durga in the Bhagur home had for a while acted as some sort of mother figure, but Yesubai had quickly taken up that position with her affections, her unwavering support for him and his brother Narayan, and her steady encouragement. She had helped Vinayak to pick up the pieces after his father's and uncle's deaths and the plague epidemic which had briefly threatened the survival of the household, and in times of difficulty she had provided him with a constant supply of panhe (raw mango juice with a bit of jaggery thrown in) and watermelons – Vinayak's favourites during Nasik's sweltering summers – and thalipeeth, of course, a Maharashtrian delicacy made of gram flour and eaten with a dash of chutney.

Many years later, when Savarkar was locked up in the Andamans, so great was the uncertainty surrounding his return home that some of his mates asked Yesubai to pen her memories of her (then still young) brother-in-law. The troubled woman wrote of how Vinayak had, as a schoolboy, asked her if she could read or write, and on finding out she could not, had proceeded to teach her to write; he also read out newspapers to her in the mornings so that her desire for learning was fulfilled without any delay. 'He gave me the highest respect and ensured I was well looked after,' she wrote.[13]

Yesubai died soon after she had written her memoirs, following a brief illness. When Savarkar received news of her death in the Andamans – he'd had no intimation of her ill-health – he was stunned; it took him a while to recover from the shock.

4

Matchsticks for a bonfire

Before he departed for Fergusson College in Pune in January 1902, Savarkar looked back contentedly at the work done by the Mitra Mela in Nasik over the past two years. Nothing spectacular had been achieved, but they had laid the groundwork for the growth of a revolutionary outfit. They had brought the spirit of the age to everyone's notice in their district and created a stir. People of different castes avoided having food together at the time, even when the question of 'untouchability' didn't arise. But the members of the Mitra Mela – Marathas and Prabhus (kshatriyas), Brahmans and Vaanis (vaishyas) – made a powerful statement by their refusal to accept segregation of seats and insisted on eating together at public functions. In some places orthodox onlookers objected to their having the young poet Darekar eat with them as he was a Dalit, but they had not given in.[1]

The members of the Mitra Mela were not delusional,

Savarkar said. They knew they were a very small bunch and were making plans to take on a mighty foreign power with barely a few sticks at their command. 'But these were matchsticks, and a matchstick, rightly placed, could set off blazing fires and reduce whole empires to ashes,' he told his compatriots. It was no mean feat to have at least spread some awareness that freedom could not be gained without a formidable and united effort; if, say, just two lakh of India's (then) population of thirty crore rose in revolt, the Raj's game would be up, he said.[2]

In Pune he got down to the task of expanding the organization's invisible footprint, tapping fellow students on the campus and in the college hostel where he was staying. He got in touch with students from other educational institutions such as the Deccan College in a bid to win them over to the nationalist cause. The city turned out to be fertile ground for recruitment, which was not surprising, as Tilak, Gokhale, Ranade and other argumentative editors had created an atmosphere of intense political ferment, and in two years the group's membership swelled to 200, going by the count at the Mitra Mela's first conclave in Nasik in 1904. Youngsters from various regions – the island of Mumbai, the Western Ghats around Pune, the town of Solapur in the south and Khandesh in the north – were drawn in. Savarkar had by now sharpened his oratorical and persuasive powers, so the strike rate was good. At least three of those who joined him at this time would go on to acquire national public profiles in their own right: J.B. Kripalani was eventually elected president of the Indian National Congress, B.G. Kher, who also joined the Congress later, became premier of Bombay Province in 1937, and P.M. Bapat gained the honorific 'Senapati' for his spirit as a revolutionary and in subsequent years made a name as a key follower of both the extremist Tilak and the pacifist Gandhi.

At the conclave, Savarkar changed the organization's name to Abhinav Bharat (New India), which sounded far more ambitious than the anodyne Mitra Mela. The renamed body's annual conferences were organized in different regions to give it an inclusive character: so if one year Kothur near Nasik played host, the next year it would be Sion on the margins of Mumbai or a site near Aurangabad in Nizam-ruled Hyderabad. Quite a few meetings were held in modest houses – for example, in the chawl tenements of Shastri Hall near Grant Road in Mumbai or those of Chikhalwadi in nearby Tardeo. By a curious coincidence, a boy from Chikhalwadi was invited in the 1980s to inaugurate a plaque in London in Savarkar's memory. He was no political revolutionary, but by standing up to the most dangerous pace bowling attack in history without a helmet, Sunil Gavaskar inaugurated a little – or as cricket-mad India would say, a not-so-little – revolution of his own: he gave the country's cricket a spine.

Savarkar, like many other leaders of the time, wrote prolifically during his college years for Pune's famously vibrant newspapers and periodicals and, during the year he spent in Mumbai after graduating from Fergusson College to prepare for the London law entrance exams, for a weekly called *Vihari*. He met the *Kaal* editor S.M. Paranjpe, finally, at his Pune office and impressed him with his intelligence and wit and became a close friend of Paranjpe's son Krishna. His poems published at the time drew a lot of attention, and one of them, 'Jayostute', a paean to liberty's patron goddess, subsequently set to music by Hridaynath Mangeshkar, brother of India's favourite singer of the post-Independence era, Lata, continues to be played on big occasions in his home state in the twenty-first century. He won the first prize in a poetry contest for his lament on the state of widows in Hindu society and topped an essay competition with his take on why historical figures ought to be feted by society.

But not everyone found Savarkar and his associates' unapologetically assertive patriotism to their liking. A Mumbai-based lawyer and Tilak aide, D.A. Khare was so discomfited by the ballads for Tanaji and Baji Prabhu sung by Savarkar's friends at Raigad fort during the Shivaji celebrations in the early 1900s that he asked Tilak to wind up proceedings in view of the blatantly 'unconstitutional' renditions. Tilak did not do so, but told the audience that Khare, chairing the event, wished to leave early as he was exhausted, and S.M. Paranjpe presided over the remainder of the function.

Another luminary, the eminent historian V.K. Rajwade whose contribution to Maratha historiography was seminal, was impressed with Savarkar's skills at a debate in the early 1900s when the latter spoke of the course of Italian history, but Rajwade openly disapproved of his attempts, in the same debate, to bring in the contemporary Indian political context.[3]

Nor did Savarkar have a taste for every light of the freedom movement. A self-proclaimed holy man who had taken the name 'Agamya Guru Paramahansa' and was asking youngsters in Pune to mobilize funds for the fight for freedom was introduced to Savarkar by some of his friends. Savarkar took an instant dislike to the 'saint' and, after abruptly ending a brief conversation with him, told his confidants not to waste time on such 'charlatans'. Some years later the 'guru' was arrested in London for sexual misconduct. Years later, in 1918, the report of a Sedition Committee headed by British judge S. Rowlatt stated, falsely of course, that Savarkar owed to this man his initiation into the revolutionary movement. Just as baselessly, the committee called Savarkar's elder brother, Babarao, the founder of Abhinav Bharat.[4]

The development that made Savarkar, for the colonial authorities, a young man to keep a really close eye on took place in 1905. Viceroy George Nathaniel Curzon's move to set in motion the partition of Bengal in October that year unleashed a storm of protest in that province. Curzon publicly said he wanted 'to rivet the British rule more firmly on to India' and 'postpone the longed-for day of emancipation'.[5] He claimed that the purpose behind dividing Bengal was to make administration easier, as the province, which apart from Bengal then included Bihar, Orissa and Chhota Nagpur, was home to more than a quarter of India's population. But Indians saw in the move a policy of divide and rule: according to the plan, Hindus would become a minority in East Bengal, to which Assam would be joined, and West Bengal would get to keep Bihar, Chhota Nagpur and Orissa and have a Hindu majority, but its Bengali speakers would be far outstripped by those who spoke Hindi and Oriya.

Curzon's move gave the Congress, and especially the Extremists led by Tilak, the opportunity to pull out the twin weapons of Swadeshi and boycott of British goods that would neither breach the limits of constitutional agitation – the Lakshman Rekha set by the Moderates – nor be ineffectual the way measures suggested by the Moderates (petitions, representations and pleadings) had been until then. Tilak had spoken out aggressively in favour of the Swadeshi platform years ago, so when the movement was launched with a boycott resolution passed at a Calcutta Town Hall public meeting on 7 August, he urged Indians to take it across the land. He called upon the people of Maharashtra in particular – Maharashtra here is defined as the broad Marathi-speaking region and not the state that came into being in 1960 – to support their Bengali compatriots by organizing boycotts in every district. The notion of Swadeshi, he stressed, had emanated from Maharashtra, and so many of Tilak's generation cherished vivid memories of its pioneer, the khadi-clad G.V. Joshi or Sarvajanik Kaka of the Poona Sarvajanik Sabha. If the Bengalis had recognized its importance, people of other regions must join hands with them, he said in an editorial in *Kesari* on 22 August 1905[6] and took the protest movement to Mumbai and Pune in spite of the Moderate leader and sitting Congress president Gokhale's desire that it be kept confined to Bengal. Lala Lajpat Rai simultaneously carried it to Punjab, and some prominent Moderates like Surendranath Banerjea too lent their support.[7]

According to Tilak's biographers A.K. Bhagwat and G.P. Pradhan, Tilak did not prefer the 'alternative line' of the revolutionaries to the methods of the Moderates but believed that the revolutionary line was a result of 'the futility of the constitutional effort' that typified the Moderate line. Savarkar was convinced that Tilak was a closet revolutionary who positioned himself as an Extremist respecting constitutional means in order to continue to lead a mass organization like the Congress and stay above ground. Tilak had, in truth, long thought of organizing a 'civil revolt' – that was not as radical or violent as what the revolutionaries wanted but not as vanilla as the methods the Moderates had been pursuing. Tilak saw in the 'Extremist' concepts of Swadeshi and boycott a chance to 'find fresh channels for the energies of the revolutionaries'.[8] He was right, for the revolution-minded in Pune were the first to respond to his call.

Savarkar, along with a few friends, met Tilak and suggested that a bonfire of foreign-made clothes and other foreign material be organized in the city. Tilak was amenable to the idea, provided the youngsters assembled a cartload so the impact could be significant. So Savarkar and the others embarked on a drive to collect clothes and other items and were assisted in this endeavour by the editor of the Marathi paper *Bhaala*, B.B. Bhopatkar, who asked students at his family-run school to pitch in. On 1 October 1905 the students met to work out the details. An intelligence agent of the Bombay police who was present recorded that 'one Savarkar spoke strongly urging his countrymen to despise everything that is English and to abstain from purchasing foreign goods. He suggested that all students should burn their clothes made of English and foreign cloth on Dassera day at Lakdi pool.'[9]

The Pune bonfire of 8 October was 'the highlight of the western Indian movement'.[10] The students led by Vinayak first placed all the collected stuff in a cart near the New Preparatory School and marched through the city wheeling it, with a music band at the head to attract as much attention as possible. While the *Kaal* and *Bhaala* editors accompanied Savarkar and the others from the start of the march, Tilak joined along the route. By the time the march culminated at the Haveli, a deserted spot near Fergusson College, the crowd was 5000-strong. The clothes and other material, which included umbrellas, velvet caps, lead pencils and even buttons, were piled up in a heap in the empty field, and when they were set ablaze, 'the eyes of the spectators sparkled with patriotism'. The Bombay police agent reported that 'the Inspector General of Police was present with the idea of hearing the speeches, but nothing was done until he had left when the leaders remarked that now that the cloud had passed they might begin'. Tilak spoke impressively on why the boycott was necessary. The police agent stated that Tilak had made it clear that 'although it had been proposed to give the European clothes to the poor instead of destroying them by fire, still it was not right to do so from the point of patriotism and religion, as what is bad for one is bad for all'. He told the students 'the boycott had created anxiety in Lancashire and Manchester' and advised them 'to be resolute thereafter in purchasing Swadeshi articles'.[11]

Paranjpe added a dash of his own drama to the occasion. In the middle of his speech, he lifted a jacket from the heap which the flames had still not touched, displayed it to the crowd, searched its pockets to indicate he was looking for the money Britain had drained from India, and contemptuously threw it into the fire, saying that that is where it deserved to be. Tilak, always so good at roping in and enthusing ordinary people, finally urged the crowd to walk around the fire three times, apply ashes to their foreheads and take a vow that they would never again purchase British cloth. The meeting ended with the gathering hailing the great Shivaji with cries of 'Jai'.[12]

This episode – as well as the many other such bonfires that were reported from across India – was described as totally unacceptable by the Raj loyalists, and *Indu Prakash*, a paper that reflected the views of the Congress Moderates, went to the extent of labelling Savarkar 'an ill-tongued messenger'.[13]

Gokhale disliked the term boycott because of its 'unsavoury associations' and felt it conveyed 'a vindictive desire to injure another'. Though he admitted that the stir at an all-India level had been 'immensely effective', he told Congress delegates at its annual session in December 1905 that 'a weapon like this must be reserved only for extreme occasions . . . as it is bound to rouse angry passions on the other side'. Moreover, if only British goods were boycotted, those of other countries could be bought, so how would it help India's own growth, he asked. He sought to differentiate Swadeshi from boycott, saying the former was 'a patriotic and an economic movement' and called its very idea 'one of the noblest conceptions that has ever stirred the heart of humanity'. On a visit to Britain soon after the bonfire, however, Gokhale told the people of that country that Manchester was hurting Indian manufacturing, and a few months later explained to Indians why they needed to embrace their own products. 'Every year about 100 crores worth of goods come to us, and we part with 150 crores . . . If a 100 rupees come into your house every month and 150 rupees go out, will you be growing richer or poorer?' This had been happening year after year to India, for decades in fact, and no country, however rich, could stand such bleeding, he said.[14]

Savarkar's admiring biographer Dhananjay Keer wrote in the 1960s that Mohandas K. Gandhi, a disciple of Gokhale then fighting for the rights of Indians in South Africa, was similarly critical of the boycott movement. That is incorrect. Gandhi praised the boycott agitation in Bengal and wrote that it 'has spread with an intensity never known before'. His fealty still to the British, he stated, 'If the Anglo-Indian administrators, who have really built up the Indian Empire, and who depended for its continuance on the goodwill of the people, were to rise from their graves today, they, in our opinion, would be the first to encourage the boycott agitation, at the same time, conciliating public opinion, which has become so excited. What can be more natural than for the people to wish to clothe themselves, to feed themselves, and to supply their luxuries out of home-grown products and home manufactures?'[15]

But the Fergusson College management was upset that one of its students had taken the lead in organizing the bonfire. It imposed a fine of Rs 10 on Savarkar and expelled him from the college hostel, forcing him, not for the first time, to seek shelter in the house of a family acquaintance. And F.G. Selby, principal of the state-run Deccan College, wrote an article questioning the propriety of students' involvement in such protests.

A furious Tilak issued a rejoinder headlined 'These Are Not Our Gurus' in *Kesari*. While it was natural for a government-run college such as Deccan College to drill into students' minds the idea of mental slavery, he baldly stated, it was incredible that a private institution such as Fergusson, India's first privately run college, had punished a student for participating in the nationwide Swadeshi movement. Tilak had serious authority to comment on Fergusson – not just because he was an educationist himself but because he was one of the college's founders. He, along with his friend the radical social reformer and rationalist Gopal Ganesh Agarkar, had set up the Deccan Education Society in 1884 to start the private college. Tilak had quit the society in 1890 following differences with colleagues such as Gokhale, and the brilliant and sensitive Agarkar had unfortunately died young, but Gokhale, a defender of Swadeshi, was still one of Fergusson's leading lights.

Full of praise for Surendranath Banerjea, Tilak cited the example of the Bengali scholar who was, in his capacity as principal of a private college, imparting lessons on Swadeshi to his students. 'The same thing ought to have happened here, but while Prof Gokhale is defending the boycott movement in Manchester, a student of his own college has been punished for taking part in it!' he wrote.

Tilak questioned the charge of indiscipline made against Savarkar. 'We don't send our children to schools and colleges for them to remain untouched by the national movement. The idea is to actually imbue them with the nationalist spirit. When a guru motivated by selfishness, slavishness or intellectual bankruptcy harasses a student for doing the right thing, he can't be called a guru really, and defying his diktat is not indiscipline. What's going on here is oppression in the name of discipline.'[16]

To Savarkar, this indictment of the rule-enforcers by an era-defining leader and virtuoso of political evisceration was immensely gratifying. Not surprisingly, a few months later, in 1906, after he had completed his graduation and shifted to Mumbai to study law (he had already completed the first year of legal studies at Fergusson College, which allowed undergraduates to take an LLB course simultaneously with arts), it was Tilak that Savarkar reached out to for a recommendation letter. He had learnt of scholarships for Indian students offered by Shyamji Krishnavarma, a London based Indian nationalist, and wished to apply. Two recommendations were needed, and the *Kaal* editor Paranjpe had offered one. Would Tilak please give him the other?

The Extremist leader immediately agreed. Krishnavarma was a fairly well-known man who had, as mentioned earlier, set up and financed India House, a hostel and site for debate in the British capital for Indian students. He edited and published a journal called the *Indian Sociologist* and had decided, early in 1906, along with a Paris-based Indian jewellery trader and fellow nationalist, Sardar Singh Rana, to give students from his homeland scholarships named after Chhatrapati Shivaji, Rana Pratap, Bahadur Shah Zafar and others. Each winner would get a sum of Rs 2000 and would be allowed to live at India House in Highgate. An Oxford postgraduate, lawyer and scholar of multiple languages including Sanskrit, Greek and Latin, Krishnavarma was a Gujarati with radical opinions and considered the Indian National Congress to be slavishly loyal to the crown. Gandhi, who met this fellow Kathiawari in 1906, the same year Savarkar reached London, succinctly described his philosophy when he wrote in *Indian Opinion* that Krishnavarma was for 'complete *swaraj*' and wanted the British to 'quit the country, handing over power to Indians. If they do not do so, the Indians should refuse them all help so that they become unable to carry on the administration and are forced to leave.'[17]

Tilak wrote to Krishnavarma that he was fully aware of the rush of applications he would be dealing with, 'but still, I may state, among the applicants there is one Mr Savarkar from Bombay, who graduated last year and whom I know to be a spirited young man very enthusiastic in the Swadeshi cause, so much so that he had to incur the displeasure of the Fergusson College authorities'.

This naturally resulted in the application being cleared promptly, but Krishnavarma had a condition for anyone who wished to take up the scholarship: he or she must pledge not to take up any government job. Savarkar assured him in writing that he had no intention of serving the colonial administration and, in fact, wanted to do a three-year course in law in London so that he could cast a sharper light on the Raj's unjust ways.

The Gujarati patron then sent across the first instalment of the fund – Rs 400 – to Tilak so that he could hand it over personally to Savarkar. Tilak did that after inviting the young man over to his wada (home) for dinner; the *Kaal* editor too was present. That was the last time Tilak and his young disciple met. Never again would they come face-to-face over the next sixteen years (Tilak died in 1920).

When Savarkar, twenty-three years old, climbed aboard the steamer SS *Persia* in Mumbai on 9 June 1906 and waved goodbye to his wife, Yamuna, their eighteen-month-old son, Prabhakar, and some friends gathered on the pier to see him off, the thought that assailed him was, 'Will I be able to return safely to my motherland in three years' time? And will I be able to meet all my near and dear ones?'[10]

The quietly bobbing steamer anchored in the Bombay dock seemed to have obscured the tumult raging in Savarkar's mind, especially with regard to his wife and little child. He did not give voice to it then, but it rose powerfully to the surface once he was in England.

Savarkar had spent most of his time away from the family

after marriage, having headed to Fergusson College not too long after his wedding and then getting heavily involved in the Swadeshi and broader national movement.

From Pune he had travelled to Nasik intermittently to meet Yamuna, and their son, Prabhakar, was born early in 1905, the year in which Curzon's act of partitioning Bengal triggered an avalanche of protest. Swept up in the agitation, Savarkar had spent some time with the infant, but it was not nearly enough.

Once in England, he allowed himself full expression of his fatherly sentiment through the medium he took to often: poetry. He wrote some verses in which he spoke of his great, overpowering desire to 'soak in the sight'[19] of the boy taking his first baby steps. Just as this desire had gripped his mind, however, Savarkar wrote in the poem addressed to 'Prabhya Priyakara' (Beloved Prabhya, the word 'Prabhya' a shortened one of endearment for Prabhakar), it was time for him to head overseas and endure separation from those closest to his heart. Yet Prabhakar was, even on those foreign shores, continually a 'sweet, invisible presence which gladdened the heart'.[20]

But Savarkar's worst fears of not seeing his son again came true. Prabhakar died suddenly of a bout of measles early in 1909. On learning of his son's death, a shocked Savarkar wrote again from English soil, in a bid perhaps to sublimate his immense grief, that the child would forever remain in his heart, as he had been all the time until then, 'a sweet, invisible presence'.[21]

About the wives of those wedded to revolution too Savarkar had clearly defined ideas. Whether he communicated these to Yamuna, whom he missed dearly as well, we don't know, but he stated that if a radical patriot were to die in the line of duty, his wife should remarry someone worthy of her and her children and live her life to the fullest.[22] Senapati Bapat, Savarkar's fellow revolutionary, took things further: while staying underground after his return from England, and with the British authorities in hot pursuit, Bapat sent two letters, one to his wife and the other to an unmarried male friend, asking the two to get married assuming he was already dead.[23] These thoughts, of advocating the remarriage of a partner on one's death, and remarriage even in anticipation of death, were hugely progressive by the standards of the time.

On the journey to England, Savarkar's cabin was in the bowels of the ship, and when he entered it, he saw a fair, strapping, handsome young man in his early twenties unpacking his stuff. He was an Indian, Harnam Singh of Amritsar, with whom Savarkar would be sharing the cubbyhole. Like Savarkar, Harnam was off to England for legal education, and they soon became friends. Two other friendships developed – with a thirty-year-old Punjabi Hindu whom Savarkar identified in his memoirs only as 'Shistachari' or 'Mr Etiquette' and with 'Keshavananda', also not the man's real name. Shistachari was so named by Savarkar for two reasons: he came from an affluent, Anglicized Punjabi family and was a stickler for English etiquette. The other reason for not identifying either was that Savarkar was writing his account of shipboard life before India gained freedom, and Keshavananda had signed up as the first member of Abhinav Bharat outside India, while Shistachari, though not a member, had helped Savarkar send arms and books from English soil inside bundles of cloth back home; he had even assisted in the translation of revolutionary pamphlets into Punjabi and helped disseminate them throughout Punjab. Shistachari taught Savarkar and the other Indians making their first trip some strict rules of British etiquette, from how to wear a tie to how to hold a fork and knife. Savarkar had never been in favour of vegetarianism, but his surroundings in India had not given him a chance to have eggs, fish and meat. These he tasted on board the ship for the first time. Picking out and separating bones, especially without using one's hands, was initially quite a task, and while Shistachari had instructed him that the knife was to be held in the right hand and the fork in the left and all eating done with the fork, the Indian habit of using the right hand took over subconsciously, with the knife making the occasional cut on the lip.[24]

On one of the ship's ports of call, Marseilles in France, Savarkar stepped ashore and went looking for the hideout that one of his heroes, the Italian revolutionary Mazzini, had used while he was trying to evade capture by the Austrians; Mazzini, in fact, had formed his group Young Italy in Marseilles. A local guide that Savarkar hired told him he had never heard of a man called Mazzini, and a journalist at a local paper, when asked, said tongue-firmly-in-cheek that if he wished to know where Mazzini lived, he would have to check the man's home town in Italy.[25] When Savarkar was back on the ship's deck, he had no idea that the port town he had just visited would, four years down the line, come to be associated with an extraordinary incident in his life.

5

Tumult in London

To the patron of India House, the new lodger seemed the kind of young man he was looking for. He needed no mental conversion; like Krishnavarma himself, he was a strong opponent of the Indian National Congress's appeals to the British sense of justice and fair play and believed Swaraj meant complete self-rule – the total exit of the British – and not the compromise of 'self-government' as defined under the aegis of Empire. Krishnavarma's public chants of 'home rule' – the limited freedom select colonies had been granted while remaining a part of the Empire – and 'passive resistance' were intended to keep Scotland Yard and other agencies at bay and his Indian Home Rule Society legally above board. Much like Tilak, his true personal beliefs were hidden and more radical. But in the year of Savarkar's arrival on British shores, he dropped that facade too: he said if force was the only way total freedom could be had, he saw its use as 'neither immoral nor repugnant'.[1]

For Savarkar too a place more suited than India House would be hard to find in the British capital. There were two main organizations of Indians in London at the time: the East India Association and the British Committee of the Indian National Congress. The East India Association had been founded by Dadabhai Naoroji in 1866 and had subsumed another group formed earlier by Naoroji, the London Indian Society. The association had Indians loyal to the Raj and retired British officials back on home soil as its members, and its chief aims were to discuss issues related to India and provide room for Indians to make representations to the British government. The British Committee of the Indian National Congress was, as its named indicated, the Congress's London branch, and it was also dominated by Britishers and Moderate Indians who had faith in the crown. These groups would not even mention the term 'home rule', as it was linked to Irish rebels then waging a powerful, violent as well as non-violent, struggle against the London government; they feared their allegiance would be thought suspect if they uttered those two words, and they genuinely believed in the beneficence of British rule. Krishnavarma was, along with B.C. Pal, a pioneer in demanding 'home rule' when neither the likes of Congress founders Hume and William Wedderburn, then the dominant leaders of the Congress's British Committee, nor the Extremists in the Congress were talking of it (they would start speaking of it a decade later). Krishnavarma also boldly carried on the masthead of the *Indian Sociologist* a line by Herbert Spencer that read: 'Resistance to aggression is not simply justifiable but imperative.' His other big effort was to promote passive resistance; he told his compatriots that 'it was shameful to assist the foreigner in maintaining his dominion'.[2] Besides, Krishnavarma was aware that youthful energy was sorely needed in his version of the Indian struggle. He already had around him trusted aides such as Sardar Singh Raoji Rana and Madam Bhikaiji Cama. A member of the royal family of Morvi in Kathiawar, Rana had been active in London from 1898 and, in spite of his shift to Paris a few years later to start a jewellery business, his visits to London were so frequent that he was very much a part of India House's inner circle. Cama, the daughter of Mumbai businessman Sorabji Framji Patel and wife of lawyer K. Rustamji Cama, had been appalled by British atrocities during the 1896–97 plague and, after starting off as Dadabhai Naoroji's assistant in the British capital in 1901, had become a keen adherent of the revolutionary ideology. But Krishnavarma was close to fifty, and Rana and Cama were only a few years younger. In Savarkar they felt they had found an ally who could take their mission forward and translate their revolutionary ideas into action.

Soon, other similarly inclined Indian students were drawn to the Highgate address, in part because Krishnavarma had timed the launch of his scholarships well. In 1905 India had had a big upheaval owing to Curzon's policies, and while earlier it was chiefly ICS aspirants or those from affluent families seeking to serve the Raj who had come to London, those with a developed or developing nationalist mindset had now starting streaming in as well, albeit in small numbers (their count rose gradually in later years). Also, some like Virendranath Chattopadhyaya, who had initially thought of qualifying for the ICS, had become imbued with a rebellious spirit. Chatto, as he was known to friends, was the brother of Sarojini Naidu and (future) parliamentarian Harindranath Chattopadhyaya. He came to Britain in 1901–02, switched to studying law after first contemplating a civil service career and became one of the regulars at India House after it opened in 1905. He met Savarkar soon after the latter's arrival in July 1906, and they developed a strong friendship.

The air in London was much less suffocating for these nationalists than India's own: it allowed a certain amount of freedom to express one's views and to move around. Plus, nationalists and revolutionaries from other countries were present there in decent numbers, so cooperation could be sought and obtained. Already, India House inmates had reached out to members of the Irish outfit Sinn Fein and some exiles from Eastern Europe and had met Turkish leader Mustafa Kemal.

Savarkar got himself enrolled at Gray's Inn, formed his own Free India Society to act as an extension of Abhinav Bharat, took to writing a series of 'Newsletters from London' for *Kaal* and took part zealously in the debates and discussions held at the London hostel during weekends. Right from the beginning he had a rapid-fire way of speaking, a habit he would retain all his life, but the pauseless rhetoric, instead of tiring his listeners, evoked a great deal of interest as it was ferocious, buttressed with facts and figures, and it bristled invariably with a satirical enthusiasm. When the venerable Moderate leader Gokhale said, ahead of a debate on the Indian budget in the House of Commons in August 1906, that 'my nation stands expectant', Savarkar sarcastically remarked that it was not at all odd that Gokhale could actually see India's betterment in a debate meant to discuss how much Britain had looted from India in the previous year and how much more it could take. Referring to the 'Beware of Pickpockets' boards he saw plastered all over London, he wondered if similar boards shouldn't be placed across the world 'given Britain's penchant for picking the pockets of entire nations'. When Gokhale assured the British government, after the ouster of a colonial official amid the Bengal partition unrest, that Indian public opinion would now 'come to its normal state', Savarkar marvelled at the Moderate leader's inability to see the bigger picture and his satisfaction with small, irrelevant victories: 'The agitation was all about securing an official's resignation. Not to protest against the loot of crores of rupees every year, or deaths due to drought, or the hellhole of poverty our people are forced to live in.' He urged the Indian National Congress's 'lamb-like' leaders to see that the wolf was at the door, with the Congress's former British patron-presidents like Henry Cotton too denouncing India's demand for self-rule as 'disastrous'. He appealed to Indians to learn from women suffragists who had only recently stormed the British parliament for their rights after their repeated pleas had fallen on deaf ears.

The fiftieth anniversary of the 1857 revolt was a landmark event that would prove to be a turning point for Savarkar in more ways than one. As the anniversary approached and the British papers looked back on that period in some detail, Savarkar did not miss the chance to bait Gokhale once again. He stated that all those columns in print set aside for India were owing to the resistance the country had shown of late, they were not the result of 'the fruitless petitions' of the Moderate 'whiners', and he pointed out that the equipping of a few Lahore youths with lathis by the Punjab leader Ajit Singh that year had produced a far greater effect on the colonizers and the colonized than 'a thousand Gokhale speeches'.[3]

More important, after two meetings by the revolutionaries in May and June 1907 – one to mark the revolt's landmark anniversary and the other to denounce the deportations of Ajit Singh and Lala Lajpat Rai to Mandalay prison – India House would come under intense suspicion. *The Times* criticized the goings-on at India House, and other London dailies branded it 'the den' and 'the beehive' of radicalism. Interception of all correspondence to and from the address commenced, as did the shadowing of prominent lodgers by Scotland Yard sleuths.

Events would soon lead to Savarkar assuming a pre-eminent position at India House. The unfurling of the Indian national flag by Bhikaiji Cama at the International Socialist Congress in Stuttgart on 22 August in the face of fierce opposition from the British contingent accentuated the tensions, forcing Krishnavarma and Cama to shift to Paris and the US respectively (Cama too later moved to Paris).

With their exit Savarkar became the chief propagandist and organizer at India House, and he drew more youngsters into its fold with a charm offensive, in the process swelling the ranks of the Free India Society and Abhinav Bharat too. Among those who signed up to India House were three Tamilians, the scholar V.V.S. Aiyar, the journalist M.P.T. Acharya and the medical student T.S.S. Rajan (who in 1937 became health minister in the Madras Presidency); two Maharashtrians, the law student P.M. Bapat (earlier linked to Savarkar in Pune and later widely known by the honorific 'Senapati') and a judge's son, W.V. Phadke; and two Punjabis, the Oxford student Lala Har Dayal and engineering aspirant Madan Lal Dhingra.

In June 1908 Savarkar passed his law examinations and became a full-fledged lawyer with the right to practice once the governing authorities at the Inn accepted and approved his application. The event was marked in London's *Times*: both Savarkar and Aiyar were in June 1908 mentioned on the list of 106 (out of 142) students who had passed the Inns of Court general examination held that month. They had cleared the same paper, 'Criminal Law and Procedure', and had obtained the same grade, 'Class II', though they were studying at different Inns: Savarkar at Gray's and Aiyar at Lincoln's.[4]

But even after passing his law examinations Savarkar continued to stay at and remained devoted to India House. Around this time, Asaf Ali, an ICS hopeful, also visited India House frequently, and his friend Haider Riza, a winner of Krishnavarma's scholarships, was a lodger. Ali, who went on to become an eminent lawyer and whose wife, Aruna Asaf Ali, unfurled the Indian flag at Mumbai's Gowalia Tank maidan during the Quit India movement, called Savarkar 'the presiding deity' of India House and recounted in later years a curious incident where Riza had 'sought to establish his oratorical supremacy' over the weekend meetings. One Sunday evening 'Savarkar was in the chair and someone set the ball rolling,' he recalled. 'As an experienced debater, Riza waited and spoke last in order to make an impression . . . He appeared to be too histrionic to carry that conviction which pure sincerity with even halting expression and mutilated grammar never fails to do. Savarkar, on the other hand, despite his careless English, had so genuine a ring of sincerity in his speech that he almost always made a memorable impact on the audience.' Riza 'definitely suffered by contrast', Ali said. Riza ultimately moved to Oxford, and gradually Ali's own visits reduced for two reasons: the food at India House, he felt, 'defied description', and the atmosphere, 'surcharged with politics, got on my nerves'.[5]

~

Things at India House would soon take a far more serious turn. Savarkar was not happy with just making speeches and yearned to convert his philosophy into action. He insisted that rhetoric be combined with militant action and chalked out a plan in detail. Broadly, step one was to buy weapons from foreign revolutionaries in exile and ship them off to India. Step two, meant to be simultaneous, was to learn how to make small bombs and open factories in India for their manufacture. Step three involved the cultivation of Indian soldiers in the British-controlled Indian army in order to spark a rebellion within its ranks.

Thus, at one of the Sunday meetings, a chemistry student at London University whom we know only by his last name – Desai – lectured the group on the making of bombs, and Bapat and a Bengali revolutionary, Hemchandra Das (later implicated in the Alipur bomb case of 1909), got hold of a Russian-language manual on bomb-making and had it translated into English. Bapat, Das and Hotilal Varma, yet another Alipur revolutionary, set sail for India with several copies of the manual. After the connections between Abhinav Bharat and Bengal's revolutionary outfit Anushilan Samiti were laid bare following eighteen-year-old Khudiram Bose's bomb assault which had killed two Englishwomen in Muzaffarpur and the Maniktala police raid which had led to seizure of bombs from the Calcutta home of Aurobindo Ghose, Bapat succeeded in going underground, but Das and Varma failed to evade the police and were convicted and sentenced. Through his aides, Savarkar sent to India a bunch of Browning automatic pistols, sometimes through French-controlled Pondicherry and Portuguese-ruled Goa, naturally deemed much safer landing points.

Meanwhile, deeply upset by the portrayal of the Rani of Jhansi, Bahadur Shah Zafar and other mutineers of the 1857 uprising as villains in a play on the London theatre circuit, the revolutionaries decided to hold a mass meeting in honour of the 'martyrs' on the revolt's fifty-first anniversary. Invites were sent out to Indians across Britain, and on 10 May 1908 the main hall of India House was overflowing. Youngsters had turned up from Oxford, Cambridge, Reading and Cirencester. The function began with a rendering of the national song 'Vande Mataram' by a group of young girls, and full-throated cries of 'Vande Mataram' – this time as a slogan – emanated from the crowd intermittently through the proceedings as speaker after speaker dwelt on the heroism of the fallen rebels. Savarkar's personal poetic tribute, 'Oh Martyrs', circulated among those present, was a smashing success. Some Britishers had at the time launched a fund for their country's veterans of 1857. The Indians now launched a fund for a memorial for their own heroes. Some students pledged to give up smoking and drinking for a month in order to be able to contribute; others said they would fast on certain days; and still others vowed to stay away from the theatre and other entertainments.

The launch of the martyrs' memorial fund was followed by a flurry of activity. Two students of the agricultural college in Cirencester – the Sikh Harnam Singh and the Muslim R.M. Khan – quit the institution to protest the principal's description of the 1857 revolutionaries as 'murderers'. Both were honoured with silver medals and the title of 'Yaar-e-Hind' by a plucky London-based Punjabi woman, Dhan Singh.

But in 1908 Savarkar made a far more significant contribution to the cause of the 1857 revolt which has stood the test of time. Three months after his arrival in London in 1906 he had completed a Marathi translation of the Italian revolutionary Mazzini's autobiography; it had sold more than 2000 copies in India as it had flown under the radar of government censors, and Savarkar's preface, despite its implied meanings, had passed muster. After that he had been busy pounding the streets of London for more than a year and mining records at the India Office Library for material on the revolt. The result was the very first account of the uprising from an Indian point of view. The title of the book, written in Marathi and later translated into English (by W.V. Phadke and V.V.S. Aiyar) and into French (by Cama and M.P.T. Acharya), was *The First Indian War of Independence*. In it Savarkar vigorously contested the colonial theory of a mere 'sepoy' rebellion and hailed the uprising as an outstanding example of Hindu–Muslim unity. He cited mainly English sources to corroborate his arguments. In 1909 Scotland Yard obtained the still-unpublished first chapter through a mole – a Maratha by the name of Kirtikar – whom it had planted inside India House.

Kirtikar's first name remains unknown, but what we do know is that he was about thirty years old and had earlier worked as a translator in the Bombay High Court. He was recruited as a spy and given a year's leave to be in London, where he was told to take up lodgings at India House. He met Savarkar there without any letter of introduction and told him in their common language, Marathi, that he was from an aristocratic Maratha family. He was going to study dental surgery, he claimed. Savarkar accepted him as a lodger at India House without reservation, and Kirtikar even took admission to a dentistry course at a London institute. He would go out every morning and return late in the evening. That he was a spy was later discovered by Savarkar's comrades Aiyar and Rajan. But by then Kirtikar had done much damage.

Scotland Yard also got to know, perhaps from Kirtikar again, that a copy of Savarkar's yet-unpublished book had gone out to his brother Babarao in Nasik. The text was, in July 1909, immediately proscribed in India under the Customs Act, earning the distinction of becoming one of the earliest twentieth-century books to be banned even before it was published. Savarkar protested vehemently that pre-publication proscription, legal or not, was indubitably unfair.[6]

There was no ban on the text in Britain itself – the colonizers had one set of rules for the homeland and another for a colony. This is what made London such an ideal ground for the revolutionaries. While the civil liberties of Indians could be short-circuited by the British anywhere, it was harder to do that in London.

But no printer in London would touch the manuscript. Attempts to print the book in France and Germany also failed, but the owner of a press in Holland finally agreed in the second half of 1909, and some copies were smuggled into India, allowed in at the ports because they came bearing beautiful dust-jackets of Charles Dickens's *Oliver Twist*, *David Copperfield* and *Great Expectations*.

Quite a few reviewers of the time criticized Savarkar's ornamental style of writing, and those loyal to the crown in particular had a problem with its content. London's *Times* felt that the book was 'in its way a very remarkable history of the Mutiny, combining considerable research with the grossest perversions of facts and great literary power with the intensest bitterness'.[7] Yet the book profoundly stirred Indian emotions. Those inclined towards revolution were evidently impressed, but so too were those like Jawaharlal Nehru, at the time pursuing his education in Britain and warned by his father, Motilal, not to involve himself in political activities. A student of Trinity College in Cambridge, Nehru never set foot inside India House but described Savarkar's account of 1857 as 'a brilliant book though it suffers from proxility and want of balance occasionally'. Well after his return to India and plunge into the freedom struggle, Nehru wrote, 'I have often felt that a new edition [of Savarkar's book], more concise and with many of the oratorical flights left out, would be an ideal corrective to the British propaganda about the events of 1857.'[8]

~

After the anniversary of the 1857 revolt, Lokmanya Tilak's imprisonment in Mandalay in July 1908 for six years on charges of sedition for allegedly inflammatory writings in *Kesari* and the clampdown on many other editors, including Paranjpe of *Kaal*, united all shades of Indian opinion – revolutionary, Extremist and Moderate – in the UK, and provided fresh energy to the Indians in London. At a joint meeting, they condemned the curtailment of press freedoms. The only Indian leader then visiting England who refused to attend the meeting was Gokhale, and Savarkar accused him bluntly of a 'lack of civility'. Soon afterwards, a crackdown began on the Indian 'sedition-mongers' in the UK, but quiet compliance from the Indians was still not easily forthcoming. When the train carrying Tilak's aide G.S. Khaparde, who was set to make an appeal for Tilak's release, entered London station, the welcome from the sizeable Indian crowd gathered on the platform was riotous, with cheers and slogans renting the air. The Bengali Extremist leader B.C. Pal too was in the British capital, and Indians turned up in substantial numbers every day to listen to his series of lectures at Caxton Hall; during one of these lectures, Cama, who had come down from Paris, once again unfurled the national flag.

To pacify inflamed Indian sentiment, some Britishers with long-time links to the subcontinent organized a meeting of Indians and Europeans at the same venue, Caxton Hall. Here Lord Lamington, the former governor of Bombay, was heckled and booed as he was holding forth on the Raj's 'noble intentions'. The *Daily Chronicle* reported that 'the hissing and the derisive laughter were tremendous, and the chairman had to call for order'. The *Evening Standard* wrote of 'grossly seditious leaflets' being sent out to India in large quantities 'by Indian residents in England . . . to sow among their young men the seeds of rebellion' and accused the Home Department of very poor vigilance. And Valentine Chirol, the highly influential foreign correspondent of *The Times* whose writings often had a bearing on determining British policy, concluded, after a conference of Indian nationalists in December 1908 had passed resolutions for complete freedom and boycott of British goods and two Bengali youths, Kunjalal and Basudeb Bhattacharya, had assaulted an India Office administrator, William Lee Warner, early in 1909, that it was the Maratha Brahmans who were at the root of all the trouble. 'The emotional Bengalee calls along the whole world to witness his deeds. The Chitpavan Brahmin, whose bent of mind is far more practical, works in silence, and he persists . . . Even in Bengal, the Bengalees did the shouting; it was Poona that provided the brains that directed the Bengalee extremists,' he wrote.[9]

The steady build-up of events resulted in the assassination of Curzon Wyllie on 1 July 1909. That the killing came twenty-three days after Savarkar's brother Babarao was sentenced to life for publishing seditious poems has caused some speculation among historians. Some have suggested that Vinayak 'swore revenge on the British' on hearing of his brother's conviction.[10] That might indeed have worked as a trigger of sorts, but the fact is that the revolutionaries were anxiously looking to strike as the Indian sentiment then aroused was fast reaching fever pitch, and in the absence of a hit any time soon, they would have found it hard to sustain morale within their group. We also know that Madan Lal Dhingra had sought to make an attempt on Lord Curzon's life in London on the day Babarao was sentenced (8 June). Dhingra went to the Colonial Institute, where Curzon was to preside over a meeting, but returned disappointed because he reached late and found the gates shut.

News of Babarao's sentencing reached London only the next morning.

Another reason for the urgent offensive, though Morley's political aide-de-camp was a far less spectacular target than Lord Curzon, may have been internal dissension. India House members were increasingly getting divided. In May the hostel's resident members were down to four, and many of the visitors had not paid their basic minimum subscription fees. News of Babarao's conviction certainly helped to bury differences and galvanize the group. Savarkar was satisfied that Wyllie's assassination had not just united the India House band once again but also overshadowed all other subjects of discussion across the British Isles and captured a huge amount of space in the press. 'Leave alone other topics, even discussion on the game of cricket has stopped,' he wrote.[11]

A rare few Britishers also came out in support of Dhingra. The British anarchist and socialist Guy Aldred, who would soon be arrested along with Arthur Borsley and handed a one-year sentence as printer of the 'inflammatory' *Indian Sociologist*, was a fearless advocate for the rights of colonized peoples. He also wrote regularly for Krishnavarma's journal and, amid the outrage surrounding Wyllie's killing, minced no words while denouncing what he saw as Britain's hypocrisy. He said 'the British Government glories in its association with the Czar, the cowardly murderer of many, whilst executing Dhingra, the political assassin of one', and called it 'the duty of the English military rank and file to refuse to bear arms equally against the Indians, the Egyptians . . .'

This withering verbal strike against the Raj was much after Savarkar's own heart. But among those who disapproved absolutely of any kind of violence, however, was the leader of the Indians in South Africa, his status reinforced by a third prison term he had just completed in Pretoria.

~

Mohandas K. Gandhi came to London on 10 July, nine days after Wyllie's assassination, and termed it 'a terrible thing'. Going further, in an article for *Indian Opinion*, Gandhi wrote that Dhingra had 'acted like a coward. All the same, one can only pity him. He was egged on to do this act . . . It is those who incited him to this that deserve to be punished . . . Mr Dhingra himself is innocent. The murder was committed in a state of intoxication. It is not merely wine or *bhang* that makes one drunk; a mad idea also can do so.' Afraid that 'some Indians will commend this murder', the proponent of peaceful civil disobedience roundly criticized the revolutionaries and their sympathizers. 'Those who believe and argue that such murders may do good to India are ignorant men indeed . . . Even should the British leave in consequence of such murderous acts, who will rule in their place? The only answer is: the murderers . . . Under such a rule, India will be utterly ruined.' Gandhi was also sure that those who had incited the youngster 'will be called to account in God's court, and are also guilty in the eyes of the world'.[12]

Promptly after Wyllie's killing, the sleuths of Scotland Yard put the locks on India House – now described by *The Times* as the headquarters of 'the most dangerous organisation outside India'.[13] When a crowd of indignant Englishmen marched in protest to B.C. Pal's lodgings, where Savarkar had moved after the controversial hostel had been shut, the young radical was compelled to leave from there as well. For the next few months Savarkar moved from one minor lodging house to another, worrying somewhat that B.C. Pal's tone towards the British seemed to have moderated. There was no evidence to pin Dhingra's crime on him even though the Secret Service had been maintaining a file on Savarkar from 1907, but his reputation as the hostel's leading spokesperson, his public opposition to the resolution condemning Dhingra and the lurking doubt that his influence hung heavy over the condemned man's statement published by the *Daily News* meant that Gray's Inn was going to think twice before taking him in. Savarkar had cleared his bar exams already, but the benchers of the Inn – that is, members of the advisory panel that formed the Inn's governing body – at a meeting held on 14 July, resolved that he was not 'eligible for call to the Bar'[14] and instituted an inquiry to find out if he was indeed instigating Indians to launch an armed rebellion. Nothing came of the investigation, yet the authorities communicated to Savarkar that he would not be permitted to practise until they were fully convinced that he was keeping his distance from all kinds of suspicious activities. Savarkar was bereft of both support and shelter: Tilak was away in a prison in Burma, Pal didn't want him at his place in London and hardly anyone was lobbying or speaking up for him in official and unofficial quarters.

So Savarkar shifted to a place 'over a small and dirty Indian restaurant in Red Lion Passage', which David Garnett, Savarkar's eighteen-year-old friend, described as one of the filthiest slums in London. He was joined there by Sukhsagar Dutta, 'who had quarrelled with Mr Pal'. It was Dutta who had introduced the British teenager to Savarkar. The budding young writer had at once been struck by the Maratha's 'broad cheekbones', his 'refined mouth and an extremely pale skin, which was almost as pale as ivory on the forehead and cheekbones but darker in the hollows'. Witness to a meeting where Savarkar read to a very small group from his book on 1857, Garnett thought that 'his was the most sensitive face in the room and yet the most powerful. I watched how he spat out his words, with almost convulsive movements.'

Coincidentally or not, Garnett had arranged to have food five days a week at the Red Lion Passage lodging house where Savarkar had moved and had paid the Jewish owner four shillings per week for the purpose. So he was able to form deeper impressions of the Indian. Garnett wrote:[15]

> There was an intensity of faith in the man and a curious single-minded recklessness which were deeply attractive to me. The filthy place in which he was living brought out both his refinement and also his lack of human sympathy, both characteristic of the high-caste Brahmin. The windows of the room which Dutt[a] and Savarkar shared as a sitting-room looked across the narrow, filthy alley of Red Lion Passage . . . In the room opposite lived an appalling slattern with four young children. Often she was screaming, frequently drunk, sometimes one could see her through the open window, lying insensible upon the floor.
>
> Dutt[a] often spoke of her and her children with horror and pity. But Savarkar was indifferent to her existence and indeed oblivious to his environment. He was wrapped in visions. What was his vision then? . . . I believe it was that

> India was a volcano, which had erupted violently during the Mutiny and which could be made to erupt again . . . until Indians regained their manliness and their mother country her freedom. All the sufferings involved were but a fitting sacrifice to her.

Despite their starkly different opinions about how best to fight the good fight against injustice, Gandhi and Savarkar met in London in October that year and developed what the Mahatma later recalled were 'pleasant relations'. On the occasion of Dussehra, a feast was organized by the local Indian community for the first time, and Gandhi was requested to preside over it at Nizamuddin's Indian restaurant in Bayswater. Savarkar was invited as one of the prominent speakers. Asaf Ali was one of some hundred-odd young Indians who turned up. Introducing Savarkar to those gathered, Gandhi spoke of his 'selflessness and patriotism' and hoped that India would benefit from these qualities for all time to come. He extolled the virtues of his favourite mythical figure, Ram, on the day that marks the victory of Ram over Ravan, but Ali recorded that Gandhi's speech 'was very brief – just a dozen sentences or so – and tepidly moderate'. The would-be Mahatma 'concluded abruptly with the words, "I should not like to stand between you and the speaker of the evening, Mr Savarkar."'

Savarkar was then of the same opinion as Gandhi on the issue of Hindu–Muslim relations: he felt that peace and unity were both possible and desirable. As Gandhi's biographer Robert Payne later wrote, 'It was perhaps the only belief they held in common.' It was as if Savarkar's vandalism at a mosque in Bhagur had been a childhood aberration, the cause of it nothing but momentary mass hysteria triggered by the communal violence of 1894–95. As a matter of fact, Savarkar had in his revolutionary avatar first in Nasik and Pune and subsequently in London consistently and unswervingly called for Hindu–Muslim togetherness; his sole enemy, he emphasized, was the Raj. 'Hindus are the heart of Hindustan,' Savarkar said in his forty-five-minute-long speech that evening. 'Nevertheless, just as the beauty of the rainbow is not impaired but enhanced by its varied hues, so also Hindustan will appear all the more beautiful across the sky of the future by assimilating all that is best in the Muslim, Parsi, Jewish and other civilizations.'[16] Asaf Ali came away from the function thinking that Savarkar's speech had been 'dazzlingly brilliant' and the comparison of the Ram–Ravan conflict with India's own struggle against British rule 'dexterous'.[17] Savarkar, in his own report on the event for *Kaal*, returned Gandhi's generous compliment for him by describing the South Africa-based lawyer-leader as a 'desh bhakt'.[18]

On his way back to Cape Town, the Dhingra case and the overall approach of the Indian revolutionaries in London seemed to be uppermost on Gandhi's mind. For, on the steamer, he wrote in precisely nine days *Hind Swaraj* (Indian Home Rule), a sixty-page book which spelt out his vision for his homeland. It contained twenty imagined dialogues between the Editor, Gandhi himself, and the Reader. The Reader, who was modelled on the Mahatma's benefactor Dr Pranjivan Mehta, then living in London, is a believer in violent tactics, and he tells the Editor that his preferred route to freedom is by assassinating a few Englishmen and striking terror, then getting a few armed men to fight openly and following that up with guerrilla warfare. The struggle would entail great sacrifices, he says. The Editor responds in the spirit of chastisement, telling the Reader that people like him 'want to make the holy land of India unholy', and asks with plain disbelief, 'Do you not tremble to think of freeing India by assassination?'

In the book, Gandhi also denounced the railways which, he is convinced, will only help to spread plague and famine owing to the speed of travel, denounces doctors for their surgical practices and affirms the ideals and centrality of village life as against the 'satanic', increasingly urban western civilization. But the text is mostly remembered and referred to in the twenty-first century not so much for Gandhi's attack on industrialization as far his espousal of the non-violent way of life.

Savarkar had his own reply to make. He wrote in November 1909, 'We feel no special love for secret organizations or surprise and secret warfare . . . It would be . . . a crime to talk of revolution when there is a constitution that allows the fullest and freest development of a nation. Only because you deny us light, we gather in darkness to compass means to knock out the fetters that hold our Mother down. You rule by bayonets . . . It is a mockery to talk of constitutional agitation when no constitution exists.' He also believed that Gandhi's method of non-violent resistance was sure to fail 'because it presupposes all men to be selfless and [that they] will not cooperate with the aggressor'. Perhaps worse, it 'blindly presumes that the aggressor has a high sense of morality'.[19]

~

Scotland Yard detectives were meanwhile unrelenting in piling up pressure on Indian agitators and especially on Savarkar, convinced that he was deeply implicated in the Dhingra affair. The strain of being shadowed and of anxious movement from one lodging house to another told on Savarkar's health, and he decided to travel down to the seaside sanctuary of Brighton for a bit of a breather. There, staring at the waves that hit the shores, he gave uninhibited expression to his mental and emotional landscape. With his friend B.C. Pal's son Niranjan or 'Nanu' by his side, he composed a Marathi poem in which he gently and movingly asked the sea to deliver him to the shores of his matrubhoomi or motherland. There was, he wrote, a terrible restlessness, an impatience in his soul, for a glimpse of his own land. The poem would prove to be his most celebrated and most enduring. Set to music in post-Independence India by the composer Hridaynath Mangeshkar and rendered by all four of the illustrious Mangeshkar sisters – Lata, Asha, Usha and Meena – it acquired a unique position in the historical and cultural memory of Maharashtra.

While the authorities in Britain had Savarkar on alert, in India things were no less tense for his family. In November 1909, a few days before Babarao's appeal against his life sentence was rejected, two bombs were hurled at the carriage of Viceroy Lord Minto in Ahmedabad but failed to explode. On 21 December, the Nasik collector and district magistrate A.M.T. Jackson was shot dead by a youth from Aurangabad, Anant Kanhere, when he entered a local theatre to witness a performance by the celebrated thespian Bal Gandharva. Jackson was a distinguished Sanskrit and Marathi scholar and conversed with locals in Nasik in their own language. For this, many

Indians even called him the 'good topiwala',[20] but he had also been responsible for arresting and prosecuting Babarao Savarkar even as he had released from custody an Englishman accused of shooting an Indian for paucity of evidence. The correspondent for London's *Times* reported that Jackson's killing, 'which is indubitably political, follows with sinister rapidity upon the sentence of transportation for life upon Ganesh Damodher Savarkar'. 'This Savarkar,' the correspondent wrote, 'has a brother, who made himself notorious in London.'[21] *The Observer* suggested that the actual assassin, once again 'a decadent youth', seemed to be 'the tool of more subtle and cowardly villains'.[22]

Savarkar was recovering from an attack of pneumonia at a sanatorium in Wales when he heard of the killing. Shortly afterwards he got to know that he had been named prime conspirator in the Jackson murder and his brother Narayan had been implicated in the bid to kill Lord Minto.

The British appeared to have obtained, finally, the piece of hard evidence they had been looking for against the pre-eminent Indian 'conspirator' in their own capital. Savarkar had, in 1908, as briefly mentioned earlier, dispatched twenty Browning pistols to India with the cook at India House, Chaturbhuj Amin, 'a short thick-set young man, very dark, with protruding eyes and short fat fingers adorned with several rings'. One look at him, and David Garnett, the young English friend of the revolutionaries, had 'divined instantly' that he was 'an unpleasant fellow, and directly he spoke to me I knew that I was right'. One of the pistols was recovered from the house of an accused in the Jackson murder, and his questioning led the cops to Amin. He was arrested and quickly became an approver – in simple terms, a participant in a crime who, in addition to admitting his role, agrees to give evidence against his accomplices in order to establish their guilt and get for himself a lenient sentence. Amin told the police that Vinayak Savarkar had handed over the pistols to him. 'I was disgusted to hear that Savarkar should have trusted him [Amin],' Garnett later wrote.

During the police investigation, a bomb manual was found at Babarao's house in Nasik; it contained, among other things, the formula for the explosives that had been seized from Aurobindo Ghose's garden house in Maniktala, Calcutta.

Days later, CR or Chanjeri Rao, a policeman from Coimbatore in service of the Raj, landed on the Mumbai coast after a brief stay in London. A search of his trunk revealed he was carrying 'seditious' pamphlets. They had been given to him by Savarkar, he told the police. Savarkar had administered the oath of secrecy to him and told him that he could be highly useful to their group as a member of the police department, Rao told his interrogators. One of the pamphlets seized from him was titled *Vande Mataram*. 'The pamphlet strongly advocates political assassination in India,' the Bombay police stated in their report, 'and whether or not it is from the pen of Vinayak Savarkar, it, at all events, represents doctrines which he was anxious to disseminate in India.' The pamphlet was truly a crisp explainer of the aims of the revolutionaries. 'Terrorise the officials, English and Indian, and the collapse of the whole machinery of oppression is not very far,' it said. 'The persistent execution of the policy that has been so gloriously inaugurated by Khudiram Bose, Kanailal Dutt and other Martyrs will soon cripple the British Government in India. This campaign of separate assassinations is the best conceivable method of paralysing the bureaucracy and of arousing the people.' Rao confessed that the idea of the 'anarchists' was 'to continue political assassination until the (general) revolution takes place in about two or three years'.[23]

With the net closing in around him, Savarkar was persuaded by his friends to move immediately to Paris, which he did. There he lived for a couple of months in Bhikaiji Cama's house at Rue do Ponthieu. Labelled by the British as 'the notorious lady' and by her supporters as 'the de facto mother of the revolutionaries', the feisty Parsi woman took great care of Savarkar and helped him to regain his health and to resume work. From her home he wrote many articles for *Madan's Talvar*, a monthly magazine bearing Dhingra's first name started by Chatto, who himself had moved out of England at the same time as Vinayak and gone on to Berlin. Savarkar also got to move freely around Paris and to meet, in Cama's company, radicals from Russia, Egypt and Turkey.

Then, quite inexplicably, he decided to return to London despite unambiguous advice to the contrary. Cama, Chatto and Krishnavarma all urged him not to go, for Scotland Yard was on the lookout for him. Chatto's brother Harindranath later wrote, 'Viren [Chatto] advised him [Savarkar] against such a step; other friends dissuaded him from such rank stupidity and crass rashness. But Savarkar left nevertheless . . . in the fond confidence that he would be able to live and work there undetected and unsuspected.'[24] The cops apprehended Savarkar the moment he alighted from the Newhaven boat train at the Victoria railway station on 13 March 1910, led him to the waiting room and showed him the arrest warrant.

That he would be caught in London was inevitable, but the

way the arrest was carried out begged a question: had someone tipped off the police in advance about Savarkar's arrival? Harindranath Chattopadhyaya hinted at this when he wrote, while discussing the episode in his autobiography: 'Walls have ears and there are spies everywhere, yes, even in quarters where one least expects to find them. I am here reminded of a high-born well-bred Indian in London who, years ago, betrayed, in a weak moment, some of his very dearest friends for "a mess of pottage." He is now one of India's most well-known sons, after a period of true repentance and the turning over of a new leaf.'[25] Who was this person, 'one of India's most well-known sons'? Harindranath did not reveal.

The other question is: why had Savarkar not heeded the warnings? V.M. Bhat, his aide from the Nasik days, said that some of Savarkar's critics among the revolutionaries had accused him of issuing directives from behind the scenes while the militant acts were carried out by others. Bhat was suggesting that Savarkar wanted to dispel all doubts about his own role by embracing big risks himself. Another theory is that some of the Indian revolutionaries who had stayed back in London told Savarkar that in his absence their group was on the verge of collapse, which is why he was keen to return. A third theory is that Savarkar was mortified at the thought that he was a free man in the beautiful capital of France when his mates in London were doing their utmost to evade arrest and continue their activities, both his brothers were languishing in prison, and Khudiram Bose and Madan Lal Dhingra had already laid down their lives, hanged for their anti-colonial deeds. Besides, France had its own limitations when it came to carrying out the work of the Indian revolution; London, on the other hand, was core enemy territory, where propaganda and action were required the most and would have the greatest impact. Was there a fourth possibility? Some people thought there was. They stated that Savarkar was in love with an English girl, Margaret Lawrence. Could he have come all the way to meet her? According to a biography of Savarkar by one 'Chitragupta' that was published in 1926 and that covered his life until 1911 (many of Savarkar's followers and critics believe he himself wrote this book, though what their claims are based on isn't clear), among the 'rumours' floated in the British papers was that he had come back for 'an interview he was to have with a girl that had fallen in love with him'. Krishnavarma, it said, 'silenced many of these conjectures by his letter' to the British press, 'nevertheless the police sedulously went on encouraging the belief that Savarkar . . . fell a victim to a false letter they sent him in the name of his intimate friend. But nothing of that sort ever happened. We have Savarkar's word for that.'[26]

Whichever of the reasons is true, the fact is that the decision to go back changed Savarkar's life irrevocably. Krishnavarma stayed outside of England and died in relative obscurity in Switzerland in 1930, aged seventy-three. Bhikaiji Cama returned to India from European exile in 1935, her health completely broken, and died at the age of seventy-four the following year. Chatto joined the Indian National Congress in the early 1920s and became a Berlin-based confidant of Jawaharlal Nehru; he enrolled as a member of the German Communist Party and moved to Moscow afterwards, only to be arrested in July 1937 during Stalin's Great Purge, and was executed by one of Stalin's murder squads two months later. Neither Krishnavarma nor Cama played a central role in nationalist affairs in the latter half of their lives, especially after Gandhi assumed the leadership of the national movement with Tilak's passing in 1920.

Savarkar's three years in London had been quite turbulent, especially since the inauguration of the bomb cult in Bengal in 1908. The political storm clouds would hover over him more menacingly in the years to come. Even when he was in British captivity, he would exert an immense pull on patriotic Indians, and later he would mount one of the most powerful challenges to the mainstream nationalist movement.

6

The escape and the global trial

Savarkar was produced in the Bow Street court and charged on five counts: (1) waging war or abetting the waging of war against the king, (2) conspiring to deprive the king of sovereignty of British India, (3) procuring and distributing arms and abetting Jackson's murder, (4) producing and distributing arms in London and waging war from London, and (5) delivering seditious speeches in India in 1906 and in London in 1908 and 1909.

After a few initial hearings, Reginald Vaughan, the counsel engaged by Savarkar's friends in London and Paris, made an application for bail. It was rejected, and Savarkar was transferred from the custody of Bow Street police to Brixton jail. The case dragged on through March and April 1910. The principal argument of the prosecution – its team included S.A.T. Rowlatt, a name that was to gain much notoriety in India – was that Savarkar must face trial in India. The reason was evident: the laws there were much more stringent and the courts little more than handmaidens of imperial authority. The defence urged that Savarkar be tried in London itself as any trial in India would be unfair.

The statements of the India House cook Chaturbhuj Amin, of C.R. Rao (the Coimbatore policeman who was caught in possession in Mumbai of seditious pamphlets allegedly given to him by Savarkar), and of another hostel lodger, Harishchandra Korgaonkar, went against Savarkar. According to the correspondent for the London *Observer* who covered the proceedings, the prosecutor A.H. Bodkin 'went through a formidable mass of documentary police evidence' from both England and India. While the testimonies of Chaturbhuj and the others established that Savarkar had founded the Mitra Mela, made incendiary speeches and sent 'parcels' (meaning revolvers) from the UK to India, the special branch of London's Criminal Investigation Department (CID) had found in Savarkar's trunk two copies of *The Indian War of Independence*, *The Life of Mazzini*, the manuscript of a book called *The Lion of the Punjab*, a booklet titled *Bande Mataram* and 'several printer's proofs of sheets in the Mahratti language'. Inside the same trunk, the CID officials said, was a copy of a pamphlet 'largely circulated in London in 1909' and 'afterwards prohibited by a notice published in the India Gazette'. And portions were read out from two of his letters. In the first, dated 11 February 1910, Savarkar had written, 'Perhaps you will be pleased to know that two Sundays ago I read an essay on "How to Organise a Revolution" at our meeting, and I had some difference of opinion about it . . . The difference arose because I hold that we should not hesitate to be loyal outwardly and to work secretly.

Our friends took a great objection to that. In Bengal there are many societies which are working splendidly with this policy.' A passage in the second letter read, 'I have almost finished the Life of Garibaldi and part of the third volume of Mazzini. I discussed our propaganda with another gentleman in the last fifteen days, and have succeeded in converting him to our views, though he has not taken any oath to work for the benefit of his country. But I am confident he will take the oath in a few days. I am very disappointed with two other gentlemen. Still, they are very frequently visitors to our place, and I haven't given them up altogether.'[1]

A heading commonly used by Savarkar while writing letters, Bodkin said, was 'May the Goddess of Independence be pleased'.

On 12 May 1910 Magistrate Albert de Rutzen ruled that the undertrial prisoner be taken to India under the Fugitive Offenders Act of 1881 but allowed him fifteen days to appeal. This appeal, along with a habeas corpus plea, was filed before the higher divisional (two-judge) court by the lawyers K.C. Powell and J.M. Parikh. Both were turned down, and in mid-June, one more appeal filed before the Court of Appeal was shot down. On 21 June 1910, the judge, Vaughan Williams, speaking for a three-member bench, concluded that 'in a case connected so much with India as this is, the prima facie right to trial in England is overridden by the facts of this case, which show that India is the locality of the seditious conspiracy which resulted in murder'.[2] For most Americans of the period, India was all about snakes, elephants, magic, mantras and of course tantra. A newspaper in New York reporting on Savarkar's imminent extradition wrote, 'Savarkar is accused of being the member of the Indian society that urges the natives to kill Europeans and offer their heads as a sacrifice to the goddess Kali.' The paper further said that the movement of which Savarkar was one of the leaders 'is considered the most destructive of English rule in India'.[3]

In the meantime, the Raj had set up, through an ordinance, a special three-member tribunal for Savarkar's trial in India. This placed the defendant acutely at a disadvantage: there would be no jury, and there was no provision of appeal against the tribunal's findings either. Yet ironically, while rejecting Savarkar's last appeal the judge had rosily noted: 'I decline entirely to hold that Savarkar is likely to get an unfair trial before the special court of three judges.'[4]

While the legal battle in London had moved forward slowly, Savarkar had spent his first few months inside a jail. We have a fairly good idea of what this time was like for him, from accounts left behind by some of his friends. Aiyar, Krishnavarma, Cama and Chatto had pooled in funds and made arrangements for his defence. Aiyar visited him a number of times in Brixton prison. Chatto too travelled back from the French capital and, according to British government records, saw Savarkar fourteen times. These visits were risky, as the more frequently these friends came, the greater were their chances of landing behind bars as accessories to the crimes Savarkar was accused of.

After one of his early visits to the prison, Aiyar informed Krishnavarma in a letter that Savarkar 'was the same as ever except that we had to converse through the iron bars'.[5] Savarkar told Aiyar that the jail superintendent and other officials 'treated him with due attention and care and that he had nothing to complain [about] under the circumstances'. In a letter Aiyar sent in April, though, there was a note of frustration at the pace of proceedings. 'The case is still dragging its weary length along,' he wrote to Krishnavarma. 'So dear Savarkar and his friends have to bear the suffering as they can every day. Some friend or other is going and visiting him and he is as cheerful inside the jail as he was when out. Necessary books and papers are given to read.'

Yet, beneath the cheery exterior that both the undertrial and his visitor demonstrated, there were unmistakably feelings of torment and anguish. 'I felt it deeply – too deeply – that he [Savarkar] should be interned in the English jail,' Aiyar wrote and, quoting partly a line from Aesop's lion and the mouse fable, described the sight of the prisoner as 'a lion in the coils of his hunter!'

Aiyar feared that if Savarkar were sent to India to face trial, 'we shall see no more of him and one of the dearest and most devoted sons of the Motherland would be rotting away in [the] cells of a malarious island'. Savarkar had said that 'if he were to be taken to the Andamans, he would have the happiness of seeing his elder brother'. Aiyar fervently hoped that Savarkar would be denied such a 'melancholy sort of happiness' and that he would be 'released and will work out the salvation of his country according to his lights'. Through Aiyar, 'Deshbandhu Savarkar', as the genial Tamilian referred to his comrade, had sent a message for Krishnavarma: could he please pay him the rest of his scholarship amount 'so that he might send it, along with what little he has here, to his brothers' wives, and they might be kept above anxiety for some time at least?' Aiyar was totally devoted to Savarkar, and in these trying months he took to wearing a bushy beard and a generally unkempt look. This was quite a drastic change, for Aiyar had always taken care to be, in Savarkar's words, a 'neatly dressed fashionable gentleman'. In a letter that Savarkar wrote him from Brixton closer to the day of the verdict of his second appeal, he gently pulled Aiyar's leg while attempting to make light of the situation. Addressing him as 'My Dear Rishi', Savarkar said, 'I am in excellent health and have added two pounds to my weight (not by growing a four-pound weight beard!).'[6]

Savarkar may also have drawn some solace from the fact that the Glasgow anarchist and socialist Guy Aldred was in the same prison at the same time, serving his one-year sentence as printer of the 'seditious' *Indian Sociologist*. One other person who provided him comfort and even a faint glimmer of hope by thinking up a plan of escape was the effervescent David Garnett.

Any perceived proximity to Savarkar could potentially be crushing for Garnett's career prospects, and the teenaged writer was indeed one day subjected to a 'searching questioning' by Inspector Edward Parker of Scotland Yard. Sukhsagar Dutta, through whom Garnett had got to know the whole India House batch, had recently told Garnett that he 'wanted no more to do with Savarkar or any of his group'. Still, fired by an adolescent enthusiasm, Garnett went 'practically every week to Brixton Gaol to see Savarkar'. Most of the times he took with him clean collars for the prisoner, as that was 'all he wanted at the moment'. Garnett noted with curiosity that the size of Savarkar's neck was only 13.5 – that of a schoolboy.

He was, besides, convinced that the delay in the case was deliberate. He wrote an article for the *Daily News*, arguing that if the basis for the trial was going to be just the proof in the Jackson murder plot, Savarkar would have to be tried in London as the murder had occurred when he was in London. In that case, he would get a sentence of two or three years. If Savarkar were tried in India, it would be another matter altogether, so in order to be able to extradite him, the authorities 'had to dig up, or manufacture, evidence of crimes committed while he was in India', and this was taking time, Garnett said.

He wasn't off the mark. The prosecution had, as the case had proceeded, pulled out Savarkar's speeches from his Nasik days and got, among others, G. Guider, a first-class magistrate from the temple town, and one Jaffar Ali, again from the same town, to depose and 'verify' the seditious speeches. In one of these, delivered in 1906, Savarkar had said, 'Are there no weapons except arms? There are many which need not be fully explained here.' In another, he had told the listeners, 'we require arms . . . When we have determined to overthrow the government, we want weapons . . . Let us fight with weapons.' In yet another speech Savarkar had said, 'Before you, you have the image of Maruti [Hanuman]. In his hand there is a club. Below his feet there is a demon. It is white – no, it is red. Give your attention to it. Its hands are red. Maruti is trampling the demons. You must do such deeds.'[7]

The defendant's lawyers, Powell and Parikh, argued that the Fugitive Offenders Act could not apply to Savarkar at all. For it to apply, 'a man must have committed an offence and then have left the country', they contended. The alleged offences of 1909 had taken place in England, and Savarkar was present at that time in England, so he ought to be tried on British soil, they said. As for the alleged offences of 1906, they were related to certain speeches, but then no proceedings had been initiated by the British authorities in India so far in that regard, they pointed out. 'In the circumstances of this case it would be unjust and oppressive to send Savarkar back,' Powell told the court, and Parikh, quoting the relevant sections of the Indian Penal Code and the Code of Criminal Procedure, said if Savarkar were tried in India 'he would not be entitled to give evidence on his own behalf'.[8]

When there remained, in view of the judges' observations during the hearings, 'not the slightest doubt' about which way the second appeals court verdict would go, Garnett suggested to Savarkar one morning, when the warder walking up and down the jail corridor was out of earshot, 'Why not try and escape? I have an idea how it might possibly be managed.' The plan, in short, was to intercept the police vehicle in which Savarkar would be taken once a week to court for extension of his remand at the prison gates, overpower the two cops who normally guarded him, push him into a car waiting nearby and drive off speedily to the waterfront, where a boat would have to be kept ready for Savarkar to be transported to France. But those who engaged the two policemen would definitely be arrested. Who would volunteer for that?

Garnett soon met a friend of Savarkar whom he identified only as 'C.C.' This friend told him 'there were two men in Paris who would willingly go to gaol for long periods in order to rescue Savarkar'. Once Savarkar had okayed the idea, instructions were issued to a third man, 'A.A.', in Paris to hire a boat. When Garnett went to Paris and met A.A. to finalize plans, the Indian told him 'that two rescuers were perfectly prepared to come, but that he [A.A.] had taken no steps to hire a boat'. Garnett 'realised it was a betrayal' but did not say anything and volunteered to organize a boat himself. He took some money from A.A., went to the Havre port outside of Paris and hired a big smack. On his return to A.A.'s hotel in the Rue de la Boetie, Garnett found the man 'luxuriating . . . in a comfortable bed'. On being told the boat was ready, A.A. said, 'But it's all off. It's impossible. Your father's here. He's going to the French police.'

Edward Garnett, worried that his son was up to no good, had rushed to Paris. A.A. gave the teenager the address of the place where Edward was staying, and father and son returned to London. There, Garnett immediately 'sent off a warning to C.C.' about A.A.'s treacherous behaviour, and 'half an hour before the rescue was timed to take place' went to the Brixton prison and met Savarkar to tell him that the plan had to be aborted. 'The moment he saw me,' Garnett wrote afterwards, '[Savarkar] knew that the plan had miscarried. But as I told him the details, he was already trying to console me for my failure. There was not a single sign in him of reproach, of bitterness, or even of shock.' Garnett informed Savarkar that 'it was obvious that A.A. didn't want him to escape, but to keep hold of the party funds' and also that he had been 'frivolously betrayed' by the man after he had booked a boat. Savarkar told Garnett, 'You have done wonderfully and there was no reason why you should have done anything at all. Do not worry about me. I shall escape somehow. I have a plan worked out already, in case your plan failed.'

At the end of this 'painful experience' with A.A., Garnett, on sober reflection, felt 'I had played a fool's part in the affair'. By that time, Garnett wrote, 'I cared nothing for Indian

Nationalism and my feeling for Savarkar was personal. I could not endure to see a man with such intense vitality spending his life in prison. [But] I shared none of his ideas.'[9] He quickly cut off his links with the Indian radicals and never met Savarkar again. And he never revealed the identity of the mysterious A.A. either.

Not too long after the abandoned escape strategy, however, Garnett opened the paper one morning and found it to be full of Vinayak Savarkar's story. On reading it, he understood what Savarkar had meant when he had spoken of an alternative plan.

When the court quashed Savarkar's appeal, the Government of India sent three policemen to bring him back to Mumbai. One was C.J. Power, the CID's deputy superintendent of police, and the other two were head constables Mohamed Siddik of the Pune CID and Amarsing Sakharamsing of the Nasik police. The government had asked the London metropolitan police commissioner if Detective Inspector Edward Parker of Scotland Yard could accompany the three India-based cops on their journey home with the prisoner. The commissioner readily consented, and on 1 July 1910 the police squad, along with a handcuffed Savarkar, climbed aboard the SS *Morea* from Tilbury. The ship was divided into saloons of various classes, and though Inspector Parker had been given a 'first saloon passage', he chose to travel in the second-class saloon to help the other policemen keep a watch on Savarkar. The two seniormost police officers, Parker and Power, and the prisoner occupied the same cabin. It had four berths. Savarkar and Parker took the lower ones, and Power the one right above Savarkar's. After a brief halt at Gibraltar on 5 July, the ship reached Marseilles at around 10 a.m. on 7 July.

The Bombay government's records, which include statements of all four cops, make it abundantly clear that the Raj had obtained reliable information – was it A.A. at work again? – that Savarkar might make a run for freedom with the help of his friends in Paris. Hardly had the SS *Morea* moored alongside the quay in the dock when a French police officer, Henri Leblias, got on board and informed Parker that the London police commissioner had sent a letter to his counterpart in Paris. The letter had requested that 'precautions be taken to prevent any demonstration or attempt on the part of Savarkar's friends resident in France to interview him or to facilitate his escape during the time the *Morea* remained at Marseilles'. Leblias promised all assistance and even took Inspector Parker ashore and introduced him to other local French policemen stationed on the quay.

According to official British documents, the morning after (8 July), Savarkar woke up at six and got off his berth. Parker too was up, and sitting on his own berth, he asked Savarkar what time it was by his watch. 'It's six-fifteen,' said Savarkar, and went back to his bed. After about fifteen minutes, the prisoner asked the half-awake Parker if he could go to the water closet. The inspector wouldn't let him go alone: he unlocked the cabin, led Savarkar himself in the direction of the bathrooms and shouted to the two head constables, Siddik and Amarsing, who stood near the kit boxes in the passage about twelve feet from the bathrooms, asking them to accompany him and keep an eye on Savarkar. After removing the manacles and allowing Savarkar to enter one of the stalls at the far end of the communal bathroom, Parker waited till the Indian had closed the door and then stepped on the platform of a urinal on the opposite side of the room to take a good look within (there were three-inch openings atop all the closet doors). He saw that the porthole of Savarkar's stall was shut. Directing the constables to keep a strict vigil outside the door, the inspector returned to his cabin to put on his clothes for the day.

Constable Amarsing peeped under the closet door – there was an opening at the bottom too – and saw two slippers, 'as if the person who wore them was seated'. To be doubly sure, he climbed the platform on which Parker had stood earlier. The sight from there threw him into utter panic: Savarkar had squeezed himself halfway out of the small porthole. As Amarsing shouted and rushed to force open the door, he saw, along with the other constable, when the door gave way, that Savarkar had passed through the porthole entirely and slipped into the waters below. The two constables raised the alarm and ran on to the deck and from there in the direction of the quay. A guard on the deck too had seen the thin young man jump, and he tried firing a couple of bullets. The swimming skills Savarkar had honed in Nasik helped him dodge the fire somehow and he proceeded at a swift pace. There are various versions of how far the ship was from the quay, ranging from an unlikely one kilometre to a more realistic thirty yards. The most conservative estimate, that of the colonial police, is that Savarkar had to swim twelve feet to reach the quay. As soon as he got on to it, he started running, and the constables and some crew members on the ship launched into a chase, the cops shouting, 'Catch! Thief! Stop! Thief!'

According to the police, Savarkar ran for about 200 yards straight before he stopped for breath, 'partly from exhaustion and partly owing to his progress being blocked by a number of Frenchmen who were employees of the dock'. The official version later put out was that a French gendarme or marine police officer, who had joined in the pursuit, was the first to get hold of the fleeing prisoner, and he handed him over to the constables. The version in the original police records of the incident is somewhat different: it says that Constable Amarsing seized Savarkar by the back of the neck, the ship's steward held his right wrist, and the French gendarme the left. Though the original police report said the three chasers 'all came up together', Amarsing's act of seizing Savarkar by the neck likely suggests that the two other men who followed held the prisoner's wrists only once he was in the constable's grip. The opening up of the possibility of a Raj policeman getting hold of Savarkar ahead of the others raises a major question, which we will discuss soon. But for the moment, a return to the denouement of the drama on the quay.

At once Savarkar, still slightly out of breath, appealed to the French gendarme, 'Take me into your custody. Take me in front of a magistrate.' The gendarme unfortunately had no knowledge of English, and the constables of the Raj told him that Savarkar was a runaway prisoner and needed to be taken back to the ship. The gendarme promptly let go of the captive, no questions asked, and Savarkar was dragged back to the *Morea*.

Krishnavarma, Chatto, Cama and Aiyar had all warned Savarkar against going back to London, and they were mighty upset that he had so easily allowed himself to be arrested by the British police. Chatto's brother Harindranath wrote of their anguish also at his thwarted attempt at escape, but he wrote that there was absolutely no feeling of sour bitterness in

Chatto or in the others about Savarkar for having disregarded their words urging caution. Instead, with their sense of unity regained, the Indian revolutionaries in Paris realized that they had a really powerful legal argument to make. Savarkar had landed on French soil and had the rights of a man in France, perhaps he was even entitled to political asylum. This is why the question of who got to him first was so crucial. If it was a British Indian constable who had arrested him, it could be said to be in contravention of the law. What authority did that constable have on French territory to effect a capture? And if it was the French gendarme, then how did he have the right to hand Savarkar over to the British? Especially since Savarkar had explicitly asked for asylum and to be taken before a magistrate. This was a matter for deliberation between two nations. An individual marine police officer had no authority to act as an arbiter in a case with international implications. The irrepressible Cama got in touch with Jean Longuet, a young socialist in Paris, to launch a campaign through the press for Savarkar's release. Longuet, the grandson of Karl Marx, regularly wrote signed pieces for the socialist paper *L'Humanite*, and the issues he raised were frequently taken up by other sections of the socialist press in France as well as by elected Socialist members of the French national assembly, known as deputies. After the Paris edition of the *Daily Mail* had carried a very small report on the Marseilles incident, Longuet in the real sense broke the news to the French public in *L'Humanite* and began a series of strongly worded articles that immediately unleashed a political storm in at least three countries: his own, Britain and India.

Two distinct illegalities had been committed, Longuet said: one by the British, who had misled the Marseilles maritime police by the 'outright falsehood' that Savarkar was a thief, and the second by the French gendarme, who had handed the man over to the British when he should have taken him to the chief of the port.[10] The senior socialist leader Jean Jaures, a member of the Chamber of Deputies and mayor of Marseilles, amplified Longuet's voice by terming Savarkar's extradition as illegal and underlining his right to political asylum, and so did the deputy mayor of Marseilles, M Cadenat. Marseilles mayor Jaures had 'espoused Savarkar's cause' with 'ardour' and 'force', the papers reported.[11]

The French socialist press protested strongly against what it described as a violation not merely of the country's territorial jurisdiction but of 'the rights of man'. The response from the *Observer* was sarcastic. The London paper remarked that the indignation of France's socialist papers 'knew no bounds' and said the average French socialist, with his 'specially tender spot for the swarthy agitator', 'weeps over the prospective fate of Savarkar'.[12] Soon it was not just the socialists protesting. Most other French newspapers, including the eveninger *Temps*, seen at the time as a government mouthpiece, joined in the clamour, saying that the British had no right to pursue, let alone arrest, anyone on French territory and that the fugitive must be returned immediately to France.

The conservative *Times* of London, arguing Britain's case without any *Observer*-like sarcastic touch, insisted that the prisoner was 'de facto in the custody of the authorities of his own country' and that the 'alleged irregularity' upon which the French representations were based 'was committed not by a British subject but by a French official'. From the point of view of international courtesy, the paper said, it would be better if the French government assumed full responsibility 'for the mistake of their agent' instead of asking the British government to 'surrender a British subject charged with the gravest acts of sedition and abetment of assassination'.[13]

The French press's counterargument to this was that even if the maritime or dock policeman was at fault and even if it were to be concluded that Britain had every right to take the prisoner, an extradition treaty between the two countries had laid down the procedure to be followed in such cases. Any informal handing over was simply unacceptable. The *Journal des Debats* said Britain 'cannot take advantage of the blunder committed by a French policeman, and Savarkar ought to be sent back to France and there restored to liberty',[14] and *L'Humanite* and *Libre Parole* of Paris urged the French minister for foreign affairs to ensure that Britain either freed Savarkar or handed him over to the French.[15]

With pressure thus mounting, the French government wrote to the British Foreign Office demanding Savarkar's return. This communiqué went out a few days before the team carrying Savarkar, after a change in steamer at Aden, disembarked on the shores of Mumbai on 22 July.

An American newspaper at this point reminded the British government of some home truths in the matter of political offenders demanding sanctuary. 'England,' it remarked, 'has always shown herself exceedingly tolerant of all sorts of . . . conspirators belonging to nationalities other than her own. Thus, when Orsini tried to blow up the Emperor of the French, England persistently declined to hand over his accomplices, who had taken refuge in London . . . although France very nearly went to war with her in order to compel her to do so.' A 'more recent case' was 'of the Chinese reformer Sun Yat Sen, who also took refuge on British soil, and whom likewise England refused to surrender, although the Chinese Government insisted'. The Chinese authorities had then 'kidnapped and imprisoned' Sun Yat Sen 'inside the Chinese Legation in London, where it was intended to hold him a prisoner until he could be smuggled on board a mail steamer bound for China'. But news of the kidnap leaked, and the Chinese had 'perforce to deliver' the captive after they received 'a curt order to that effect signed by Lord Salisbury'. The 'same principle holds good today' in Savarkar's case, the paper argued.[16]

The aggressive stance of conservative London papers like *The Times* notwithstanding, the Raj itself did not speak in one voice in the beginning. Even before the Marseilles incident there was dissension on whether Savarkar should have been sent back to India. On the day the *Morea* sailed out of British waters, the relatively liberal Secretary of State for India Lord Morley complained in a letter to the Bombay governor Lord Sydenham about the extradition proceedings against Savarkar, prompting Sydenham to respond that 'Savarkar was one of the most dangerous men that India has produced'. Despite the legality of the proceedings having been examined at length in England and Savarkar's role in dangerous activities well established, the governor wrote disapprovingly, 'all this and more Lord Morley seemed not to know'.[17]

After the Marseilles incident the disagreement seems to have been amplified. The other India Office mandarins took a view different from their boss Morley's: they were firmly of the opinion that Savarkar should not be sent back to France, and in this they were backed by the Secret Service and Scotland

Yard. For Home Secretary Winston Churchill, 'nothing' was more important than that Britain should be seen as an upholder of the law of nations. To keep this image 'the petty annoyance of a criminal escaping may have to be borne', Churchill said.[18]

Keir Hardie, the founder of the Labour Party, its first MP and first Labour parliamentary party leader, moved a special resolution at the 1910 International Socialist Congress in Copenhagen in September demanding that Savarkar be sent back to France. He contended vociferously that England had in the past 'afforded protection to Garibaldi, Mazzini, Kossuth and Karl Marx', but 'contrary to all her traditions', the country had now violated the right of asylum of 'the revolutionary Hindoo, Savarkar, who, in an unprecedented manner, has been arrested on French soil and extradited without any legal formality'. Hardie added, 'The trial of Savarkar had not been a fair one. He had been condemned as though he were a mere criminal, no recognition of the political purpose of his action being allowed.'[19] The resolution was passed unanimously.

Other left-wing elements in Britain stood solidly by Savarkar. Guy Aldred, just released from prison after having served his term, formed a 'Release Savarkar Committee' and launched a 'Savarkar Release Tour' across England, Scotland and Wales. H.M. Hyndman, founder and chief of the Social Democratic Federation, felt 'it can scarcely be regarded as democratic justice that Savarkar should have been packed off to India' and noted that 'faith in British equity has been completely shaken by these proceedings'.[20] The *Manchester Guardian*, a champion of the working class, wrote that 'the mere fact of his landing on foreign territory releases him from British jurisdiction'. It asserted, 'an important point in international law, the right of asylum, on which Great Britain has always been the first to insist, is at issue'.[21] The London paper *Justice*, considered 'the organ of social democracy', said under the headline 'The Infamies of Liberal Rule in India' that Savarkar had been taken to India so that 'innocent or guilty, his condemnation could be officially ensured' and noted that the London socialists 'heartily sympathise with the legitimate efforts of Indians of all races, castes and creeds to emancipate themselves finally from the monstrous domination under which they suffer today'.

Valentine Chirol, the celebrated journalist with the London *Times*, reacted furiously to these pro-Savarkar comments. He complained that what the *Justice* had published was 'outrageous' and asked if it was right 'to allow language of this kind to be used and circulated with impunity' when, in India, the same language would 'at once give rise to a criminal prosecution'.[22] It was a case of a journalist demanding a crackdown on journalism. The British editor of the then British-owned *Times of India* similarly had concerns that went well beyond the legal complexities of the matter. He was appalled at the 'sheer levity' of the police force, which seemed not to realize that 'they are not playing at an afternoon tea party but are dealing with bold, resolute and resourceful men'. The paper said the police had 'made popular heroes of political criminals and brought contempt upon themselves. The Marseilles incident is the last straw.'[23]

As the government in London continued to stall France's demands and the regime in India, with scant regard for all the protests, announced that it would go ahead with Savarkar's trial, the French politician and head of the League of Human Rights, Francis de Pressense, suggested a way out of the diplomatic impasse. Calling upon France to carry out its 'obligation' of 'reclaiming Savarkar from the British', he asked the French foreign minister, M Pichon, to refer the vexed issue to the international tribunal at The Hague for arbitration. Britain and France had in any case agreed to go in for arbitration should any such disagreement arise, he reminded the minister.

This appeared to suit the French government, which did not quite want to antagonize Britain whom it saw as an ally against the perceived threats of Russia and Germany. The British too consented in October, but maintained that the trial in Mumbai, which had already opened in the middle of September 1910, would proceed regardless. The Indian radicals and left leaders and liberals in London and Paris thought it manifestly odd that a Mumbai court should try Savarkar when The Hague was to decide on a vital question of global law. The Committee of the International Arbitration and Peace Association issued a statement to leading European newspapers to register its protest 'against the continuance of the trial until the decision of The Hague Court has been given'.[24]

But the special tribunal in the Bombay High Court – comprising two Englishmen, Chief Justice Basil Scott and Justice Heaton, and one Indian, N.G. Chandavarkar – carried on with the proceedings undeterred. The prosecution team was led by M.R. Jardine, the advocate general or chief government lawyer of Bombay. This Jardine is a completely forgotten man in India today, but his son Douglas holds a secure position in the memory of cricket-crazy Indians and of the entire cricket world as the captain of the England team that controversially used bodyline tactics against Don Bradman in 1932–33. From Paris, Cama engaged Joseph Baptista, East Indian lawyer, fervent nationalist and long-time Tilak confidant, as the head of the legal team that would defend Savarkar.

When Baptista asked for permission to see Savarkar in Pune's Yerwada jail, where he was lodged after spending a few days in custody in Nasik, the inspector general of police laid down tough conditions for the interview: a police inspector would be present throughout and would hear the full conversation, and the conversation itself would have to be restricted to the case in the high court.[25] The idea evidently was to prevent the undertrial from finding out about the furore generated by his extradition abroad and from taking the position that he was not answerable to a local court till a verdict on the status of his extradition had been reached by a global tribunal.

The Mumbai cases against Savarkar progressed swiftly as expected, with the judges dismissing Baptista's contention about the arrest being illegal and asserting that Indian courts could still try the accused. It was decided, however, that if he was convicted locally, the conviction would not be executed until the order from the Netherlands came in.

In all, thirty-eight people were named as accused, and nearly 300 witnesses were examined. Jardine told the court that Vinayak Savarkar was 'the ring leader' of Indian radicals in London. He 'appeared to be a man probably of considerable ability and certainly a man of considerable influence' and he had 'made [the] most inflammatory speeches' at the India House.[26]

On 23 December 1910 the judgement in the first case (on the allegedly seditious speeches) was pronounced. Savarkar was held guilty and sentenced to transportation for life – which meant twenty-five years. All his property would be confiscated, the three judges ruled. The other accused too were convicted. One of them got a fifteen-year transportation term, three got ten years in jail, four received a four-year sentence, five got three years each, three others got two years and four – including Vinayak's brother Narayan – were sentenced to rigorous imprisonment for six months.

The second conviction, in the Jackson murder case, came a little more than a month later, on 30 January 1911. It was identical – transportation for life. Did that mean the two twenty-five-year sentences would run simultaneously? No. Savarkar would have to serve the prison terms one after the other. Fifty years was more than a lifetime for an Indian of that period (the average life expectancy in India then was less than forty years).

A fortnight after the verdict in Mumbai, the arbitral tribunal at the Permanent Court of Arbitration at The Hague began its hearings. It had five members, and most of Savarkar's supporters believed its constitution – allowed to be determined by the contending parties provided those picked were all members of the Permanent Court – was itself a compromise on the part of the French government. No one from Russia or Germany found a place on it. Its president was former Belgian prime minister Auguste Beernaert, and its other members were England's former attorney general the Earl of Desart, the eminent French legal adviser Louis Renault, a former Norwegian minister, G. Gram, and a minister from the Netherlands, A.F. de Savornin Lohman. Article 1 of the French–British agreement clearly stated that the tribunal would 'decide the following question: Ought Vinayak Damodar Savarkar, in conformity with the rules of international law, to be or not be surrendered by the

Government of His Brittanic Majesty to the Government of the French Republic?'[27]

The British government strenuously made the point that it had not in any way violated France's sovereignty in effecting Savarkar's recapture and rubbished his claim to the right of political asylum. Contrary to expectations that the tribunal's hearings would continue for at least a couple of months, if not longer, it took ten days to pronounce its verdict. It stated unequivocally that 'an irregularity was committed by the arrest of Savarkar [in Marseilles], and his being handed over to the British Police'. At the same time, it was categorical in asserting that the British were not obligated by any international law 'to restore him [to France] because of a mistake committed by a foreign agent who delivered him up to that Power'. To quell any lingering doubts about what it meant, the arbitral tribunal put it down in bold letters that it had decided that Britain 'is not required to restore' Savarkar to the French Republic.[28]

The order was assailed by Europe's liberal intelligentsia. The Berlin *Post*, for instance, widely recognized at the time as an 'influential moderating force in German politics', wrote scathingly that 'the real issue of the Savarkar case' had been 'passed over' by The Hague tribunal 'in complete silence' and with 'an exhibition of touching naivete and pure folly'. Describing the outcome as 'a very cold bath for enthusiasts of arbitration in Germany', the *Post* commented that 'it is known that the Tribunal gave its decision in obedience to the wishes of the British and French Governments'.[29] This, in its view, was 'a crass breach of international law' and 'proof [of] how far the subservience to England has brought France'.[30]

Britain was also criticized by various journals for its

unwillingness to uphold democratic traditions. And one of the most devastating attacks on the judgement and on England's and France's approach to the issue came from a leading politician from within Britain, Josiah Clement Wedgwood. The maverick long-time Labour MP from Newcastle, who in later decades stood out for his stern opposition to Nazism and Britain's appeasement of Hitler, wrote in the *Manchester Guardian* that The Hague tribunal, 'a cooperative law court' founded by 'the nations of Europe':[31]

> is finally closing down the hatches on every rebel against the existing order . . . The fugitive – 'assassin' or 'patriot,' 'avatar' or that weird monster the 'Anarchist' of the newspapers – whatever he be, so long as he fails to conform to the rules laid down by the united schoolmasters of society, can find no corner of the globe to shelter him, and the only doubt is under which precise code of regulations he shall be judged, punished, and put away.
>
> . . . This triumph of organisation may be admirable, but it must give food for reflection to every individual who values freedom of speech and action.

The 'Government of His Brittanic Majesty', as it was referred to in The Hague document, was, however, more than prepared to take this new round of criticism. It had got exactly what it wanted – the prisoner Savarkar himself.

The reaction of the Indian exiles in Paris was summed up in a letter that Bhikaiji Cama wrote to M.P.T. Acharya: 'The great master Deshbandhu Savarkar is lost. The demoralised people have collapsed.' Sometime later, when a Bengali, Dr Abish

Chandra Bhattacharya, called on her, Cama, according to her biographer, broke down at the mention of Savarkar's name. 'Savarkar's powers of thought and action were incomparable. I could not imagine that the British would be able to influence the International Court so much,' she told her Indian visitor. Then, composing herself, she said, 'The British are the main enemy of freedom in the world.'[32]

'How the judgement went against France is a mystery,' wrote a befuddled Asaf Ali. He also cited the condemned man's own comment on the situation. 'Considering that a man has but one life, Savarkar asked, how could he be sentenced to two transportations?'[33]

Savarkar was in the Dongri prison in central Mumbai when The Hague verdict came in. He told a warder that it was only to be expected. His sole consolation was that he had temporarily been placed in the same cell in which Tilak had spent two prison terms, one along with his friend Agarkar and the other on his own. The prison officials told Savarkar with a certain pride how Tilak would spend sleepless nights in the mosquito-infested cell, obviously to accentuate the new prisoner's worries about having to spend fifty years in jail.

But there was one more thing on the prisoner's mind: would he get to see his family at least once before he was carted off to Port Blair? He had not seen them since he had left for London, and that was five years ago. Savarkar's chief preoccupation for a while had been to look, from the floor of the prison cell, at a nest that a pigeon had been building in a tiny gap separating the ceiling and the wall on one side. One day, while he was looking on as usual, a warder came up to his cell and told him he was wanted in the prison chief's office.

That usually meant trouble for any prisoner, but the moment he arrived there, he saw, beyond the iron bars that separated the office and the visitors' room, his wife, Yamuna. She was accompanied by her older brother, T.R. or 'Dada' Chiplunkar. A torrent of emotions ran through Savarkar's mind, the chief one being the big disappointment he had been to his wife. She had, since she waved him goodbye five years ago on the Mumbai harbour, waited expectantly for him to return in a proud Gray's Inn lawyer's garb. Instead he had on him a condemned man's prison clothes, and she might perhaps never get to see him again. There were tense moments as Savarkar nervously fussed with the fetters on him and moved slowly closer to the iron bars, but once they came face-to-face, he spoke up, clearly in a bid to assuage his own, and his wife's and brother-in-law's anxiety. 'What? You didn't recognise me? I'm still the same, only the clothes have changed,' he said.[34] That brought a smile to Yamuna's face, and the atmosphere now less heavy, husband and wife slowly got talking. On a more serious note, he told Yamuna that God willing, they would meet again; he had heard that prisoners were allowed to get their families to settle on the islands, after they had spent a few years in the Andamans. If that happened, fine, but if it did not, she must build up courage and face things as they were. She said she was more worried about him; she would be fine if he took care of himself. Soon the superintendent interrupted their talk, saying time was up, and Savarkar must return to his cell.

Turning back after saying goodbye, Savarkar attempted to walk a little less nervously; Yamuna and her dada would be still looking on, and he must not give the impression that he was having any difficulty in those fetters. Once the havildar had locked him up securely, Savarkar felt all the strength suddenly going out of him. It was, emotionally and psychologically, a draining moment, and he lay down on the dirt floor, looking up once more at the pigeon's nest. The little ones were hungry and somewhat anguished; their mother had not turned up at the hour she normally did. The next morning, he found out she had been felled by a prison official's bullet.

7

Kaala Paani

'Don't worry, the government is generous, they'll definitely release you in the year 1960,' the sipahi inside Mumbai's Dongri prison said with malicious delight, handing over what was called, in Raj lingo, 'the jail ticket'.

'But death is more generous. It could release me earlier,' said the convict.

Both laughed, the sipahi unrestrained, the prisoner with 'some effort'.

The wooden 'ticket', dangling on an iron ring, was placed around Savarkar's neck. Written on it was the year of his release and freedom. Savarkar was handed the jail uniform of a kurta, a round topee and shorts – only undertrials could wear their own clothes; he was now a convict – and as he changed into it, he said to himself, 'I can never cast this off. In these clothes I will be carried out for cremation one day.'[1] He was going to be transported to a site in the Bay of Bengal where death was always lurking round the corner. The Andaman Islands, where the Raj had created a penal colony, and the Cellular Jail there, were breeding grounds for disease, desolation and dementia. Drudgery was the lucky outcome, a fatal collapse the more ordinary one. A slightly sensitive prisoner was in real danger well before he had even set foot in Port Blair, the main island on which the jail was situated.

Marched in fetters on to the steamer SS *Maharaja* from the coast of Madras, Savarkar found out why. He was huddled among scores of transportees, many of them hardened criminals. One, from Sindh, had smashed in a young man's skull and was making his third trip to Kaala Paani – as the penal settlement was called after the black waters surrounding the islands. Another was a nineteen-year-old who had stabbed his sister to death for having complained about his bhang addiction. Some had served terms previously for dacoity and thievery. The convicts' usual way of reconciling themselves to the reality of being spirited away to a notorious colony was to be loud, noisy and vulgar. Being brought down to the lower deck amid such cacophony and the clanging of chains was in itself an uneasy experience for Savarkar; the cramming in of fifty prisoners in a space fit for thirty, barricaded by iron bars, made it far worse. Savarkar had contracted bronchitis in England, and its after-effects sometimes made breathing hard inside congested spaces, which in turn caused chest pain. So the doctor on the steamer asked him to take up a spot at the far end of the enclosed space. That was of no help. As the convicts all lay down on their spread out blankets, one man's head touching another's toe and shoulder brushing shoulder, there wasn't an inch to spare. The portholes were way above, so there wasn't enough air either. Soon, in addition to the musty smell all around came a genuinely repellent stench. It was from a bucket placed in a corner, close to where Savarkar was seated. A man had just squatted over it. The bucket served as the toilet, and as night fell many more prisoners descended upon it. Filled with nausea, Savarkar shut his eyes and, just as many others had done with their shouts and manic laughs, found his own way of reconciling himself to the situation: he got philosophical, telling himself that purging was a bodily function no one was spared of, and if one could deal with one's own waste, one could deal with others' waste as well, as spiritual giants such as Ramakrishna Paramahamsa and Samarth Ramdas indeed had.[2]

After four nauseating days on the sea, a bunch of islands was spotted, and the *Maharaja* wound its way towards the only one which had a settlement at that time: Port Blair. Like the other islands around it, Port Blair had plenty of hills and forests, but unlike the others, the mass of green here was punctuated by many structures that had come up ever since the British, led by Lieutenant Archibald Blair of the navy, first colonized the island in 1789. The standout structure on the island's south had the look of a fortress, and Savarkar initially thought it must be the residence of the islands' chief commissioner. Convicts taken off the steamer were asked, one by one, to climb in the direction of the fortress with their fetters and scolded when they slowed down because of those fetters. The realization dawned that that was to be their home for the next few years: the Cellular Jail. Though the first transportees to the settlement had been the 1857 revolutionaries, the Cellular Jail had come up later, in the 1890s. By the time Savarkar entered its gates, it had over 600 cells for prisoners. At the jail's heart was a three-storeyed Central Tower. Seven blocks stood in seven straight lines radiating out in different directions from the tower. Every block had three storeys, called the Upper, Middle and Lower Corridors, and every corridor had about thirty cells. Each cell was 7.5 feet wide and 13.5 feet long and was meant to accommodate one prisoner. For ventilation, every cell on the second and third floors had a tiny window, placed at a considerable height and covered with iron bars, and those on the ground floor had shafts. All the rooms had a rough wooden plank for a bed, an earthen pot for a water closet, and a door that could be shut only with the iron bolts and bars on the outside. Each floor had a veranda, and every block had in front of it a courtyard where prisoners had their workshops. In the courtyards stood a smallish tank with taps and a single toilet.

What distinguished the Cellular Jail most from any other prison in India was its system of rules, or the lack of it. Rules were framed towards the end of the nineteenth century, when complaints were first made that the prison functioned outside the Indian criminal justice apparatus, but they had stayed pretty much on paper, and David Barry, the jailer and chief overseer, was effectively the system. This was the twentieth-century British version of the US's twenty-first-century Guantanamo Bay. Barry's whims represented Kaala Paani's flexible and ever-shifting set of rules, and his lackeys were the prime enforcers. These sidekicks were placed in three categories, in order of descending hierarchy: jamadars, warders and petty officers. All three were drawn from among the convicts themselves and were often more zealous in implementing Barry's diktats than any English officer.

'The goat does not fear the tiger half so much as the prisoners feared this king of the Black Waters,' wrote Aurobindo Ghose's brother Barindra who, along with six other convicts in the Alipur conspiracy case, had arrived at the jail a year before Savarkar. Barry was short and fat, with a 'ghee-fed belly', rotund eyes, flat nose and a spiky moustache. His typical way of introducing every new set of captives to the Andamans, according to Barindra Ghose, was to say: 'You see the wall around, do you know why it is so low? Because it is impossible to escape from this place. The sea surrounds it for a distance of 1000 miles. In the forests there are savages [a reference to the native Jarawa tribe]. If they happen to see any man, they do not hesitate to pierce him right through with their sharp arrows.' As for his own authority, he would say, 'If you disobey me, may God help you,' and remind the listener in the same breath that 'God does not come within three miles of Port Blair.'[3]

Barry met and had his first conversation with Savarkar separately; he did not address him during his customary sermon to the new batch of convicts. The reasons were obviously the brouhaha caused by the young man's escape from Marseilles and a directive from the Raj's Home Department asking the jail authorities to 'keep a careful watch over him lest he may try to escape'.[4] Barry tried, at first, to act as avuncular adviser, telling the twenty-six-year-old Savarkar that he himself was Irish and had at one time participated in the movement to free Ireland, but he had changed his mind with age and experience. Savarkar had his whole life before him and must not waste it, he said, stressing that 'murders are murders and they will never bring independence'. The Indian replied that he would not have hated Barry even if he had been an Englishman and that he had spent some years in England and was an admirer of the qualities of the English people. Savarkar added that it was odd that Barry hadn't dished out similar advice to the Irish Sinn Feiners and wrongly presumed that Savarkar had advocated political murder. Seeing that Savarkar could not easily be won over, Barry changed tack. Savarkar should not violate prison rules, he said; if he did, he would be punished. The next line was the unsettling one the jailer used for all: 'Don't try to escape, or you'll be lean meat for the savages.'[5]

Barry's I'm-a-law-unto-myself policy had been buttressed by the government's stand in the wake of a series of recent revolutionary acts in India that political prisoners were 'dangerous' and deserved harsher treatment than ordinary ones. The Raj had made clear they were not to be allowed to work together or given clerical work but, 'as a rule', made to do hard or 'gang labour', a term borrowed from slavery for intensive work carried out under constant supervision. Political captives were denied the rights granted to ordinary prisoners. Political prisoners could be beaten, even flogged, if they did not complete their quota of work. Verbal abuse was a constant; the only way it varied was in the richness of vocabulary. No newspapers or books were allowed, and God help if a piece of paper or pencil stub was found on them, let alone anything scribbled. The amount of food given was reduced for certain infractions (it was known as 'invalid diet', meaning insufficient diet), and they were allowed to go to the toilet 'only at three fixed hours a day'.[6] Unlike common criminals, they did not have the right of remission, that is, their sentences could not be reduced on the grounds of good conduct in prison. And if they crossed the line in any respect they could be given 'standing handcuffs', 'chain-gaug fetters' or 'crossbar fetters'. (We'll just come to what precisely these are.)

Prisoners were made to take their bath in seawater, which made the skin irritable and hair rough. Once Savarkar had his bath near the water tank, the jamadar assigned to look after him, a Pathan, took him to Block 7. Its Upper Corridor had been emptied to prevent any communication between him and other convicts, and he was placed in one of the isolated cells and the door bolted from outside. Three warders attached to the block – two Baluchi Muslims and a Pathan – would keep an eye on him round the clock.

If bathing wasn't a good idea, eating was an equally bad one, no matter the level of hunger. The food was neither of good quality nor sufficient. The warder or petty officer who stood guard invariably took the bread allotted daily to a convict, as also the curd given once a week; those who refused to hand things over got blows on their back with sticks. The rice served would be 'as good as raw' or at best half-boiled, the dal or curry altogether devoid of taste and the conjee – a kind of rice porridge – occasionally came drizzled with kerosene oil. As if all this wasn't bad enough, the food was prepared in unhygienic conditions in the common kitchen by a handful of sweat-drenched convicts, exposing the prisoners to the risk of contracting various diseases.

Sequestered from the beginning, Savarkar was kept on his own inside his cell. After a fortnight, though, he was brought down to the yard in front of his block and given the task of pounding coir. The Andamans were full of coconut trees, all on government land, so trade revolved around items made from this resource. All prisoners had to work from 6 a.m. to 10 a.m., after which they could take a two-hour break for lunch. They were asked to resume at noon, and time was called on their daily tasks not before 5 p.m.

Coir-pounding was a tough task for the political prisoners, mostly young members of a resurgent Indian intelligentsia with hands used to handling books, files and pens. Each one was handed the dry husk of about twenty coconuts, which needed battering with a wooden hammer until it turned soft. The husk was then doused in water. After much pounding all over again the fibre that remained had to be dried fully in the sun and cleaned. A roll of fibre weighing one to three pounds had to be prepared by 5 p.m. Savarkar had bruises and blisters on his hands, and muscle pain, at the end of almost every day; when he complained, he was told he ought to be grateful he had not been given a higher weight target as so many others had.

On 16 August 1911 Savarkar was ordered by Barry's boss, the superintendent of Port Blair, H.A. Browning, to work the oil press for fourteen days. His target: thirty pounds of mustard oil every day – way beyond anyone's capacity to grind. Upendranath Banerjee, one of the Alipur case convicts, wrote that turning the oil mill wasn't work, but a kind of 'wrestling'.[7] In today's world, it would be described as torture, inhuman and degrading. Savarkar was told a Burmese prisoner would aid him while he was yoked to the press, which was a way of saying we'll treat you horribly of course, but we'll do the same thing to someone else, at the same time.

The sturdiest could find the mill too much to handle, and Savarkar reacted the way most political prisoners did. Soon after he started turning the mill with his hands, with 'the barest piece of loin cloth'[8] tied around his waist, he felt giddy and robbed of all his strength. Banerjee described how physical disintegration would be very quick. 'Within 10 minutes, our breathing became difficult, our tongues got parched. In an hour, all the limbs were almost paralysed.'[9] Barindra Ghose claimed in jest that given the sheer weight of the punishment, they ought to have all been seen as 'bigger avatars than Ram Chandra'. Anyone who doubted it could do oil-grinding and coir-pounding for just a week, he said, for 'one week would be sufficient to make him feel what another avatar felt on the cross'.[10]

No breather could be had. No extra water either. Water poured into two broken coconut shells was the quota no one could exceed, no matter how thirsty. And no breaks were allowed other than the one for food, even if going around in circles non-stop made the prisoners faint and collapse. On the first evening Savarkar felt a throbbing pain all over his body and mounting fever as he lay on the wooden plank in his cell. One afternoon the pain got more excruciating than ever while still on the oil press, he suffered stomach cramps, and he realized he was going to faint. He sat down with some difficulty, supported himself against the wall and lost consciousness for a while.[11]

For Savarkar there was one consolation. He had earlier been kept in complete isolation; grinding oil meant he spent his day in the company of other political prisoners doing the same task before returning to his cell, and although talk was barred and rewarded with blows of the fist or baton, or both, he and the Bengali nationalists interacted for some time every day, a couple of them not engaged in the conversation keeping vigil lest a petty officer, warder or jamadar turn up all of a sudden.

A fortnight later he was assigned to rope-making. A bundle

of coir would be thrown to prisoners. Step one was to convert the fibres into wicks by rubbing them on to the ground with one's palms. Step two was to complete a pile of these. Then a couple of wicks had to be picked up at a time, and with one end of each held solidly on to the ground with the feet and the other firmly placed in the palms, deft use of hands and fingers was needed to twist it tightly into a small rope. 'Then repeat the process by joining other two bits of wick to the two ends and twist again. And so on. As the rope becomes longer and longer, you throw it behind you and hold the last joint under the toe and join again another wick and twist.'[12] Initially very difficult for all prisoners, the skill could, however, be learnt, and Savarkar and the other 'politicals' did eventually get the hang of it. But while other prisoners could sit together in the yard to make ropes, Savarkar was forced to sit in isolation in the corridor outside his cell on the third floor.

Right from the time he had come in, Vinayak had been keen to see his brother Babarao, who had been given transportation for life in 1909 and sent to Cellular Jail in 1910. During the first few days Savarkar asked Barry and other prison officials, all of whom peremptorily dismissed his questions, saying they could not even confirm if Babarao was in the same prison or, more cruelly, that he should mind his own business and not make gratuitous queries about other prisoners. Finally, a warder agreed to help, but clandestinely. Every evening, prisoners of each of the blocks were herded together in the yard in front of the Central Tower to assess how much work they had done. One batch came in at a time, and when it returned, another trooped in. But there were occasions when a batch was brought in before the previous one had disappeared inside its block. The warder engineered such a crossing of paths one evening by letting Savarkar's batch into the yard a bit prematurely. As the brothers looked each other in the face, all that a stunned Babarao could mumble was, 'Tatya, how did you land up here?' Before either of them could say a word more, they were separated by the warders and petty officers and instructed to go their own ways. Soon Babarao somehow succeeded in smuggling across to Savarkar's cell a letter to the younger brother. 'My imprisonment was made bearable by the fact that you were still free to carry on our work outside. How did you fall into their clutches when you were in Paris? What about our youngest sibling Bal [Narayan], who's going to take care of him?' he wrote. The letter 'pierced my heart', Savarkar later wrote.[13] Babarao had seen him after five long years and suffered the same disappointment Yamuna had – where he had hoped for a lawyer's wing collar hanging down the neck, there was that notorious jail ticket. In his reply Savarkar tried to comfort Babarao, stating that those who died unsung in a dungeon were as critical to the national movement as those who stood centre stage in the public sphere, but he knew these words could scarcely provide any reassurance.

On 20 August 1911 Savarkar was dealt a fresh blow. According to the official 'Jail History Ticket of V D Savarkar' maintained by the Home Department, he was on this day sent to six months' solitary confinement 'until further orders'. The jail ticket does not mention why he was thus isolated. The sight from 'Convict No. 32778' Vinayak Savarkar's 'Cell No. 52', where he would be alone, held out another threat: it looked over the gallows where three men could be hanged at the same time.

The jail history ticket shows that after six months of solitary confinement, he was, in June 1912, once again given 'one month's separate confinement for writing letters to others without sanction'. On 10 September he was given 'seven days standing handcuffs for having in possession a letter written to another convict'. This meant standing against a wall inside the cell, hands extended above the head and held in handcuffs tethered to the wall, for eight hours a day. During this time the prisoner could not use the toilet. Most of them passed urine on the walls and stools on the floor and endured the stink until a jail worker cleaned it all up while hurling abuses at the person who had 'dirtied' the floor.

In November 1912 Savarkar was placed, for the third time, in separate confinement for a month 'for being in possession of a note written by another convict'. For three days – from 30 December to the first day of the year 1913 – he 'refused to eat his food all day'. But in December came the only silver lining that year: he was allowed to send his first letter from the Andamans to his brother Narayan, who was studying medicine in Calcutta. Savarkar tried to sound light-hearted, asking Narayan if he had already lost his heart to a Bengali girl and forgotten the Marathi language, while emphasizing that he was a staunch advocate of 'inter-provincial marriages among the Hindus'. He explained the jail routine in some detail, said he was of sound health and inquired, 'In your letter inform me – how is our dear Motherland getting on? Is the Congress united? Does it pass the resolution for the release of the political prisoners from year to year as it did at Allahabad in 1910? Any remarkable Swadeshi enterprise like the iron works of Tata or Steam Navigation Company or new Mills? How is the Republic of China? Does it not sound like Utopia realised? . . . And Persia, Portugal and Egypt? And are the Indians in South Africa successful in getting their demands?'[14] He wanted to know if any important law, such as the one Gokhale wanted introduced on compulsory education, had been passed, and when 'the great Tilak' was due for release. In this and every subsequent letter he could send home once a year, he poured forth his affections for the three women he most cared for: wife Yamuna, 'Vahini' (sister-in-law) Yesubai, and Bhikaiji Cama.

In his first letter from prison, he said pithily, 'Man can never go out of it [jail] exactly as he came in.'[15]

Savarkar's annual letters to Narayan were but a brief respite from an otherwise miserable existence of lurching between solitary confinement and Chinese torture. When Port Blair officials noted in the prison record in December 1913 that he was 'absolutely refusing to work', he got one more month in solitary confinement. From 17 January 1914 he was given the task of rope-making and, on 'absolutely refusing to work' again on 8 June, was made to stand handcuffed for a week, a second time. The day the handcuffs were taken off, he still refused to work, and was ordered to be placed in a 'chain gaug'.

Barely had that punishment begun when, two days later, on 18 June, he was given ten days in 'crossbar fetters' for defying work orders. A crossbar fetter was a metal triangle, 'tied at three points, the ankles and the waist', which, once fixed, ensured you couldn't bend and had to keep your legs spread apart all the time.[16]

The jail ticket clinically states that the day after the crossbar fetters were fixed, Savarkar asked 'for work' and was 'put in rope making'. The fetters, though, were removed only after the ten-day period. In mid-July 1914 he was back to the chain gaug, and those chains were removed only three months later, in October.

Savarkar's public prominence, his escape bid and the case at The Hague made him a central figure among the ranks of the revolutionaries imprisoned in the Andamans. That he had made a substantial impression on them is clear from a dream that Ullaskar Dutt, an Alipur case convict, had during his stay there. Ullaskar himself was a prominent revolutionary, initially sentenced to death; the Calcutta High Court, on his appeal, changed it to transportation for life. He described in his book how, when he was threatened with thirty lashes by Barry, each of which would 'cut into your flesh one inch deep', he vividly saw in his dream Savarkar engaging in a duel with the notorious jailer on his behalf. 'He [Savarkar] threw one [blow, from a gloved fist], with such unerring aim at him [Barry], that it fell squat on his face and made him smart, looking quite the fool that he was,' Ullaskar wrote.[17]

Yet dreams were one thing, reality another. The torture techniques had deadly effects. On 29 April 1912, Indu Bhushan Roy, a young Maniktala case convict or 'Convict No. 31555' in the Raj's bland bureaucratic lingo, hanged himself by the window grille inside his cell with a torn piece of his kurta. Dr F.A. Barker of the prison hospital refused to admit or tend to any political prisoners and instead promptly recommended they be flogged. Indu Bhushan was found hanging by the warder a little after 2 a.m., and Dr Barker came in to take a look six hours later.[18] Savarkar, who in his most widely read book, *Majhi Janmathep*, recalled in harrowing terms his years in Cellular Jail, wrote he knew that Indu Bhushan's spirit had been crushed by the cruel treatment (they were in the same Block 7) and that he had tried to dissuade the young man from self harm when Indu had spoken to him once about putting an end to his life.

Indu Bhushan's was the first suicide by a political revolutionary in the jail, and Savarkar wondered if his own would be next; he had fought off suicidal thoughts with real difficulty the day he had fainted in the oil press yard.

Less than two months later, on 15 June 1912, Savarkar woke up to very loud cries from Block 5. Ullaskar Dutt was being dragged out by jail staffers. 'Ullaskar has gone insane!' one of the warders shouted. The prisoner was taken to the lunatic ward. His father, a retired professor, sent nine frantic letters to the Viceroy asking about his son's condition and the reasons for it; after the ninth letter, he got a terse reply from Port Blair's chief commissioner, Browning: 'Patient's insanity is due to malarial infection. His present condition is fair.'[19] Six months after that, Ullaskar was moved to a lunatic asylum in Madras.

The tragedies of Indu Bhushan Roy and Ullaskar Dutt drove the political inmates to organized protest. While two of them, the editor of *Swaraj*, Ladha Ram, and a seventeen-year-old Nani Gopal Mukherjee, went on a hunger strike in September 1912, the others struck work. They demanded they be given three rights accorded to ordinary prisoners: work outside jail after the first six months of imprisonment, clerical responsibilities and remission in sentences. The fourth demand was for books and newspapers.

The strike continued till December 1912, with Ladha Ram and Nani Gopal being force-fed through tubes and the latter being subjected to 'standing handcuffs' in that condition and ordered to spend an additional year in prison as punishment. When the superintendent finally promised corrective action and asked them to await the Government of India's decision, many of the prisoners withdrew the strike, but almost an equal number would not budge. Their firmness even after various kinds of fetters were imposed on them compelled the Raj to send Parcey Lukas, director of the Indian Medical Service, to talk to them. Lukas soon brokered a truce, and the strikers agreed to return to work on the assurance that they would be granted light labour and permitted to work and live outside the jail after six months. Certain kinds of books too would be allowed.

Babarao had joined the strike from day one and endured serious humiliations. Vinayak Savarkar did not go on strike right away. His position, he explained in his memoirs, was that all political prisoners ought to wait until they got their letters from home. They were, at the time, allowed to write and receive just one letter in a year. As October had almost dawned, a reply was due for most of them. That was their sole way of finding out what was going on back home. Their family members of course needed to be careful while writing back, as any letter that smacked of politically sensitive information would not be passed on after screening, but it was nonetheless possible to write of broader political developments so that those who were incarcerated and deprived of any other source of information got the general drift.

Besides, Savarkar wrote, the letter he got from Narayan, who had been released after six months in jail, 'always contained fuller news of events in India, and that had afforded to all of us ample matter for discussion later on. It used to be circulated throughout the prison for perusal by political prisoners. As the time was near for receiving the letter, I had decided to postpone going on strike till the receipt of that letter.'[20]

When the letter came, Savarkar was told it could not be

handed over to him because it contained 'objectionable content'. He then struck work himself. When Nani Gopal's health turned precarious towards the end of December, Savarkar went on a hunger strike. This was not to join Nani Gopal but to persuade him to give up his own agitation. Savarkar had requested earlier that he be allowed to speak to Nani Gopal, but had not been allowed to.

Savarkar said that he regarded hunger strikes as self-defeating. 'I was always against the suicidal policy of [a] hunger strike, as I regarded it as ruinous to the individual and ruinous to the cause,' he wrote and recounted the entire episode:[21]

> That [hunger strike] was not the way to fight the enemy, I maintained strongly. My view had its desired effect on the minds of our friends and they gave up the hunger strike. The hardest nut to crack was Nani Gopal. He would not yield. He was on the verge of death. I, therefore, employed an extreme measure to overcome his resistance. I threatened him with hunger strike if he would not give up his own. And the following day I acted up to my word. I went on a hunger strike. The news that I had stopped taking my food went like wildfire round the prison . . . I was tried for this new offence. But in the trial, instead of punishing me, they [the authorities] exhorted me to break the fast. I told them why I had gone on hunger strike, and asked them to permit me to speak to Nani Gopal. When Nani heard the news that I had declared three days' hunger strike, he was stricken with grief. I was taken to his cell by Mr. Barrie. I saw him and he agreed to break his fast.

Savarkar told Nani Gopal that death by obstinacy was not glorious and said, in terms that will surely be regarded as politically incorrect today, 'Do not die with a feminine stubbornness; if you must die, die fighting.'[22]

Savarkar was not on the list of nineteen political prisoners eventually allowed to work and live outside the jail as part of the agreement; he had to continue making ropes in the prison yard. All the nineteen too were in August 1913 abruptly summoned back to the prison. The superintendent alleged they had formed a secret society and were plotting to kill one of the officials by manufacturing a bomb and hurling it at him. They got locked up again.

By now, the Indian population on the mainland had become aware of the ordeals these men were facing. The *Bengalee* had published three articles in 1912 on the subject after an inmate, Hotilal Varma, had almost miraculously succeeded in smuggling a letter out to Calcutta. The *Tribune* of Lahore, the *Maratha* of Pune and Guy Aldred's *Herald of Revolt* in London had taken up the issue in earnest, and the campaign had acquired a momentum the Raj could no longer ignore. Yet it deputed its home member (equivalent to home minister), Reginald Craddock, not so much to inquire into the prisoners' situation but to discuss the superintendent's proposal to keep them within the jail's confines (as opposed to allowing them to live and work on the island) till the end of their term. Craddock met five prisoners, including Savarkar, in November 1913 and concluded that once out on the island they could not only conspire among themselves but also win the sympathy and support of ordinary prisoners as well as the common population settled in Port Blair. Some prisoners, Craddock warned, 'were of a specially dangerous type and had shown qualities of leadership by guiding political and revolutionary movements'. They could 'easily use thousands of convicts as their tools' and must not be allowed to step out of jail, he said.

Savarkar, in particular, deserved no liberties at all, Craddock stated in his report. 'If he is allowed outside . . . he would certainly escape. His friends could easily charter a steamer to one of the islands and a little money distributed locally would do the rest. In case he is sent to an Indian Jail he would certainly manage his escape from there also,' the home member said.[23] Craddock's recommendation was to keep Savarkar and the other 'life convicts' (prisoners serving life terms) in the Andamans and send the others back to Indian jails 'where their sympathisers were not large in number'.

The Raj agreed to repatriate the 'term convicts' to jails in their respective provinces, but sixteen political prisoners then launched another strike against the rejection of remission of sentences and continued their stir even after the term convicts had left for India. Angry and upset by the show of defiance, the superintendent referred to Savarkar as 'the ringleader of all the political prisoners' and wanted him confined in his cell 24x7 to quell the agitation. He also suggested Savarkar be taken away from the Andamans altogether as it was 'dangerous to keep him near other political prisoners'.[24]

The rigours of prison life stayed more or less the same for those left behind following the repatriation of term prisoners. With the outbreak of the First World War in 1914, Port Blair authorities clamped down on political convicts out of concern that Britain's adversaries might make an attempt to wrest the Andamans with their assistance. Not too long after the conflict began, a German submarine, *Emden*, was found plying in the waters around the Andamans, so a regiment was hurriedly dispatched to Port Blair as rumours swirled that the Germans planned to storm the island, free the political activists – the inmates, all taken together, could outnumber the prison squad – and with their help take Burma and from there enter the rest of Indian territory (the British had made the Buddhist kingdom of Burma a province of India in 1886; it was separated from British India in 1937).

The influx of hundreds of new political prisoners during the war period and their resistance to Barry's tactics fed into these fears, ensuring that the severity of the clampdown remained unvarying. Members of the Ghadar Party came in significant numbers, as did those convicted in the Lahore conspiracy case. Ghadar had been launched in California by the revolutionary Lala Hardayal, and fired by his ideas Sikhs based in the US came back secretly to the Punjab when war broke out to try to oust the British from India; most of them were arrested and transported to Cellular Jail. The Lahore conspiracy was the brainchild of Rash Behari Bose and V.G. Pingley. They wanted Indian soldiers in army contingents based in the north to launch a rebellion which would be backed by military assistance they had already sought from foreign powers. Their plan too was busted.

Among the Lahore case prisoners was Bhai Parmanand from Punjab. Finding Barry's abuses intolerable, Parmanand, along with Ashutosh Lahiri of Bengal, lifted and flung Barry to the ground. For this they got thirty lashes each. Another inmate, Ram Rakhan, killed himself because he was not allowed to wear the sacred thread, and Prithvi Singh was kept in solitary confinement for years at a stretch. To add to the atmosphere of conflict and suppression, the prisoners launched one more strike during the war, for which Savarkar was again held responsible by Barry and named as prime instigator.

Savarkar indeed was a nationalist icon for Ghadar members, for at least one of them confessed to having turned to revolution after seeing a cartoon of Savarkar yoked to the oil press in the party mouthpiece in California. Another revolutionary had landed in Port Blair after he had read Savarkar's book on 1857 and tried to emulate the revolt's heroes.[25] A one-time Ghadar member, Nawab Khan of Ludhiana, who had worked closely with Hardayal in San Francisco, turned approver later and told a probe panel in Lahore that when the group had met in America and made up their minds to launch the mouthpiece *Ghadr*, they had decided 'to translate into Urdu the history of the Mutiny written by Savarkar in English'.[26]

Savarkar himself wrote much poetry inside his cell, scribbling stuff on walls with nails hidden inside door bolts or with a plant's thorny leaves. All lines were committed to memory before being wiped out, so that they could be 'rescued' later. Two poems, 'Bedi' (Fetters) and 'Kothadi' (The Cell), were autobiographical, one a paean to Rabindranath Tagore on his winning the Nobel Prize in 1913 and yet another, 'Kamala', a leap of the imagination with its rich imagery about a garden and the flora of the psyche.

As war drew gradually to a close in favour of Britain, the political captives intensified efforts to secure a better deal for themselves and, if possible, a way out of the island.

8

A conditional release

Savarkar was from the outset revolted by the conditions in Cellular Jail. The prospect of spending fifty years in that dungeon was spirit-destroying. There wasn't much hope of coming out alive, considering the damage the jail inflicted on its inmates physically and psychologically and that the average lifespan of an Indian of his time was under forty. Whether he would ever see his home and homeland (India's mainland) and family again was just as uncertain.

Several prisoners, even those with five- and ten-year terms, contemplated and, in some cases committed, suicide. Savarkar, we have seen earlier, had thought of ending his life at the oil press – he had done so earlier too, when he was being brought back to India on the steamer following the failed escape bid – before he pulled himself back, but he was powerfully opposed to the idea of killing oneself. He thought it a colossal waste and akin to granting the adversary a walkover. Whenever an inmate he knew turned suicidal, Savarkar would try to talk him out of it and suggest he obtain whatever concessions the Raj was willing to give and get out of that hellhole at the earliest opportunity. Prisoners, whether allowed to live outside jail in the Andamans or sent back to a prison on the mainland or released altogether, had to abide by certain conditions. Savarkar was all for accepting those conditions so long as 'certain core principles', as he defined them, were not compromised. Even if barred from participating in political activities for a certain period, he argued, a person could prove himself useful to society in various ways and work towards his own, and society's, advancement. To survive, return home and restart life was to give oneself and one's ideas, opinions and ambitions a chance; death meant the end of it all.

The theory of self-survival as the most precious thing that he put forward had its critics, and it attracted controversy, as did his whole political career. Savarkar's critics pointed to what they saw as an obvious contradiction in his approach. Hadn't Savarkar repeatedly belittled Gokhale and the other Congress Moderates for their petitions to the British? Hadn't he openly called for sacrifice and martyrdom for the Indian cause, they asked. This paradoxical stand, again, had its roots in his notion that his own skills were in leadership, oratory and strategizing. He would not shy away from acts of courage – proof of that included his protest for Swadeshi in Pune, his time in London, his political journalism, him raising the lone resistant voice at a public meeting to condemn Dhingra and above all him plunging into the waters at Marseilles. But putting himself out as a foot soldier when the need, as he perceived it, for his talents was greater elsewhere – specifically for the framing and articulation of a nationalist ideology and a political plan – was, in his view, not sensible. Not everyone was convinced of that, and we will get to the stinging criticisms soon, but first a look at Savarkar's attempts at release.

These were manifold – and they were made throughout his stay at the Cellular Jail even when he was refusing to work, joining protests and strikes, and writing letters and notes to fellow inmates that resulted in solitary confinement and other torture.

Savarkar filed his first 'petition for clemency', the jail history ticket tells us, on 30 August 1911 after nearly two months of being in the Andamans. It was rejected in four days.

After having faced sixteen months of incarceration and a series of punitive measures such as solitary confinement, work on the oil press and 'standing handcuffs', he filed on 29 October 1912 a second plea for release, stating his 'conduct has been better'.[1] The authorities were not convinced: not only had he been found 'writing letters to others without sanction' on two recent occasions, a 'pencil', purportedly a dangerous item, had also been seized from him. Two more petitions were sent out in the next two years – in November 1913 and September 1914. Before the 1913 request, Savarkar mentioned in his letter home that he ought to have been released and allowed to work and live on the island by this time. But neither he nor Babarao, who had been brought to the Andamans before him, had been let out. Referring to the practice of permitting prisoners, after some years, to bring in family members and stay with them in Port Blair, Savarkar wrote that for him and Babarao 'the authorities here can do very little' probably because 'orders we suppose directly come from the Indian Govt.'. So Narayan was also urged to 'send a petition to the Indian Govt.'.[2]

By the second half of 1914, as mentioned earlier, all term prisoners had been sent back to India. Only the political ones with life terms remained, and some of these too had been lucky enough to leave the Andamans following King George V's 'proclamation' of royal amnesty, his so-called grand gesture at the 1911 pageantry called the Coronation Durbar.

The outbreak of the First World War in 1914 created the impression in England as well as in India that things could no longer go on as usual, and as Indian nationalists took the opportunity to push their case, Britain, under pressure, began speaking of new constitutional reforms. These would be the Montagu–Chelmsford reforms of 1919. In his 1914 plea Savarkar volunteered to go to the war front if Britain freed all political prisoners, provided colonial self-government to India and allowed for the Imperial Legislative Council to have a majority of Indian representatives.[3]

Before the government had taken a call on his 1914 petition, he wrote to Narayan asking him to send a public petition 'at the end of the war' for the release of political convicts, suggesting that he was not hoping for a positive reply to his petition immediately. If a journey back home was not likely soon, Savarkar was willing to accept the next best thing. 'At any rate,' he told his brother, 'you may ask for us to be sent out of this jail just as all other prisoners . . . are allowed to go and settle on the island and bring their family here.' He felt that 'by repeated petitions from both you and us both' at least such concessions, well within the jail regulations, could be won.[4]

In February 1915 his sister-in-law Yesubai and wife, Yamuna, wrote separately to Lord Hardinge, Minto's 'liberal' successor as Viceroy. Yamuna's contention was that her husband had not defended himself during trial as he believed that, having landed in France, he was fully deserving of political shelter; if he had, he may have proved himself innocent. The colonial bureaucracy returned both pleas, saying they must be routed through the governor of Bombay, Lord Willingdon. That was done, and Willingdon said a firm no; the Viceroy endorsed his view.[5]

Savarkar himself made a fresh appeal for amnesty to the Viceroy in 1915 and then again in 1917 – his sixth such plea – this time addressing it also to Edward Montagu, who had just taken over as Secretary of State for India. The Viceroy too had changed by this time, with Lord Chelmsford coming in, and the statements of both, appearing to be a great deal sympathetic to Indian aspirations, sparked fresh hopes.

While speculation was rife on the nature of constitutional reforms the two would propose, Savarkar wrote to them that if home rule were granted without all political prisoners being liberated, it would not 'touch the real roots of discontent in the land'. But, ever political, and with an eye on the greater prize, Savarkar added, equally non-assuring would be the release of convicts without any sincere effort at forming responsible government, by which he meant 'at least a substantial majority' for Indians 'in the Viceregal Council' without a Council of State in England 'presiding over it and mixing a curse with every blessing'. Provided such an arrangement were made 'then I for one and many whom I know would consciously adopt such a constitution' and 'would, if thought fit by our people and given a chance to do so by the Govt. work under it and try to fulfil the Mission of our life through the council chambers which have up to this time been bearing nothing but ill-will towards us'. Asserting that it was rare to find a patriot who would prefer bloody revolution if 'the path of constitutional progress' was open to him, he wrote that it was a 'mockery to talk of constitutional agitation where there is no constitution' but 'a crime' to talk of revolutions 'even when there is as elastic and progressive a constitution as, say, there is in England or America'. And he emphasized in the petition that as the whole idea was one of 'general' amnesty, 'I should be the last one to be dissatisfied if that could be done by omitting my own name, if that alone be a thorn in the way of its fulfillment.'[6] This was significant, because it indicated he was willing to give up the revolutionary path and become a constitutionalist.

Finally, with Montagu and Chelmsford together putting out their report on a reforms scheme involving 'self-governing institutions' and 'responsible government' in mid-1918, some in India began to raise the demand for freeing those still rotting away in prisons. Among the first to speak up were the provincial conferences of the United Provinces and Andhra. The latter, in particular, came in for big praise from Savarkar for its 'very definitely and comprehensively worded' resolution which, he said, 'showed that the heart of the Andhras beat in thorough and honest sympathy' with captives who had worked for 'the great deliverance' of the homeland. The Maharashtra and Bombay conferences passed an equally strong resolution.[7] The Indian nationalist papers and periodicals too pressed the point forcefully. The *Bombay Chronicle*, a nationalist paper, reported that home rule advocates had in a meeting in Dadar resolved that not only must a general amnesty be declared for all political prisoners 'at an early date' but 'an enquiry by a non-official agency must be forthwith instituted into the health and jail treatment of the suffering prisoners and internees, especially in the case of Mr Vinayak Damodar Savarkar . . . about whose health much anxiety is being felt as reported in the papers'.[8]

If Savarkar felt relief that at least some noise was being made, it came mixed with a sore disappointment: the Congress's silence. He wrote in a letter to Narayan that he wondered why the Congress was still 'trembling to utter a syllable that might smell of sympathy' and mentioned its 'conveniently' framed resolution of the previous year that had spoken only of releasing internees (those confined not in a prison but in a particular area). He found the silence all the more baffling because so many provincial conferences had already made their views known, and if the organization wanted to be a 'Congress' in the real sense, he said, it was required to voice the sentiments not 'of the few that dominate its proceedings but of the many who give it its weight and support'.

But what had in particular caused this sudden public outpouring of support for Savarkar's release? Of course there were the petitions initiated by Savarkar's wife and by his brother. But there had also been troubling reports in the nationalist press on Savarkar's health. His health had held up until 1915, despite the wretched diet, dismal environment, claustrophobic cells and dismissal of most health complaints by jail officials. Babarao had suffered equally badly, if not more, as he had a persistent problem of migraines, and the prison staff not merely refused to believe these could be disabling but accused anyone who did not have any visible health issue such as fever, vomiting or diarrhoea of making excuses not to work. For Savarkar, the inevitable crack-up of his health came not as a sudden hammer blow but as a gradual, quiet invasion.

In mid-1916, the jail history ticket states, he was admitted to the prison hospital for digestive ailments and recurring fever, a result of the unhealthy diet served to the prisoners. Savarkar's suffering was made worse by the fact that no family members had been allowed to visit him yet, when the normal practice was to sanction visits after five years. In mid-1918 Savarkar admitted to Narayan that his health was 'utterly broken'. Chronic dysentery and the resultant debilitating weakness 'has reduced me to a skeleton', he wrote. His weight, 110 pounds or just 49 kilos the previous year, had dropped to 98 pounds or 44 kilos (Babarao's was just slightly better at 106 pounds or 48 kilos). For eight years, he stated, he had stood firm and borne it all, the 'innumerable and unknown hardships' and 'an atmosphere of frowns and threats and sighs, of demoralising and disheartening stench'. But now, 'I feel the flesh has received wounds that are hard to heal and is day by day pining away,' he wrote. Of late the medical superintendent had been giving him 'special attention', perhaps because of his precarious situation, and he was slightly better as he got hospital food (albeit still working and not hospitalized), which was better cooked, and he was offered milk and bread too. But he feared that 'what is likely is that this constant debility may end in some fatal malady or that inevitable friend so well known in jails, especially in Andamans – the Pthysis [pulmonary tuberculosis]'. Tuberculosis was not curable in those days, not until antibiotics were discovered in the 1940s. The rich dealt with it by living in sanatoriums on the hills or other places where the air was good, but for those whose surroundings were unclean, such as those in Port Blair, there was not much help on hand.

And yet Narayan should not make himself overanxious, he wrote, indicating that he would not give in so easily. His spirit was 'still willing and able to dominate the quivering flesh, willing to suffer even further . . . not only ungrudgingly but unflinchingly', he reassured his brother.[9]

Towards the end of 1918, reports on the state of Savarkar's health began appearing in some Indian newspapers. The following year the physical breakdown was more rapid. Attacks of malaria became frequent, and 'not a fortnight passes without a fever or some attack of stomach complaints', Savarkar wrote. His weight was now 43 kilos, and things would have been worse, he pointed out, if not for the hospital food and exemption from rigorous work he had been granted owing to his 'weakness and chronic malarious inroads'.[10]

In March 1919, Narayan Savarkar, by now a qualified physician, travelled to Delhi to see if any relief could be obtained for his two brothers. In the capital he stayed with G.S. Khaparde, who had recently been elected to the Council of States and who met 'Mr Macpherson', an official in the Secretariat, on Narayan's behalf and inquired about the brothers. But a response was not forthcoming. A couple of days later, Narayan met Vithalbhai Patel, the elder brother of Vallabhbhai.[11] Perhaps as a result of Narayan's efforts, at the end of May 1919, he, his wife, Shanta, and Vinayak's wife, Yamuna, were finally given permission to see Savarkar and Babarao in the Andamans. They had two meetings with them over two days, one for an hour and the other for an hour and twenty-five minutes, according to the jail history ticket. Savarkar was extremely relieved to see his loved ones after more than eight years. The three Savarkar brothers were coming together after a gap of thirteen years – the last time they had all met was when Savarkar had left for England in 1906, though Vinayak and Babarao had had a few quick face-to-face exchanges in Cellular Jail (in one of his letters he had told Narayan that 'while together for a minute or so'[12] he had spoken to Babarao) and had also swapped written notes, sometimes with, but mostly without, official permission.

Savarkar was also allowed a separate and private half-hour meeting with his wife. He had been longing to see her. In his first letter home from prison, he had asked Narayan, the tone of impatience evident, 'Did you show my letter [this one] to my beloved Yamuna? Please translate all to her.' It was 'only a few years more – not more than 5, when a better day will dawn', he had assured her, citing the rule that allowed a convict's family to settle on the island five years into his prison term. 'So my beloved wife, hold on as nobly as you have done,' he said. In other letters he had, apart from voicing his feelings of love for her and making inquiries about her well-being, wished her 'a thousand glories' for her 'silent and yet intense fixity of purpose' and asked what she had been reading, once even ribbing her by telling Narayan that though he must not trouble his own wife over reading and writing, 'do trouble as much as you can my friend Yamuna on that score – she has promised me to act as a typewriter and a clerk – of course without any pay and out of sheer patriotic fervour!'[13] To his 'Vahini', Babarao's wife, Savarkar had sent in every letter his 'respectful pranams' and never tired of stating that she was for him 'a mother, a sister and a friend at the same time'. It was to her that he had addressed what he called his 'will and testament' after his arrest in London in 1910 and compared her, a 'hero's better-half', to 'the divine Uma [Shiva's wife Parvati] practising severe austerities in the snow-clad Himalayas' and to the women of Chittor who, with 'young smiles playing on their lips' had entered the flames rather than giving in to Allauddin Khilji or his men. In early 1915, when some hope had momentarily arisen of the government allowing Narayan to meet him, Savarkar had advised him not to bring his Vahini along. He was 'firmly of the opinion' that 'dear Vahini should not be put to troubles of the voyage this year' because the facilities for travel, and for stay on the island, were far from adequate. 'You should come alone and when you see all the facilities or otherwise here and know the best way to bring her, then the next time . . . you may bring her, and dear Mai [his sister Maina] too . . . I feel it a duty to forgo the inestimable pleasure of seeing those dearest ones this year for the sake of their convenience,' he wrote.[14] Almost throughout 1918, Yesubai had not been keeping well, suffering from repeated bouts of fever and weakness. But surely she would have come a year later? Not that he had been aware even of her illness the previous year; the family had not let him know of it. He asked Narayan why he hadn't brought his Vahini along and was told that she had died just days before the Savarkars got a letter from the authorities saying that she too had been granted permission to go and visit her husband and brother-in-law. The news was shattering for Babarao of course, but equally so for Vinayak, for whom she was 'a source of inspiration'.[15] Yesubai had been the one who had looked after him after his mother's death, and what he had imagined would be a moment to cherish was abruptly turned into a terrible tragedy.

~

Before the landmark Montagu–Chelmsford reforms kicked in in 1919, the government in Delhi communicated to the Port Blair superintendent its 'desire to extend clemency to prisoners on the day of Signature of Peace' marking the end of the First World War. The superintendent wrote back with a brief history of the two Savarkars: Vinayak was 'punished 8 times during 1912, 1913 and 1914 for refusing to work and possession of forbidden articles', he reported. His behaviour had been 'very good' for the last five years, and he was 'always suave and polite but like his brother, he has never shown any disposition to actively assist government', so 'it is impossible to say what his real political views are at the present time', the superintendent noted. The government in Delhi informed the Bombay government in December 1919 that the Secretary of State wanted the passing of the reforms legislation to be accompanied by 'an act of Royal clemency to political prisoners'. The idea was that 'whatever exceptions [to giving clemency] are made they should be as few as possible'. But the Bombay government did not think amnesty to the Savarkars would help at all given the political atmosphere: of late, public feeling had been 'aroused as a result of proceedings of [the] Hunter Commission [appointed to probe the April 1919 Jallianwala Bagh massacre], [the] return of Tilak [from imprisonment in Mandalay] and [the] announcement by him of [the] policy of intensive agitation'. It agreed to accept the central government's general policy and grant 'free pardon to all such prisoners . . . with [the] exception of [the] Savarkar brothers'. Those in the seat of government in Delhi, of course, were fine with that.

Aghast, the *Mahratta* of Pune remarked that 'a cruel wrong has been done' and sharply criticized the Viceroy for acting 'against the Royal Mandate'. The Savarkars 'are not keeping good health and are losing in weight considerably', so 'these considerations also demanded their release', the daily commented. As the *Mahratta* had listed some of the assurances that Savarkar had made to the government, the most significant among them promising he would stick to constitutional means to secure his goals once the Montagu–Chelmsford reforms were introduced, D.V. Belvi asked a question in this regard in the Legislative Council.[16] The government's plain reply was that it had got 'no such representations as are referred to in the article'. Khaparde asked if at least Babarao could be released or sent to an Indian jail. Barindra Ghose, Hemchandra Das and one more Bengali revolutionary had been recently released after having sent petitions similar to those of the Savarkar brothers. So had Bhai Parmanand. But no, the provincial regime did not want Babarao out of the Andamans either. In its responses it was backed by the latest report of the jail committee appointed by the Raj to recommend prison reforms; the panel had categorized the brothers as 'dangerous'.

Indians serving in high positions in the colonial judiciary too were careful not to step over the line laid down by the Raj. For instance, Narayan Chandavarkar, one of the judges who had awarded transportation to Savarkar, published in July 1919 an appeal to the Viceroy for mitigation of the life sentences given to Lala Harkishenlal of the Punjab and some others for fanning the anti-Rowlatt-Act agitation; Savarkar did not figure anywhere on Chandavarkar's list. The East Indian nationalist leader and Savarkar's lawyer Joseph Baptista wrote, in response, an angry letter to the *Bombay Chronicle*, a paper edited by an Irishman, B.G. Horniman. Not only was Horniman sympathetic to the Indian patriots' cause, but he was also the editor who brought to the attention of the Indian people the full horrors of the Jallianwala Bagh massacre which had been sought to be suppressed by the British and Anglo-Indian dailies. (Horniman was deported to Britain immediately after he had published Jallianwala's details.) Chandavarkar, wrote Baptista:[17]

> sent Savarkar to the Andamans for 'attempting' to wage war against the king. The attempt consisted in placing on a book-stall for sale, for three months or thereabouts, some poetic effusions of the youthful Savarkar. These poems were all the Armies, the Navies and Airies and the Munitions and Machine-guns with which the poet or protester 'attempted' to overthrow or overawe the British Government!!! . . . Is it not possible for Sir Narayan to try to mitigate the cruel severity of his own sentence on Savarkar by appealing to H. E. the Governor of Bombay to include him in the coming amnesty as an act of clemency?

As a final appeal, Narayan Savarkar early in January 1920 wrote to the Viceroy and also to the Andamans chief commissioner. From the former he received no reply, and the latter sent a telegram saying, 'No order received from India.' According to Narayan, nearly thirty political bodies had wired the Viceroy since the general clemency order was issued, and he himself was 'receiving nearly half a dozen letters daily inquiring whether my brothers are released'. The people were 'getting anxious', he said.[18] The Home Department finally replied to him, reiterating the brothers' release was not part of the plan.[19]

The *Bombay Chronicle* then ran a campaign of sorts for the brothers' release. In an editorial, the paper, whose guiding spirit Horniman had still not been allowed to return to India, asked the provincial government of Bombay if it was not time for it 'mercifully to recollect' that the Savarkars had 'more than paid for' their guilt. In Bengal three Alipur case convicts were out, and in Madras, C.S. Sitharama Iyer of the Chingleput treason case, convicted of having corresponded with German generals, too had been freed. One of the Savarkars had only 'written a series of inflammatory verses', and 'the brothers have had their portion, and we ask Government to remember them', the daily wrote.[20]

His own hopes not fully extinguished yet, Vinayak Savarkar sent one more petition on 30 March 1920 – his seventh. In addition to the points he had made in the earlier pleas, he clarified that he and his brother were willing to pledge not to participate in politics 'for a definite and reasonable period that the Government would indicate' or even to stay in a particular province or report their movements 'to the police for a definite period after our release'. He was sincere, he said, in expressing 'my earnest intention of treading the constitutional path and trying my humble best to render the hands of the British Dominions a Bond of Love and Respect and of Mutual help and such an empire as is foreshadowed in the [royal] Proclamation with my hearty adherence'.[21]

Why did Savarkar pledge to stay away from politics for a specified period? Because the other political prisoners (such as Barindra Ghose and the other Bengal convicts) granted amnesty that year had been asked to sign exactly such a bond. If they broke it, they were told, they would be sent back to Cellular Jail to serve the rest of their sentence.

In his book on his Andaman experiences, Savarkar has recorded the powerful opposition of many of the inmates to the signing of such a bond. He, for his part, tried to persuade them to go ahead and sign:[22]

> A hot discussion went on among us whether we should at all sign such a pledge for procuring our release. My advice to my friends was that there was nothing wrong in it, as it referred to a future contingency and was in the best national interest. I quoted to them instances from the life of Shivaji, of his dealing with Jay Singh and Afzulkhan; I told them of Guru Govind and his flight after the incident of Chamkore; nay I drew upon the life of Lord Krishna himself, in order to convince them of the correctness of the step they were taking. The most obstinately proud among them would not be persuaded even by these parallels from the past. Their stubbornness on this subject, after all that they had suffered for the cause, inspired me with great hope for the future of the country. But, at last, I could convince them of my point of view, and they all signed the pledge without demur, and thus broke open the lock of the jail in the Andamans.

The Bombay government, asked by the *Chronicle* if it would at least now 'rise to the occasion',[23] said it did not believe in

Savarkar's promise and flatly rejected the parallels he had drawn with Barindra Ghose's case. But it did say, apparently as a concession of sorts, that it was willing to consider the matter a year later.[24]

These sarkari replies were challenged again. The National Union, based in Mumbai but with members from across India, had sent the government and the Secretary of State what the *Chronicle* described as a 'monster petition'[25] signed by 5000 people. Questions were raised in the Imperial Legislative Council by Rangaswamy Ayyangar and Khaparde.[26]

The very vision of constitutional reform was brought under question by the non-release of the Savarkars. At the Provincial Political Conference representing various shades of Indian thought that met in Solapur, attended among others by Annie Besant, a unanimous resolution was passed saying it 'viewed with utter disappointment the non-release of the Savarkar brothers' and condemned 'the illiberal construction put upon the terms of the amnesty clause in the Royal Proclamation' by so-called safeguards such as compatibility with public safety.[27] The Kanara Provincial Conference, meeting in Karwar, passed a similar resolution after it was moved by 'Mr Majali of Belgaum' who 'spoke with a real feeling'[28] and most other provincial bodies followed suit. Referring to the brothers' assurances to the Raj, the *Gujarati Punch* asked, 'Will the Government . . . prove by action rather than words that they are anxious to maintain the liberty . . . of those who do not advocate violent methods of political agitation?' The fact that Babarao Savarkar 'has been a victim to tuberculosis and stands in danger of losing his life . . . is an additional reason the Government . . . should put an end to its wrath towards the Savarkar brothers', it said.[29] And the *Chronicle*, hammering home the point once more, said the Raj's stand on the Savarkar–Horniman cases had created 'a disagreeable impression' and 'so long as such acts of injustice remain unaddressed, the public will . . . refuse to believe in the changed angle of vision of our "rulers"'.[30]

The Congress Working Committee too ultimately adopted a resolution demanding that the Savarkar duo and two other prisoners from the Punjab be set free.[31] The Marathi historian and Savarkar critic Y.D. Phadke has hinted that this might have been the result of Narayan Savarkar's efforts within the Congress. Indeed, as Phadke states, while Vinayak and Babarao did not ever go anywhere close to the Congress, Narayan had joined it soon after he settled in Mumbai after obtaining his degree in medicine. The Bombay and Maharashtra Congress units were at the time still dominated by Tilak aides such as N.C. Kelkar, despite Mahatma Gandhi having inaugurated a new era of politics in India following his return from South Africa, and they might have been instrumental in Narayan veering towards the organization.[32] The youngest of the Savarkars also got along splendidly with the Gandhians and even explained at a Bombay Congress meeting in October 1920 the meaning of Gandhian non-cooperation to the city's residents who might not have fully understood the term and urged them to follow their leader, the Mahatma;[33] and one public meeting that Narayan or 'ND' addressed at Girgaum's Shantaram Chawl – a popular venue for meetings by Indian nationalists – was presided over by 'Mr M.A. Jinnah, Bar-At-Law'.[34]

Moreover, in May 1920 Gandhi himself wrote an article in *Young India* asking why the two were still in the Andamans five months after others had been given amnesty. Pointing to the brothers' vow not to go down the revolutionary path and their desire to 'work under the Reforms Act',[35] Gandhi stated:

> They both state unequivocally that they do not desire independence from the British connection. On the contrary, they feel that India's destiny can be best worked out in association with the British. Nobody has questioned their honour or their honesty, and in my opinion the published expression of their views ought to be taken at its face value. What is more, I think, it may be safely stated that the cult of violence has, at the present moment, no following in India.

Little of what actually went on in Cellular Jail was known to the general public. But this was all set to change in 1921. The government had by this time prepared a special report on the state of the Andaman jail and its inmates but had refused to give in to demands to make it public. It took the well-meaning British politician Josiah Wedgwood to take the lid off the horrors. Wedgwood, who had slammed The Hague tribunal and the British and French governments over Savarkar's deportation in 1911, arrived on a visit to India in January 1921. On a train to Lahore he met a professor of history at the Lahore University. The professor had been a political prisoner at the Cellular Jail and had been released under the royal clemency the previous month. What he told Wedgwood about the goings-on at Port Blair convinced the gentle Britisher that he was speaking the truth, and Wedgwood wrote a piece in the *Daily Herald* of the UK, describing life on the island in its headline as 'Hell on Earth'.

Wedgwood wrote that it was shockingly from among the convicts that gangmasters in the Andamans were chosen, so 'the most hardened criminals' were 'unchecked masters of the rest'. Referring to prisoners from the North-West Frontier Province (NWFP), he said 'the border ruffians and murderers from the martial races bully till life is hell', and 'political prisoners are their special prey'. The political prisoners are 'physically less capable of heavy work, and being of the non-criminal class, are hated by the criminals'. The other victims, he pointed out, were 'the more effeminate races from Burma and Madras', who 'cannot possibly learn the Urdu of the frontiersman in less than a year – a year of incessant punishment and torture'. Worse, with few women on the islands, the Burmese were used as prostitutes. The jail authorities knew of this abuse, and their solution to it was to suggest that wives be allowed to join their husbands in the Andamans. But, said Wedgwood, even the hardened criminals did not want this; his informant had said, 'How could they protect their wives from gangmasters and other brutes in [the] shape of men?' Wedgwood concluded on a sombre note: 'One may be thankful that the patriot Ganesh Savarkar, after 10 years of this hell, is now permanently in hospital awaiting his end – a release from this world to one where there are no tyrants, no prisons, but a goodly company of men like himself who have gone before.'[36]

The former English missionary C.F. Andrews, a dear friend of Gandhi and Rabindranath Tagore, found the details provided in Wedgwood's article so 'appalling' that he wired immediately to the *Bombay Chronicle* from Santiniketan, where he had shifted from Delhi. Saying that his worst fears had been confirmed, Andrews called the punishments handed out to political prisoners in the Andamans 'a grave scandal' and 'altogether intolerable' and said a 'merciful man' like Bombay governor George Lloyd 'cannot possibly allow the Savarkar Brothers in the Andamans after this exposure by Col. Wedgwood'. The penal settlement itself, 'cruelly out of date', must be abolished immediately, he said.[37]

The paper commented that Wedgwood's revelations had made the 'further incarcerations' of the brothers, 'both highly educated and none of them directly concerned with any murderous attack', indefensible.[38]

The sustained campaign at last bore fruit, albeit only partly. In April 1921, the Raj reminded the Bombay government of the readiness it had shown in May 1920 to reconsider the matter after a year's gap. The local government was still rigid, but possibly as a consequence of the fierce criticism, it acquiesced. In May 1921 the brothers were finally shifted to jails on the mainland. Babarao was moved to Bijapur, from where he was shifted later to the Sabarmati prison. Seen as much less of a threat than his brother, he was released unconditionally in September 1922.

Vinayak Savarkar was taken to the Ratnagiri prison. Days before he was brought back to the mainland, Gandhi wrote to the Bengali leader C.R. Das, 'The Savarkar brothers' talent should be utilised for public welfare. As it is, India is in danger of losing her two faithful sons, unless she wakes up in time. One of the brothers I know well. I had the pleasure of meeting him in London. He is brave. He is clever. He is a patriot. He was frankly a revolutionary. The evil, in its hideous form, of the present system of Government, he saw much earlier than I did. He is in the Andamans for his having loved India too well. Under a just Government, he would be occupying a high office.'[39]

As Savarkar, still very weak physically, quietly kept track of various big and not-so-big developments from Ratnagiri jail by poring over the morning papers, the likes of Jamnadas Mehta, the noted lawyer, Vithalbhai Patel and above all Narayan Savarkar kept up their efforts to get him out of there.

Sometime in the second half of 1923, Savarkar was transferred to Yerwada Central Jail in Pune. It was here that J.H. Murray, who had been superintendent in Port Blair earlier and had established a good rapport with the revolutionary, was by a lucky coincidence serving at the time. Savarkar held Murray in high regard. In his letter to his brother in 1915, he had written, 'Captain – now Major – Murray is superintending the jail affairs. As long as he is here, you may rest assured that nothing that evinces a personal rancour will be done or said; no underhand pin-pricks, beyond what the regulations require.'[40] Given that demands for Savarkar's release were still being made publicly from time to time, the newly appointed home secretary in the Bombay government, A. Montgomerie, asked Murray if he felt Savarkar would create trouble if he were set free. The national movement had completely transformed in India during the years that Savarkar was locked up. In the early 1920s, the greatest focus was on Gandhi. Revolutionaries across the country had taken a back seat and constitutional agitation was the focus of the nationalists.

When he got Montgomerie's note, Murray was unaware that Savarkar had already arrived at the Yerwada prison. Murray said he had seen Savarkar a lot when he had been superintendent in the Andamans for seven years, and Savarkar had at that time appeared sincere in his commitment to work within the bounds of the Montagu–Chelmsford reforms and the constitutional/legal framework for government. But in the past three years, they had not been in touch. It was hard to say what Savarkar's thinking might be at the moment. He would speak to him and let Montgomerie know about Savarkar's current line of thought. In any case, Murray believed, Savarkar had spent more than twelve years behind bars, and it was unlikely that if allowed to leave prison, he would imperil his freedom straight away by doing something rash. It was but fair that Vinayak, like Babarao, be given a fresh chance, he stated. But Murray also wanted some truly tough conditions to be laid down, such as non-participation in politics for at least five years, and a return to Cellular Jail if any violations were noticed.[41]

Murray's meeting with Savarkar in Yerwada ended with the superintendent writing to Montgomerie that the prisoner would not object to conditions that did not impinge on his sense of self-regard. Perhaps wanting to check things for themselves, the then Bombay governor George Lloyd and home member Maurice Hayward met Savarkar separately soon after. Both came away thinking that they could not trust him but had vastly different opinions on the course of action to be adopted: Hayward was dead against release, fearing that Indian nationalist elements disillusioned with Gandhi following his withdrawal of the non-cooperation movement might get attracted to Savarkar, while Lloyd was in favour of Savarkar's release simply because he thought of it as sound policy that would in fact assuage popular sentiment.[42]

As these deliberations continued, the Nasik Congress Committee resolved to organize public meetings across the district to ramp up more pressure and demand Savarkar's 'early release'. After Babarao and some others visited Savarkar in the Pune prison, the Poona Sarvajanik Sabha on 13 October 1923 held a public meeting condemning his continued incarceration.[43] According to the *Bombay Chronicle*, the issue was also 'forced on the attention of the Indian National Congress' at its annual session in Kakinada in December 1923, with members lending their 'powerful support' to it.[44]

The consensus that emerged in the British establishment after much deliberation was that Savarkar be permitted to leave jail with stringent conditionalities in place disallowing him from taking part in politics and leaving the confines of Ratnagiri district for five years. Ramping up its assertion of powers, the Raj decided it could extend the five-year period if a review deemed it necessary. Two more promises were sought to be extracted, though the government stated that 'it was explained to him [Savarkar] that it was in no way made a condition of his release': the first was an 'acknowledgement' that he had 'had a fair trial and a just sentence', and the other would be one in which he would express his 'abhorrence of methods of violence'.[45]

Savarkar consented to both clauses but asked if he could live in Nasik, his home district; he knew there was no way he would be sent to Mumbai or Pune, both places which would give a revolutionary of his standing the highest visibility. The government refused, lest he team up with his Abhinav Bharat aides again. In the event, Savarkar accepted Ratnagiri as his new destination and stepped out of jail on 6 January 1924, a little less than thirteen years after he had been dispatched to the Andamans and nearly fourteen years after his arrest in London.

Narayan came to pick him up and the two brothers took the Poona Express to Mumbai, where they stayed at Narayan's new home in Kirloskar Bhavan, Girgaum, for a day, before Savarkar proceeded to Ratnagiri, 350 kilometres to the city's south along the Konkan coastline. The *Bombay Chronicle* reported that on 7 January, a Monday, Narayan's Girgaum residence 'was besieged by a large number of people – men and women – eager to congratulate the brothers Savarkar on their happy reunion after a separation of eighteen long years'. The paper in its editorial mentioned that the patriot's release from jail was among the steps that showed 'the magnitude of the change which has taken place, if not in the heart of Government at any rate in its head' and wished Savarkar 'many years of happiness and useful citizenship, to compensate for all the years that have been lost to him'.[46]

Two things emerged into the public domain soon. One was a public request made by several local newspapers to collect a purse of a decent amount for Savarkar, since his health was so precarious that he would be unable to do strenuous work for some time and would have to depend on his Mumbai-based brother. The other was information in reports in the *Indu Prakash*, *Kesari* and other Marathi dailies listing the conditions imposed on Savarkar and his acceptance of them.[47]

The reactions were swift. Many among the pro-self-rule Indian commentariat were slack-jawed, others deeply saddened that a well-known patriot had been made to sign such things under duress. The Bombay home secretary wrote in his correspondence with relief that some of the Extremist-minded publications had been completely taken aback by Savarkar's signed statement.[48]

From his new home in Ratnagiri, Savarkar before long began writing the story of his incarceration. It was published in serialized form in *Kesari* through 1925 and 1926 and then in *Shraddhanand*, a Marathi weekly edited from Mumbai by his brother Narayan, in early 1927. Published as a book in May 1927, it included, among several other things, Savarkar's explanation – which went along the lines already delineated – of why he did what he did.

In a blistering attack on Savarkar, however, the editor of the Kanpur daily *Pratap*, Ganesh Shankar Vidyarthi, wrote to *Shraddhanand* in 1928 asking why people who fancied themselves 'martyrs' for the Indian cause had in the first place pleaded for 'pardon'. 'Why didn't they embrace death in prison? What was the need to send petitions to the government at all?' he asked indignantly.[49]

Deeply wounded by the criticism, Savarkar immediately wrote a response which *Shraddhanand* carried on its pages. 'From Punjab to Pondicherry and Sindh to Bengal, scores of revolutionaries set fire to their homes so that their nation could free itself and entered into a spirited battle with the adversary in what was virtually the valley of death. When they collapsed on to the battlefield, overpowered and bearing massive wounds, and underwent incredible torture for years, they decided to accept the enemy's condition that they temporarily withdraw from battle and sought freedom so that they could live to fight another day for their motherland,' he emphasized.

Citing Shivaji's example, Savarkar argued that even the Maratha hero had not summoned the 'suicidal courage' to end his life when he was held hostage in Agra. He had sent a flurry of pleas to Aurangzeb to secure release and then, after escaping from the Mughal emperor's clutches, defied the empire to create an independent state. 'In fact, in front of Afzal Khan he appeared with hands folded – the same hands in which he held the tiger claws,' Savarkar remarked.

The year before, the Hindustan Republican Army (HRA) based in north India had attacked a train carrying government funds in Kakori close to Lucknow. In 1927 four of its members were sentenced to death, five transported for life and four given jail terms. In his response to Vidyarthi, Savarkar pointed out that Ramprasad Bismil, one of the four condemned to hang, HRA leader Sachindranath Sanyal and several others in the Kakori and other such cases had sent pleas to the government to try to secure their release, but it was fortunate that 'no wise man had come forward to ask them why they hadn't preferred death instead'. Only 'a person truly petty could be so audacious as to ask those who'd made huge sacrifices why they hadn't died', he wrote and underlined, using an English adage in the otherwise Marathi piece, 'Fools rush in where angels fear to tread.'

Savarkar's lawyerly instincts also seemed to come to the fore. He said that he had read in Calcutta's famous *Swatantra* daily a report on 4 August 1928 revealing how the editor of *Pratap*, Vidyarthi, slapped with a contempt of court notice by a local court, had offered an 'unconditional apology' to get himself discharged from the case. 'Forget about any danger to his life – there was none at all – this editor couldn't even bear the prospect of one or two years in jail,' he wrote.

Savarkar clarified that he was not ridiculing the editor over the apology – it may have been apt in the circumstances. His intention in pointing to the court case, he said, was simply to show that Vidyarthi's criticism was born entirely out of prejudice, and if the prism of prejudice were cast aside, a just and balanced view of the matter was possible.

Vidyarthi had in his own piece also referred to Savarkar's serious differences with Gandhi. To this, Savarkar said it was impossible to argue with someone who did not understand that criticism of non-violence 'didn't mean criticism of Gandhiji as a person'. He and Gandhi, he suggested, knew each other and could discuss things themselves 'without some Tom, Dick and Harry intervening'. Gandhi was at the time engaged in the landmark satyagraha in Bardoli. For now, Savarkar wrote, 'the fight which that great patriot is fighting in Bardoli befits an able commander, and as we believe it is right to fight shoulder-to-shoulder in the national struggle to the extent we all can, our words and our conduct will only be in support of Mahatmaji. It's only when we believe national interest is compromised that we place ourselves in opposition, and that too for the national cause,' he concluded.[50]

The controversy over Savarkar's petitions continues to this day. The Congress and the BJP have had a slanging match over Savarkar more than once, but often it is the mercy pleas around which the discussion revolves. Opinions are sharply divided on the issue. But some things stand out.

Some of Savarkar's followers insist he never wrote any pleas, and one article in a Marathi newspaper in 2018 maintained that even if he did, he certainly did not ask for clemency.[51] That is simply not true, for Savarkar himself did not deny writing the pleas.

Savarkar's modern-day critics, for their part, claim Savarkar never spoke or wrote about his mercy pleas all his life – not even in his tome on the Cellular Jail years – but in fact attempted to conceal this episode of his life. These claims are also absolutely wrong.

9

The new credo of Hindutva

Savarkar had entered the Cellular Jail a passionate promoter of Hindu–Muslim amity, having, among other things, lavished fulsome praise on the Muslim heroes of 1857 such as Awadh ruler Wajid Ali and Rohilkhand rebel chieftain Khan Bahadur Khan. But he came out of prison driven by a desire to remake his country in the name of Hindutva or Hindu nationalism – the Indian nation seen as a nation based on Hinduness.

What explains this change of heart? Part of it may have been due to Savarkar's experiences in the Andamans. His interactions with the jailer Barry's Pathan, Baluchi and Sindhi lackeys had left him bitter. The British believed that any staffers belonging to India's majority community might be sympathetic to political prisoners, most of whom were Hindus, and so only Muslims were tasked with supervising the inmates. To Savarkar these overseers appeared fanatical and overzealous, and not just in their mistreatment of the prisoners. They also converted non-Muslim prisoners to the Islamic faith by way of threats, coercion and inducements. Savarkar described the Pathans, Baluchis and Sindhis as the most fundamentalist of Muslims he met in prison, followed by the Punjabis. The Tamil, Marathi and Bengali Muslims in prison were neither cruel nor anti-Hindu, but the others would taunt the Hindus as 'kafirs' (infidels), he said.[1]

These subordinates of Barry, Savarkar claimed, were in the business of converting, on an average, three to four prisoners every couple of months. Physical and sexual abuse, especially of the very young and the weak, was rampant, and it ensured they yielded to conversion quickly, he said. Many others, Barindra Ghose included, spoke deliberately of their 'ambition to become one day Mussalmans' in front of the worst tyrants such as the jamadars Khoyedad Khan, Mirza Khan and Gulam Rasool to try to get them to show some leniency. Khoyedad had a reputation as a namazi – one who would pray the requisite number of times a day – and a few of the Hindu inmates would routinely extol his 'religious fervour' and offer their own share of milk as a 'bribe' to 'appease' him.[2] The prison regulations forbade any 'undue interference' in religious matters and allowed the inmates to wear sacred symbols, but Upendranath Banerjee wrote that nobody 'dares to touch the beard of the Mussalman or the hair of the Sikh' while being 'only too prompt to take away the thread of the Brahmin'.[3]

While Savarkar thought the 'appeasement tactics' of fellow inmates were understandable given the overall scale of persecution, what seemed to irk him no end was the Hindus' absolute silence on the matter of forced conversions.

There was a lack of unity among the Hindus, Savarkar felt,

and he was irritated by their orthodox beliefs and notions of purity which made it hard for them to come together as a group. He recorded in his memoirs that any Hindu who so much as sat and dined in the company of Muslims – their food was apparently prepared separately in the canteen – was immediately boycotted by the rest as having been 'polluted' by the eating of meat and, possibly, beef. He accused the Muslim warders as well as prisoners of taking undue advantage of the belief widely prevalent among Hindus that seven generations of one's family were defiled and corrupted if one ate cow's meat.

Savarkar found that the baang, or the muezzin's call to prayer, at the break of dawn inside the jail was a serious disturbance to everyone's sleep. He believed the Muslims' prayer time was also a convenient cover for them to take breaks from work. He said they extended their namaz for as long as possible to be able to take some time off from the punishing work. But the Hindus were unable to cite a single such injunction mandated by their faith.

Both Barry and the superintendent turned a deaf ear when he complained to them of the sleep deprivation and disruption, Savarkar wrote, so he took it upon himself to end what he called the free run of the Pathans.

The Hindu religion is not into proselytizing, but Savarkar was fully in favour of welcoming back anyone who had left the fold and wished to return, and indeed of facilitating their re-entry in every way. The Arya Samaj of Dayanand Saraswati had been something of a pioneer in this regard – it had even coined a term for this practice, shuddhi, or purification. Savarkar sought to push this idea in the Andamans. He also suggested that the Hindus 'respond' to the baang with their own loud early-morning prayers, and when the jail officials told him that such a ritual was hardly universally observed among the Hindus, he came up with an ingenious alternative, blowing the shankh or conch shell. The blowing of the conch shell was a time-honoured religious practice that no one could object to, and soon the din created by the two different and competing groups reached such levels that the jail authorities decided neither could any more be allowed, Savarkar claimed.[4]

Similarly, when Savarkar was shifted to Ratnagiri prison in 1921, he reported seeing the same Islamic practices there and wrote, that year, inside his prison cell, a tract titled *Hindutva*, regarded as the seminal text for Hindu nationalists. It was then that the term 'Hindutva' entered India's political lexicon – but it acquired entirely different meanings for different groups. For believers in a Hindu Rashtra it was, and is, the earliest and clearest delineation of their theory of Indian nationhood, inextricably linked to the country's purported Hindu ethos and history. For those prizing India's absorption of multiple faiths and cultures and its assimilation even of confrontational forces as its distinguishing essence, it was, and is, the defining text of exclusionary divisiveness and the scapegoating of non-Hindus, especially Muslims.

Various saints and political leaders from Swami Vivekananda to Dayanand Saraswati and Lokmanya Tilak had publicly called for a Hindu revival before Savarkar did. The major difference was that Savarkar defined his idea of a Hindu resurgence in political terms, not religious. He defined the nation as based on the unifying Hinduness of its people. And called as much for a combative spirit as a cohesive one if India were to retain its essence, which in his opinion was its Hindu civilization and Hindu way of life.

At the very outset, Savarkar made it clear that Hindutva was not the same as Hinduism. It had nothing to do with religion or rituals. The term in English which came closest to the one he was using, he wrote, was perhaps Hinduness. As a principle, Hindutva formed the basis of India's national character, he maintained, and, to provide greater clarity, offered his own definition of who was a Hindu. The word Hindu was as ancient as the Vedas, he contended, and explained that the letter 'Sa' in Sanskrit was often turned into 'Ha' in the Prakrit languages. Thus the land of the people known as the Sapta Sindhus, which had acquired for itself the name Sapta Sindhu, was referred to as 'Hapta Hindu' in the Avesta of the ancient Persians, he said.

Savarkar wasn't really setting out to create a Hindu nation. India was, he asserted, citing some ancient and medieval texts, a Hindu nation in an organic sense. (To those who argued that no Sanskrit text mentioned the word Hindu, he replied that it was 'ridiculous to expect a Prakrit word in classical Sanskrit' and cited the example of Banaras, which too was non-existent in Sanskrit as it was the Prakrit word for the Sanskrit 'Varanasi'. He held out some other Prakrit words such as Jamuna, Sia and Kishan too as examples.) And anyone who considered this nation as his or her pitrubhu (fatherland) and punyabhu (holy land) was a Hindu. The Sikhs, the Buddhists and the Jains, in his view, met both conditions and were therefore Hindus. However, although he would concede that many Muslims and Christians living in India were true nationalists and saw the land of the Sapta Sindhus as their fatherland, their holy land lay elsewhere, in Arabia or Palestine.

Did that mean they were excluded altogether from a nation which had Hindutva as its base? 'Their love is divided,' believed Savarkar, and they would have no choice if they were asked to pick between their fatherland and holy land. It was 'natural' that they should choose the holy land, he stated, adding that he was 'neither condemning nor lamenting', merely being matter-of-fact. He wanted to keep the door open for them, nevertheless, for 'the Bohras and such other Mohammedan and Christian communities possess all the essential qualifications of Hindutva', he said, even if 'they do not look upon India as their holy land'. The 'patriotic' Bohra or Khoja, he argued, 'loves our land . . . as the Fatherland', 'possesses', in certain cases, 'pure Hindu blood', particularly 'if he is the first convert to Mohammedanism', is 'an intelligent and reasonable man, loves our history and our heroes', and 'in fact the Bohras and Khojas as a community worship as heroes our great ten Avatars, only adding Mohammad as the eleventh'.[5] Most of them thus shared with Hindus a common race; after all, their forefathers had been forcibly converted, according to Savarkar. He urged such 'long lost kith and kin', 'so cruelly snatched away at the point of the sword', to come back to the fold, and told them that their brothers and sisters 'with arms extended are standing at the open gate to welcome you'. There was nowhere else they would find greater freedom of worship as in the land 'where a Charvak could praise atheism from the steps of the temple of Mahakal', he said. If only they recognized 'our common Mother' not only as their fatherland but their holy land, they would be 'most welcome to the Hindu fold', he stated.

No one need have any misgivings, for 'we are trying our best' to 'develop the consciousness' and 'attachment to the greater whole' so that 'Hindus, Mohammedans, Parsis, Christians and Jews would feel as Indians first, and every other thing afterwards', he said, perhaps by way of reassurance.

The goings-on in the Cellular Jail no doubt played a role in Savarkar veering rightward and embracing Hindu nationalism, and some commentators have gone to the extent of doubting if the incident of the assault on the village mosque in Bhagur was a later invention of his – he wrote his childhood reminiscences *after* the Hindutva text – just to make the point that his credentials had always been sufficiently pro-Hindutva.

~

Aside from his experiences in the Andamans, another factor in the ideological turn Savarkar took was the deterioration in Hindu–Muslim relations since the revolt of 1857 and the social climate of the time. The immediate social and historical context that Savarkar inhabited can briefly be summarized as follows.

First, the Wahhabi movement was launched in India by Saiyid Ahmad of Rai Bareili in the early nineteenth century. He called for the restoration of Muslim rule (Dar-ul-Islam) over India, which had become 'enemy territory' (Dar-ul-Harb). The British must be driven out and the Indian 'infidels', the Hindus and Sikhs, must be brought to heel, Ahmad said, and built an organization to achieve his aims, seeking support from the Islamic clergy and from Muslim rulers like the Nizam of Hyderabad. Ahmad's movement was active in 1857 (he himself died in 1831) but despite his call for the ouster of the British, the Wahhabis stayed away from the Great Uprising, wanting to have no truck with the Hindus, and were soon crushed by the British.[6]

Another man with the same name, but spelt as Syed Ahmed, kept his distance from the mutineers. Ultra-loyal to the British, Syed was a court official in Bijnor, sixty-odd kilometres from Meerut, where the rebellion was most intense, and he saved a British collector called Shakespeare and some other Britishers in the province from the mob. The British knighted him in 1870 and, in order to propel the Muslims towards western-style education, he formed the Muhummadan Anglo-Oriental College in Aligarh and was rewarded with a seat in the Viceroy's Imperial Legislative Council in 1878. Here he firmly opposed elections, fearing that since they operated on the principle of representation on the basis of what the majority of voters chose, the Hindus would always be dominant in India.

Not too long after, he gave his politics an openly anti-Hindu colour. Initially totally opposed to religious orthodoxy among Muslims, Syed Ahmed was quoted as saying in 1884 that their religious differences notwithstanding, Hindus and Muslims constituted one nation. But by 1888 he had concluded that 'Hindus and Muslims were two different nations' that 'could not lead a common life if the British were to leave India'.[7] His was the very first expression of the two-nation theory, and it came as music to the Raj's ears, for it was doing its damnedest to 'divide and rule', which didn't mean inventing differences but exploiting and exacerbating the fault lines that already existed.

One of the techniques that would be employed to divide and rule and to ensure that Hindus and Muslims would not unite as one people was to introduce the notion of separate electorates, that is, Hindu voters would elect their representatives and Muslim voters would elect theirs. The corollary of this principle was that Hindus could not represent Muslim interests, and vice versa. In 1883 the demand for separate representation for Muslims was raised for the first time by Amir Ali, the leader of the National Muhammadan Association who, in the words of B.C. Pal, had been 'inoculated with the virus of Pan-Islamism' – a global Islamic movement – by Djamal Al-din Al-Afghani, the founder of the Pan-Islamic movement, during his India visit in the early 1880s. By 1887 the Secretary of State for India Lord Hamilton was saying that a 'new element of intrigue and commotion' had been introduced in India 'by the Pan-Islamic Council in Constantinople and the close connection which is being established between the [Turkish] Sultan and Indian Mohamedans'.[8] The Turkish Sultan, or the Caliph, or Khalifa, was seen by some as the spiritual head of the Muslim world and epitomized Savarkar's charge that Indian Muslims had loyalties to powers outside of India.

Syed Ahmed pitted his Aligarh movement against the Indian National Congress after the latter was formed in 1885, saying that it was looking for representative government which merely meant the rule of the Hindus. His word came to prevail over most in the Muslim community, much to the unhappiness of the Congress's third president, Badruddin Tyabji, a prominent member of Islam's Khoja sect who wondered in his presidential address why the Muslims were not working shoulder to shoulder with other fellow Indians. Similar concerns were voiced by two other top leaders: Surendranath Banerjea said the Muslims were keeping aloof from the Congress and working 'in opposition to the national movement', and G.K. Gokhale said in a speech that 'seventy millions of Muhammadans were more or less hostile to national aspirations'.[9]

Bankim Chandra Chatterjee's novel *Anandamath* centred on Hindu resistance to Muslim misrule became hugely successful in 1882, and in the same decade several Hindu–Muslim riots erupted across the country's length and breadth. The pattern continued into the next decade with big spurts in violence occasioned by clashes during Dussehra and Muharram processions, the slaughter of cows which were regarded as holy by Hindus, and the razing of temples and mosques. In the mid-1890s a number of 'Gorakshini Sabhas' or cow protection societies sprang up in quite a few regions, and their acts of blocking vehicles carrying the animals for slaughter met with resistance from Muslim cattle traders and sparked further rioting. Syed Ahmed himself requested the Muslim community to shun cow slaughter, but hardly anyone on either side appeared to be in a mood to listen.[10]

The roots of the two-nation theory penetrated deeper into the soil when a delegation of thirty-six Indian Muslims led by the Aga Khan, the spiritual head of the Ismaili Muslims, went to Simla in 1906 for a meeting with Viceroy Minto demanding representation for the community in civic and district bodies on the basis of communal electorates and in the legislative councils on the basis of a 'Muslim electoral college'. The representation should not be on the basis of their numbers alone as they were one fifth of the Indian population, they stated, but keeping in mind the 'political importance' of Muslims, their 'contribution to the defence of the Empire' and 'with due consideration' of the position they had in India just over a hundred years ago. Minto was delighted to accept their terms, and Morley in London was so pleased, he stated that 'the whole thing has been as good as it could be'.[11]

The Raj's greatest satisfaction was in knowing that it could leverage the delegation's demands as refutation of the Congress's theory of Hindu–Muslim unity and to legitimize Curzon's initiative of partitioning Bengal. The All-India Muslim League was founded in December 1906. It declared its support for the Empire, insisted on education for Muslims and asked for separate electorates, which were granted legal sanction by the Minto–Morley reforms of 1909. These were extremely limited reforms. From 1861 India had had, under the Indian Councils Act, the Viceroy's Executive Council, which acted as a sort of union cabinet with the Viceroy at its helm and his handpicked men as its members. Then there was the Imperial Legislative Council, the principal central lawmaking body (of which the Viceroy's Executive Council members or 'cabinet' members were also a part) and each of the provinces had their provincial legislative councils. A small number of elite Indians were appointed on the councils but they had no say in lawmaking; their role was merely consultative. First in 1892, and then in 1909, a small number of Indians were even allowed to be elected to these councils from certain faith-based and social groups, such as the Muslims, Anglo-Indians, landowners, high taxpayers, and officials at universities, municipal boards or chambers of commerce. Their select voters – they all had to be taxpayers, the others were excluded – too were from these same groups, and the voiceless Indian masses had no vote at all. The elected 'native' council members themselves weren't vested with powers either, so they too were simply advisers, with all Raj lawmakers and officials free to disregard their advice.[12] One young Muslim in the Congress, Muhammad Ali Jinnah, denounced the idea of separate electorates, saying it meant 'dividing the nation against itself'.[13] In just a few years the same Jinnah, a barrister in the Bombay High Court, joined the Muslim League. His change of heart had also much to do with the realization, now that he had himself been appointed to the Imperial Legislative Council, that India's Muslims would be secure if they got one-third of seats in the Central Legislature. Dual memberships being then allowed, he remained an influential personality in the Congress at the same time. During the First World War, along with the League, the Congress arrived at an internal agreement on demanding 'early self-government' based on 'a constitutional system, with direct elections and separate electorates for religious minorities'.[14]

Tilak too had turned, after his six-year ordeal in Mandalay, into a Moderate. He had formed his own Home Rule League, as had Annie Besant, the theosophy guru whom Savarkar mentioned as one of two exceptions – the other being Vivekananda's disciple Sister Nivedita – that 'proved the rule' as far as his definition of a Hindu was concerned. Tilak's League was modelled on the Irish Home League and stood for 'self-government' or 'Swaraj' for India within the Empire, like Australia, Canada and New Zealand. And he was willing to give constitutional reforms a chance.

He made a spectacular comeback to the Congress in Lucknow in 1916 and was hailed by Jinnah for playing 'a very important role in bringing about Hindu–Muslim unity'. The acceptance of separate electorates by the Congress, which is what Jinnah was alluding to, was cleared with some difficulty. It generated a lot of heat in the Congress, with both Hindus and Muslims getting agitated over the issue of communal representation, but Tilak stood 'calm as a rock', the Congress activist C.S. Ranga Iyer wrote. Tilak wasn't enamoured of the pact, Iyer said,[15] 'but if it would satisfy the Muslims, if it could bring them to the Congress, if it could replace their extra-territorial patriotism by Indian nationalism, the agreement was worth reaching'. It was at this time that Tilak uttered his oft-quoted line 'Swaraj [Home Rule] is my birthright and I shall have it'.

The Lucknow Pact, which also came to be known as the Tilak–Jinnah Pact, enunciated what the scholar Richard Cashman has described as Tilak's 'alternative Muslim policy'.[16] The pact called for abolition of the Secretary of State's Council in London and enlarged central and provincial councils, with Indians constituting 50 per cent of members of the Viceroy's Executive Council, all to be chosen by elected members of the Imperial Legislative Council. Indians must get 'equal status and rights of citizenship with other subjects . . . throughout the Empire' and 'commissioned and non-commissioned ranks' in the army and navy, it stated. Importantly, the pact supported the principle of 'positive discrimination' in favour of Muslims established by the 1909 Act, guaranteeing them one-third of all elected seats on the Imperial Legislative Council and increasing the number of guaranteed seats on the provincial councils, though, with the separate electorates they would get, Muslims could no longer vote in the general constituencies as well. Nor would Muslims have separate electorates in Bengal and the Punjab, where they were anyway in a majority. A further protection for all minorities was that 'no bill or resolution' in any council related to any of these communities could make any progress if three-fourths of a community's members opposed it.[17] For the first time since 1857, thus, Hindus and Muslims had come to a power-sharing agreement, and Tilak's stand was, after his imprisonment in Mandalay, radically different from Savarkar's following his incarceration in the Andamans. Neither Tilak nor the rest of the Congress knew at the time, of course, that the negotiations with the Muslim League and their acknowledgement and recognition of the League as a body representing India's Muslims would have far-reaching consequences in time.

Yet, for all their flexibility vis-à-vis Muslims, neither Tilak nor the Congress had mellowed enough to accept the Montagu–Chelmsford reforms. These reforms promised much but delivered little. On the Viceroy's Executive Council or the central cabinet, there were to be three Indians (instead of two allowed earlier) out of a total of six members, including the Viceroy. The Imperial Legislative Council or central legislature would be split into two: a legislative assembly, with 140-odd members, 106 elected and the rest nominated, and a Council of State, an upper house, to represent the landed elite. The governance structure was thus somewhat changed, but the Indians found that the superstructure of imperial power remained the same because the bodies were all advisory in nature, and all powers of approval and rejection stayed in the Viceroy's hands. The various bodies could not even hold the Viceroy accountable for any actions; only the London government could. The provincial legislatures, for their part, had again been promised plenty of autonomy, and while their strength grew a hundred per cent in terms of numbers, with 70 per cent of their members to be elected, they were crippled by a system known as 'dyarchy' or dual governance, which meant that the governor called the shots in the most important matters such as law and order (police), revenue, justice, labour and irrigation and towered over his ministers – chosen from among the elected members to look after the so-called transferred departments like education, public works, agriculture, cooperatives – like a prime minister with full constitutional authority. The 'separate electorates and reserved seats introduced for Muslims in 1909 were increased both in the provinces and in the centre', they were 'also extended to other minorities' like the Sikhs and Indian Christians, and the electorate itself was greatly expanded though the criteria of property and taxpayer status remained.[18]

Tilak and the Congress thought the reforms did not go far enough and were in fact intended to tighten Britain's grip on the colony, and to add insult to injury were accompanied by the repressive Rowlatt Acts which curbed civil liberties. The Jallianwala Bagh massacre of April 1919 had also brought to the fore the height of British callousness.

This sums up the historical and social context of Hindu–Muslim relations around the time that Savarkar had his change of heart.

In his final few years in the Andamans, Savarkar had been allowed some access to news, and at times news literally walked in, as it did in the form of Indians sent to the penal colony for their participation in Mahatma Gandhi's non-cooperation movement (1920 to 1922). For Savarkar the principle of satyagraha or 'truthful' non-cooperation was hard to comprehend. Two freedom fighters from Punjab, living outside their province to escape arrest, had been convinced by a prominent follower of the Mahatma to surrender in order to uphold the truth. They did, and were promptly dispatched across the black waters. Savarkar asked the two what on earth had got into their heads. 'When you were evading arrest, you weren't cooperating with the Raj, but by turning yourselves in you cooperated,' he told them, warning against blind acceptance of advice just because someone – he meant Gandhi – was claiming higher moral ground.

Savarkar differed in this respect from his younger brother. Narayan, as we have seen, was in the Congress and had enthusiastically embraced Gandhi's leadership and the non-cooperation movement, even taking pains to explain the nature of the agitation to many. When Narayan had gone to meet Vinayak in the Andamans after the launch of the movement, the incarcerated brother told him that the Indians ought not to have boycotted the new Reform Councils. Narayan told the *Bengalee* of Calcutta that his barrister brother had said, during the course of their conversation, 'With all reverence which I owe to Mahatma Gandhi whom I had the honour to know and understand intimately while we were in London, I must confess that I disagree with him in boycotting these Councils. In my opinion, it is a great mistake to forgo the partial hold on the administration . . . I am, therefore, sorry to see that the Congress too has passed a resolution to boycott the Councils.'[19]

What rankled him further was Gandhi's move of supporting the Khilafat movement in solidarity with the campaign launched by the Ali brothers Muhammad and Shaukat from the princely state of Rampur. Khilafat was the term used in the subcontinent for the Caliphate, the global seat of power in Islam. The Ottoman emperor or Caliph, deemed the protector of Islam's holy places, had allied himself with Britain's adversaries in the First World War, and the Ali brothers – one an Oxford-educated maulana and the other a cricket aficionado – opposed the British war effort and were placed in confinement for their campaign for the Caliphate. On their release at the end of the war, Gandhi made the saving of the Khilafat one of the primary aims of the Indian national struggle and also promised 'Swaraj' within a year.

Gandhi endorsing the Khilafat movement was bad enough, but linking the non-cooperation agitation to an overtly religious agenda was, according to Savarkar, taking things beyond acceptable limits. To make the wound more painful for the Tilak protégé, Gandhi, the new star on the Indian horizon, announced the launch of the movement on 1 August 1920, and that very morning Tilak died, his health wrecked by prison life. The Mahatma was now the unchallenged authority in the Congress. One era had ended, and another begun.

To many Indians the Khilafat plank seemed bizarre, especially as no other nation, including the Islamic ones, was showing any interest in saving the Sultan, and the Turkish people were in fact fed up with his misrule. The Ottomans had even carried out a genocide during the war, slaughtering an estimated 1.25 million Armenians. Gandhi was in complete denial. 'I distrust the Armenian case,' he said,[20] making several leaders wonder how saving a ruthless regime could be held up as the cause célèbre of a non-violent protest, a Pan-Islamic emblem as a platform of Hindu–Muslim togetherness, and a transnational ideology as a byword for 'national unity'.

The Jewish English journalist Henry Polak, Gandhi's friend from South Africa, wrote to him asking what was going on; his favourite cousin Maganlal accused him of political expediency;

and at a special session of the Congress in Calcutta, Jinnah and Annie Besant opposed him, only to be outvoted by the Khilafat backers mobilized by the Ali brothers, who had by now joined the Congress, and Motilal Nehru. Motilal's young son Jawaharlal, recently transformed into a staunch Gandhi follower, tried a bit of a dodge for defence, saying that the only thing India's rural peasants could understand of the controversial term was 'khilaf',[21] which meant 'in opposition', so they were thinking the fight was merely against those responsible for wrongs perpetrated against them.

Savarkar broke up the term differently. This was no Khilafat but simply an aafat, he said,[22] employing the Urdu and Hindustani word denoting serious trouble. Yet Gandhi had truly taken the Congress by storm, and the nonconformist Jinnah, who made the mistake of referring to the Mahatma as 'Mister' at the annual session in Nagpur in December 1920,[23] found himself shouted down by an angry crowd. Jinnah soon left the Congress on account of his differences with the Mahatma on the direction of the freedom movement, deciding to focus on the Muslim League instead. Swaraj didn't come in a year's time as promised, and Gandhi abruptly withdrew his agitation after a mob burnt down a police station in Chauri Chaura. The Khilafat movement for its part fizzled out, as it was expected to, and the new Turkish leader Mustafa Kemal deposed the Caliph and sent him into exile.

Joseph Lelyveld has made the case in his much-discussed Gandhi biography that the sentiments aroused by the Khilafat movement ultimately found their way into some new groups like the Tablighi Jamaat whose influence went 'beyond India' and 'played back into the Arab world in significant ways'. Carrying the argument further, Lelyveld suggested that 'a complex religious and ideological lineage could be traced over nearly a century from Muhammad Ali and other Indian proponents of the cause to present-day Islamists, including Osama bin Laden'.[24] Such a theory is controversial and indeed arguable; but what is not in any doubt is that in India the consequences of the Khilafat movement were immediate in the Malabar district in the south.

The Moplahs, a group of Muslims living along the Malabar coast, declared a 'jihad', or holy war, in August 1921 and unfurled the Khilafat flag in the region in the wake of attempts by the police to arrest their local leaders who were collecting arms for the 'religious war'. Two British policemen were killed in the clashes. The Moplahs then announced that they had established 'tiny Khilafat kingdoms' across the district,[25] and in these places the homes and temples of Hindus were burnt down or demolished, women were raped and children massacred. According to official figures, 600 Hindus were killed and 2500 forcibly converted to Islam. The full scale of the horrors emerged from reports of the Kerala Congress and local Calicut units, a statement that the women of Malabar sent to the Viceroy's wife, Lady Reading, the proceedings of a conference chaired by the Zamorin (Hindu ruler of Calicut), and disturbing details revealed in Annie Besant's journal *New India* and C. Sankaran Nair's 1922 book *Gandhi and Anarchy*.[26] Many women, some of them pregnant, had been hacked, some victims skinned and burnt alive, and some half-dead victims dumped into wells. The tanks and wells had filled up with bodies of the dead.

Gandhi's instant reaction was to speak of 'the brave God-fearing Moplahs' fighting for their religion, and the Khilafat leaders issued congratulatory messages. But as soon as Hindu refugees from Malabar narrated to the world outside their stories of the carnage, the Congress passed a resolution purportedly meant to be against the atrocities. The reality was that it sounded like an apology for the aggressors: it denied that the disturbances had anything to do with Khilafat and said 'Khilafat preachers' and 'non-cooperators' had been denied access to the area by district authorities a full six months before the violence. 'The outbreak would not have occurred had the message of non-violence been allowed to reach them [the Moplahs]. Nevertheless this Congress deplores the acts done by certain Moplahs by way of forcible conversions and destructions [sic] of life and property,' it stated. Many of the Moplahs had been arrested, and around 200 were hanged for their crimes.

Almost immediately after he had begun his period of internment in Ratnagiri district, Savarkar started work on a Marathi novel on the Moplah rebellion. The title he gave it was *Mala Kai Tyache?* or 'How Do I Care?', a comment on what he perceived as the average Hindu's indifferent approach to Islamic fundamentalism so long as it did not directly touch him or his kin. Savarkar had to write covertly for the moment because he was banned from political work. So *Hindutva* was published in 1923 under the pseudonym 'A Maratha', and the Moplah novel came out in the mid-1920s with Babarao's name as author. Subsequent editions, however, carried the real author's name.

In the previous decade, the Hindu Mahasabha had been formed in north India for the explicit purpose of ring-fencing Hindus from intimidation and assault. The Malabar violence and the subsequent communal riots that broke out in Multan, Saharanpur, Amritsar, Nagpur and Agra, among other places, gave the hitherto small organization a push, and its first national session was held in Banaras. The Mahasabha was led by Madan Mohan Malaviya, Congress leader and founder of the Banaras Hindu University, and other Congress figures such as Lala Lajpat Rai gravitated towards it.

Around the same time, a friend of Babarao Savarkar's from Nagpur, Keshav Baliram Hedgewar, was thinking of forming a new group for bringing about a Hindu renaissance. Hedgewar and Narayan Savarkar had studied medicine at the same time in Calcutta, and it is possible Babarao met Hedgewar through him. The two found themselves similarly ideologically inclined, and Babarao took him to Ratnagiri in March 1925 to meet his interned brother.[27] Once a member of the revolutionary Anushilan Samiti in Calcutta, Hedgewar had spent time in jail as a Congress worker in the non-cooperation movement but was later disillusioned with Gandhi. Savarkar's newly published *Hindutva*, on the other hand, exerted a powerful pull on him.

Hedgewar set up the Rashtriya Swayamsevak Sangh in his home town in 1925, but the man of the moment for the Hindu Sangathanists, as Hindu nationalists of the time preferred to be called, was Swami Shraddhanand. A doughty fighter against untouchability, the swami was hugely respected for the gurukul he ran in Hardwar and had got to know Gandhi through their common friend C.F. Andrews. A long-time believer in the Arya Samaj's Shuddhi movement, Shraddhanand was swept up in the Gandhian hurricane and rallied behind the Mahatma's Khilafat call. His credentials thus burnished, he was invited to address the Islamic faithful at Delhi's Jama Masjid, where all those who heard him hailed him as a messenger of peace. But the swami quickly tired of what he felt was Gandhi's arbitrary decision-making and increasing indifference to rooting out untouchability and joined the Hindu Mahasabha. As communal clashes became endemic across the land, he took the lead in the mass reconversion of Mewar's Malkana Rajputs and was roundly criticized by Muslims for forcibly making these Rajputs Hindus.

When Muhammad Ali, who took over as Congress president when Gandhi was in Yerwada prison for two years starting 1922, suggested that half of India's so-called untouchables be made Hindus and the other half Muslims, and when a fresh round of communal violence in Kohat near Peshawar forced an exodus of Hindus from the region, the swami was convinced that the Mahatma was pandering to Muslim sentiments. But before he could carry his Shuddhi campaign any further, he was murdered. Shraddhanand was recuperating from an illness in his Delhi home in December 1926 when Abdul Rashid, a Muslim calligrapher, walked in as a visitor, asked to see him and pumped two bullets into him, allegedly for his anti-Muslim rhetoric and for avenging the conversions in Mewar.

Gandhi had a genuine regard for Shraddhanand despite their many differences and refused to mourn, saying the reformer had died a warrior's death. In the same breath he called the assassin 'a brother', wrote in *Young India* that he wished to plead for the killer, and added, 'I do not even regard him as guilty of Swamiji's murder.' According to the Mahatma, it was all the newspapers' fault, they were spreading lies and fomenting hatred, and the average newspaperman had become 'a walking plague'. Leaders 'of both Hindu and Muslim opinion' too were not known to curb their 'tongues or pens', and it was the propaganda that had done its 'dark and horrible work'. 'The fault is ours,' he insisted, adding, 'we, the educated and the semi-educated class' are 'responsible for the hot fever which possessed Abdul Rashid'.

For Gandhi, the assassination had put both Hindus and Muslims on trial. If the Hindus showed any resentment at what had happened, they would 'disgrace Hinduism and postpone the unity that must come', but if they demonstrated self-restraint, they would be 'worthy of the message of the Upanishads and of Yudhisthira', the embodiment of forgiveness. 'Let us not ascribe the crime of an individual to a whole community,' Gandhi told India's majority community. 'Let us not harbour the spirit of retaliation. Let us not think of the wrong as done by a Mussalman against a Hindu, but of an erring brother against a hero.'

There wasn't any doubt, Gandhi said, that Muslims were 'too free with the knife and the pistol', and the sword, 'no emblem of Islam', was 'yet too much in evidence'. It would have to be 'sheathed if Islam is to be what it means – peace', and India's Muslims had to express 'unequivocal mass condemnation of the atrocity'.

At the end of his article, Gandhi once again castigated the adherents of both faiths and asked, 'When both are to blame, who can arbitrate with golden scales and fix the exact ratio of blame?' Savarkar's response was severe. He termed Gandhi's remarks as 'cowardly, unjust and biased' and accused him of creating a false equivalence between Hindus and Muslims. He could not see how both were equally to blame, he said, citing the recent pattern of rioting from Malabar to Kohat and elsewhere. It was indeed a crime to conceal the wrongs of one's own community, he said, but it was a bigger crime to blame one's community when it was in truth a victim of atrocities.

He threw in his customary satirical touch too. That newspapers were 'a walking plague' had been established at least in the case of Gandhi's weekly paper *Young India*, Savarkar said, alleging that Gandhi, even though he fetishized the truth, was spreading untruths to enhance his status as Mahatma. Referring to Gandhi's statements that the Moplahs were 'brave' and Abdul Rashid was a 'brother', Savarkar asked why no such noble and spontaneous sentiment had been articulated when the Bengali revolutionary Gopinath Saha had been arrested for shooting a British officer in 1924. In response to the Bengal Provincial Congress's motion of the time saluting Saha's patriotism, the Mahatma had made sure that the resolution was rejected as 'repugnant' by the All India Congress Committee and had clarified in an interview[28] that 'I would call murderers like Gopinath Saha patriots, but not without that indispensable adjective, namely, "misleading".'

Earlier in 1926, the year of Shraddhanand's murder, expressing support for the Tabligh movement, Muhammad Ali had at a Khilafat conference in Delhi called it 'the duty of every Muslim to convert non-Muslims to Islam' and 'prayed for the day when he would convert Gandhi to Islam'. Another speaker at the same meet, Barrister Amin, had called upon every Muslim to convert at least three Hindus in the next ten years so that the 'Swaraj' that would come would be 'Islamic Raj'. This kind of mindset, Savarkar wrote, was at the root of the communal troubles across India, but if Gandhi was hell-bent on making the wrong diagnosis, 'the remedy would end up being disastrous'.[29]

From 1925 Gandhi had been extensively touring the length and breadth of the subcontinent. A few months after Shraddhanand's murder, he came to the Marathi-speaking regions in the west and, after going through Nasik, Ahmednagar, Akkalkot, Pandharpur, Solapur and Belgaum, arrived in Ratnagiri in March 1927. His speech here turned out to be the most important in the coastal belt, and he began by making references to Tilak, who had been born in the district, and Savarkar. The Mahatma said he knew that Savarkar, whom he had 'known well in England and whose great sacrifice and patriotism were known', was staying in the same town. 'We had our differences then,' he told his listeners,[30] and 'we have them now but they have not affected in the least our friendship. Differences of opinion should never mean hostility.'

After the public meeting Gandhi headed straight to Savarkar's place, and the two spoke at some length. Savarkar was laid low by fever. The one-time revolutionary explained that Gandhi was at his place 'not as a political leader but as a friend' and asked the proponent of non-violence to clarify his stance on the two issues that Shraddhanand had laid the greatest emphasis on: untouchability and Shuddhi. Gandhi's secretary Mahadev Desai wrote[31] of the interaction that Gandhi cleared some misrepresentations and told Savarkar, 'We cannot have a long talk now, but you know my regard for you. Besides, our goal is ultimately one and I would like you to correspond with me as regards all points of difference between us. And more.'

Gandhi added, 'I know that you cannot go out of Ratnagiri and I would not mind finding two or three days to come and stay with you if necessary to discuss these things to our satisfaction.' Savarkar's reply, as recorded by Desai, was, 'I thank you, but you are free and I am bound, and I don't want to put you in the same case as I. But I will correspond with you.'

The differences of the two leaders on how to deal with the tricky question of Hindu–Muslim conflict were deep enough. On the point of how to take Hindu society forward, the chasm was even greater. Savarkar attacked Gandhi's relentless focus on his rules for daily living which included hours at the spinning wheel, enemas, a dogged insistence on vegetarianism and debates on whose milk – a cow's or a goat's – was more beneficial to human health. (Some of these rules, however, were meant for Gandhi's ashramites and not for his followers elsewhere or the general public.) These, for Savarkar, were non-issues with no bearing on either moral fibre or health. Their sole effect, he felt, was to fritter away people's energies and direct public debate down the wrong path. Far more crucial were attributes such as courage, Savarkar said, voicing the apprehension that India's 'Kshatriya spirit' could be in danger of dying if the Mahatma, with his insistence on absolute non-violence, continued to delegitimize the application of force essentially for self-defensive acts like the repulsing of invaders, oppressors and plunderers.

Yet Savarkar's personality was truly as complex as Gandhi's. A devout Hindu, the Mahatma sincerely believed in prayer, ritual and ritual cleansing and made much use of traditional and religious idioms in public life, holding up Ram Rajya as his ideal and the protection of the cow, a sacrosanct figure for most Hindus, as a sacred duty. For all that, and for all his glorification of village life, rejection of modern machinery and unwillingness to unequivocally condemn the varnashrama, the system of four castes, he was vigorously opposed to Shuddhi or reconversions. Savarkar was, in contrast, hardly a practising Hindu in the religious sense. He followed no rituals and thought that God, if indeed God existed, wasn't really in the habit of responding to prayer. He was all for demolition of the caste system, albeit for the purpose of Hindu sangathan or unification. He genuinely loved his fish – which he must have got a consistently rich haul of in coastal Ratnagiri – and disliked all his fellow Brahmans who looked askance at those who relished non-vegetarian food. He was keen that Hindus and Indians in general should embrace the urban life and modern scientific advances, even if they ran counter to their cherished religious beliefs. And he held, at the same time, the very strong conviction that there was no alternative to the campaign for shuddhi if Hindu society were to retain its identity and character in the face of what he saw as Islamic aggression.

On the position of the cow Savarkar deviated sharply not just from Gandhi but from the majority of his co-religionists. During his forced stay in Ratnagiri, he came across an article in the Marathi daily *Bhaala* in which the editor had posed the question 'Who is a Hindu?' and answered it himself by declaring that a Hindu was 'one who regards the cow as his mother'. Savarkar felt compelled to react. 'If the cow's a mother to anyone at all, it's the bullock,' he wrote in a piece for the Marathi journal *Kirloskar*. 'Not the Hindus. If Hindutva is to sustain itself on a cow's legs, it'll come crashing down at the slightest hint of a crisis.'

The cow was a highly useful animal but its worship made no sense, he said, arguing that humans could possibly consider as a divine being someone with superhuman qualities but certainly not an 'out-and-out animal' inferior to humankind. It was time to abandon the 'naive practice' of 'gau-poojan' also because it was nothing short of 'buddhi hatya' or 'murder of the intellect'. He was not against the nurturing of cows and in fact promoted the principle of nurture as a 'national duty', but only as long as it was predicated on broader economic and scientific principles – as it was, he said, in America – that heightened bovine usefulness.

In short, Savarkar pronounced himself in favour of 'cow care, not poojan' and abhorred the idea of consuming the animal's urine and, in some cases, cow dung. Such consumption, he believed, may have actually started out in ancient India as a form of punishment in order to allow a person to 'expiate his sins'. And to those orthodox Hindus who would cry blasphemy on reading these radical views of his, he had a sardonic response ready: 'Your blasphemy's far, far greater, just see how you've crammed 33 crore deities into a cow's belly.'

The approach, undoubtedly strictly utilitarian, nevertheless could not be divorced from the theory of Hindutva. As a matter of fact, Hindutva was at the core of it. Unlike, say, a Nehru who spoke of India's 'composite culture', Savarkar was not convinced that India had been subjugated only by the British. He viewed the many hundred years of Islamic rule as an era of shackles, submission, suppression and slavery. And one of his big problems with cow worship was that it had 'ensured' many Hindu defeats in the past.

Muslim armies had, according to Savarkar, used cows often as a shield in critical battles against the Hindus. He cited two examples of the Hindus shying away from a much-needed assault after they were threatened with defilement of the cow: the march to Multan and the eighteenth-century Maratha chieftain Malharrao Holkar's campaign to 'liberate' Kashi. Rather than backtracking at moments like these for fear of being criminally responsible for cow slaughter and the razing of temples, Hindus needed to chart a different course, he suggested. If ever the 'Hindu Rashtra' was hemmed in by non-Hindu forces and there was no other way to lift the siege and procure food, cow slaughter would have to be exercised as an option, he said. Hindus had hugely damaged their own cause by trying to save a few cows during battle; the survival of the animals had forced an ignominious retreat for their forces and ultimately led to the destruction of more Hindu shrines and 'setting up of abattoirs across the land'.

The strong reprimand for Hindus was not a go-ahead for non-Hindus who regarded cow killing as their religious duty, however. Savarkar wrote that Hindus might be naive, but they weren't cruel. In contrast, those who cut down the animal as part of their 'dharma' were brutal in their religious zealotry and had 'no right to ridicule cow worshippers for their beliefs'. In all the deliberate slaughter Savarkar saw 'excessive barbarism, ingratitude and an asuric [demonic] instinct'[32] and urged those indulging in it to give up their hate and take up 'cow care' instead.

10

Reconverting the converted, 'purifying the polluted'

Internment was a loose form of 'district arrest', and Savarkar had reconciled himself to the fact that there would be no getting away from Ratnagiri district for five years starting 1924. Briefly a flicker of hope arose in mid-1924 when Dr M.B. Velkar, backed by other members of the Bombay Legislative Council, moved a resolution calling for the lifting of all restrictions on the one-time revolutionary. The resolution was outvoted 50–37, but not before a heated debate.[1]

Velkar described the restrictions as 'vindictive' and said Savarkar had suffered 'the longest term any political prisoner had' in India. Moreover, he had been treated 'like an animal' by being 'yoked to an oil mill for days together'. Velkar urged that the house keep in mind the conditions between 1906 and 1908, when even the 'calm and level-headed' Dadabhai

Naoroji had 'lost all faith in British justice and fair play', 'engines of oppression' had been 'set into operation' and 'all channels of constitutional agitation' shut, forcing the political movement into 'subterranean channels'. Ever since the Montagu–Chelmsford reforms were introduced in 1919, Savarkar had shown his readiness to take the constitutional path, 'even if it be a path of "irritating slowness"', Velkar said. Noting that Savarkar was 'a man of uncommon abilities and talents' who had 'built a reputation as a great orator, an inspired poet and a cogent writer', Velkar went so far as to suggest that 'if the House was anxious to receive him in this Hall as their honourable colleague, Mr Savarkar would enter the Councils as a "Responsive Co-operator"'.

A.N. Surve suggested an amendment to Velkar's resolution, retaining the bar on political activities, prompting a fierce reaction from K.F. Nariman. Nariman, known for his boldly patriotic views, called the amendment 'an insult to the nation'. 'Just as Mr Surve could not separate himself from his sense of super loyalty, Mr Savarkar could not separate himself from his political feelings,' he said. And when the Raj loyalists asked why the resolution was being tabled when the internee himself had agreed to all conditions, Velkar said Savarkar's consent 'had no value . . . as he was not a free agent'.

The government argued it was too early to say anarchical societies were dead, and refused to release Savarkar from internment. In a scorching editorial the next morning, the *Bombay Chronicle* lambasted the government for its 'unreasonable attitude'.[2]

What nobody knew at the time was that the term of Savarkar's internment would stretch well beyond five years. It was extended two years at a time, four times in succession – that is, it was extended by a total of eight years. He was finally set free after thirteen years in Ratnagiri in 1937, which took the total period he had spent under some form of arrest to twenty-seven consecutive years in the prime of his life. Only twice was he permitted to leave the coastal district of Ratnagiri: once in 1924 for a few months for Nasik as the plague had struck Ratnagiri, and the second time in 1926, for just a fortnight, for Mumbai to meet his ailing older brother. Fortunately for him he was reunited during this period with Yamuna, who was much relieved to have her husband back after a long period of incarceration. Three children were born to them during Savarkar's conditional confinement in Ratnagiri, of which one, a girl named Shalini, born extremely weak, died in her infancy. The other two children, a daughter named Prabhat, born towards the end of 1924, and a son, Vishwas, born in 1928, survived, bringing much joy for the couple and helping them deal with the loss of the other girl child.

Worried how he would make ends meet during this period since he still was not allowed to practise as a lawyer, the legislator Velkar, ex-Tilak aides N.C. Kelkar and B.S. Moonje and some others set up a 'Savarkar Purse Fund Committee' and solicited contributions from ordinary citizens in Bombay Province, the Central Provinces and Berar. A sum of Rs 13,000 was collected[3] and handed over to Savarkar, who accepted it saying he was not taking it 'for the services he had done but as an earnest reward for the services yet to be rendered by him'.

The next best thing to political action, which he was not allowed to engage in, was work in the social sphere. The British had succeeded in converting Savarkar, once at the centre of revolutionary national life, into a kind of niche player. The political spotlight was now decidedly on Gandhi and his protégés. Savarkar viewed his social work through the lens of Hindutva and set himself to the task of obliterating the blights of untouchability and superstition that was taking a devastating toll on Hindu society and sought to replace these with an inclusive and scientific outlook. The inclusion was to help serve the cause of Hindu consolidation and the scientific outlook aimed at acquiring prowess that would end what he perceived as the endless cycle of invasions that had battered the 'Hindu nation' and prevented it from becoming a powerhouse. An essential aspect of the work would be reconversions to Hinduism or what, in the new millennium, is understood by the term 'ghar wapsi.' In short, Savarkar's new mantra was sangathan (unification of Hindus) and Shuddhi (purification in religious terms).

A breach of custom during the popular Ganesh festival in Ratnagiri in 1924 marked the beginning of his crusade against untouchability. (Savarkar, even during his student days in India at the head of Abhinav Bharat, had thumbed his nose at caste regulations by publicly eating with his comrades from other castes.) Idols would every year be taken out for immersion in a procession, with Brahmans at its head. Savarkar upended the order, placing the idol of the low-caste Mahars first, followed by those of the scavenger and shepherd communities. Addressing a gathering of lower-caste groups, he called for the end of caste discrimination and warned them against attempts at mass-scale conversions. Other Hindu festivals too were utilized: on Dussehra day, Savarkar along with some aides visited the lower-caste Hindus' segregated homes to mark the occasion;

at a haldi–kumkum ceremony organized at his behest, upper-caste women placed the traditional vermilion mark on the foreheads of women from the deprived castes; and on Hanuman Jayanti, he distributed in the Mahar neighbourhood copies of the Hindu texts *Ramvijay* and *Bhaktivijay* and his own novel on the Moplah atrocities. The Mahars also received a word of advice. The music band that played at weddings in the district was an all-Muslim one. The Mahars ought to have their own band, he told them, and, taking a 300-rupee loan against his own name, bought them instruments so they could get started. (Mahar drummers were in any case called to play at the time of Holi and for some ceremonies.)

To promote the inclusion of children from lower-caste families in local schools, he launched a new school in Ratnagiri in the late 1920s to facilitate their entry, with funds from the businessman Bhagoji Keer and, at a conference of Scheduled Castes, handed out sacred threads to the Mahars and Chambars (Chamars or cobbler community) and declared they had as much of a right to recite the Vedas as anybody else.

Infuriated, the orthodox Brahmans of Ratnagiri announced that Mahars would not be permitted to step into the local Vithal temple during the ten days of Ganeshotsav, when a Ganpati idol would be installed there. Savarkar's countermeasure was to install another, parallel idol in the same temple compound for all Hindus and to get it consecrated by a man who did scavenging work after he had first had a bath with water drawn from the well on the temple premises. Simultaneously, Savarkar got a plan to construct a temple for all Hindus off the ground. A trust was set up for overseeing the shrine, with four members from four different castes and one nominee of the patron Keer, himself part of a lower-caste group. The foundation stone was laid by the Shankaracharya of Karvirpitham in 1929, and in two years the Patit Pavan temple, as Savarkar named it, was opened, with a Chambar ceremonially washing the feet of the Shankaracharya.

Savarkar had by this time extended his support to B.R. Ambedkar's landmark anti-caste satyagraha at the Chawdar tank in Mahad – also in the Konkan – and organized a number of inter-caste dinners. At the Patit Pavan mandir's opening, however, the Shankaracharya set limits to his own challenge to orthodoxy: he would not be part of the inter-dining, he said, and was served food separately.

Some others were not so queasy. One enthusiastic participant at these dinners was the singer and stage artiste Dinanath Mangeshkar. The impresario had recently developed a friendship with Savarkar, and he visited the internee off and on with his family in tow. Savarkar in particular looked forward to the scrumptious vegetarian pulao that Dinanath's wife, Shevanti, better known as 'Mai', brought for him every time. On one such visit, Dinanath decided to take his five-year-old daughter Lata along for one of Savarkar's inter-caste dinners.

Her regard and affection for Savarkar notwithstanding, Mai was reluctant to send the girl along, Lata Mangeshkar said.[4] 'She's so small. Why take her there?' the concerned mother asked. First, those dinners were mostly male affairs; second, children who had barely started school were hardly ever made part of the proceedings; and third, partaking of the food there was likely to make anyone unpopular, as most Hindus were still firmly in the grip of orthodoxy. 'Baba [father] would not hear of it. He told my mother, "She needs to know right now what Savarkar is doing and why it's so necessary,"' Lata said, recollecting how she ended up becoming perhaps the youngest member of the Savarkar squad at the time.

Savarkar's sphere of influence in the matter of caste stood severely restricted by the geographical limits the Raj had set for him. Two other Indian leaders, Ambedkar and Gandhi, engaged in a similar anti-caste fight at the same time, had enormous arenas to work in. Their political star, too, was in the ascendant, while Savarkar's had declined considerably. Perhaps he hoped that his star would also rise once he was freed. Naturally the other two exerted a wider and far more powerful influence on societal currents.

All three leaders had different approaches to ending untouchability. Gandhi wished to raise all castes to the same level but was hesitant to demolish varnashrama (the system of four broad castes); for some years he would not even endorse inter-caste dining. Savarkar favoured a wipe-out of the caste order as it was iniquitous and, equally key for him, precluded unity among the Hindus. As for the Vedas, Puranas and Upanishads, he was of the opinion that the Hindus needed to 'respectfully' place these sacred texts in their closets and pick up science books instead. The approach appeared contradictory, for at the same time he distributed Hindu religious texts to the lower castes and made the opening up of temples a significant feature of his movement, but that was more to make them feel Hindu so they would be part of the Hindu nation as he had envisaged it. Ambedkar initially promoted both temple entry and inter-caste dining but, having suffered caste discrimination himself, unlike Savarkar he gradually realized these steps were inadequate and concluded that only a rejection of the Shastras would bring about the annihilation of caste. He had no interest in forging some kind of cohesive Hindu front either, though he was as sternly critical of Islam as he was of Hinduism.

Yet Ambedkar and Savarkar did think similarly on at least two issues. Both considered Gandhi's piety as showmanship rather than sincerity and, as admirers of western education, were thoroughly impatient with his viewpoint on science, surgery, technology and urban life being essentially negative forces. Both showed a genuine appreciation for each other's work despite obvious differences.

It was Ambedkar, a leader who had triggered controversy by the torching of the *Manusmriti* on 25 December 1927 at Mahad, whom Savarkar had originally invited to preside over the opening of the Patit Pavan mandir in 1931. Ambedkar, based in Mumbai, said he would not be able to make it because of an earlier commitment but wrote to Savarkar that 'I however wish to take this opportunity of conveying to you my appreciation of the work you are doing in the field of social reform. If the untouchables are to be part and parcel of Hindu society, then it is not enough to remove untouchability; for that matter you must destroy Chaturvarnya. I am glad that you are one of the very few who have realised this.'[5] When Ambedkar declared in 1935 that he was born a Hindu but would not die as one, Savarkar told him conversion would be of no help as neither Christianity nor Islam would provide equality to the Depressed Classes. As proof of his assertion, he pointed to the violence that had just broken out between 'touchable' and 'untouchable' Christians in Travancore. He was sure that untouchability was on its way out. He suggested that Ambedkar should 'fight out valiantly for equality by the side of the progressive Hindus'.[6]

For someone who envisioned a Hindu 'sangathan', though, Savarkar did not endear himself to the majority with his attempts at reform from within. There weren't too many progressive Hindus around and the rest, including those willing to embrace piecemeal change, were increasingly finding his relentless assault on ritual and time-honoured practices hard to digest. In April 1929 a group of furious orthodox Hindus tried to break up a meeting called by him in Ratnagiri's Vithoba temple, dedicated to Lord Vithal of Pandharpur. Afterwards, Savarkar's act of garlanding and touching the feet of a Mahar and his wife after they had recited kirtans in the temple – until then only Brahmans could sing kirtans and expect obeisance – sent shock waves among higher-caste groups.[7] They sent to the provincial governor a plea saying Savarkar be barred from carrying out 'anti-Hindu acts' and be asked to leave their district.[8]

Savarkar's essay on cow worship, and above all his suggestion that Hindus need not shy away from cow slaughter if their survival was at stake, caused much heartburn, as did his other writings and pronouncements. For instance, he was openly scornful of a sadhu who, in the early 1930s, declared he had covered the distance between two of Hinduism's holiest sites, Prayag and Hardwar, by prostrating himself and crawling slowly along on his belly. The sadhu touted this as an act of sacrifice for the gods, but Savarkar saw this as bizarre. He sarcastically asked who had indeed been closer to God, considering almost all religions said that God was in the heavens above – someone who was attempting to build an airplane or fly in it or someone desperate to turn himself into a maggot. In another instance, he mocked Lehri Maharaj, again a self-styled saint based in

Nasik. The oddly named godman – Lehri means eccentric – announced, in the wake of the 1934 Bihar earthquake, that to rid humanity of such disasters, he would soon release 11 lakh carefully made balls of flour, with a chit containing Ram's name embedded in each of them, into the waters of the Ganga. Wondering how all that flour was going to reach God, Savarkar said the mouths of the fishes and frogs who would ultimately consume it were not post offices from where to dispatch letters to the Lord and advised the godman to distribute 11 lakh quinine tablets instead to 'farmers, children and others'[9] afflicted with malaria.

His distancing from the general populace proceeded apace as his attacks, including the busting of long-held myths, signalled to many that Savarkar was galloping towards atheism – and that he was not good-naturedly trying to cleanse the Hindu faith of its more obscurantist elements.

Another example of this drift from the general Hindu populace can be seen from the following story. The thirteenth-century saint Dnyaneshwar or Dnyandeo looms large over western India's religious and cultural landscape as a pioneer of the Bhakti movement and child prodigy who breathed vitality into the Marathi language. He is at the heart of the annual pilgrimage to Vithal or Vithoba of Pandharpur, undertaken by half a million people annually to this day in much the same way Sabarimala draws great crowds in southern India and Puri in Odisha every year. Stories of how Dnyandeo miraculously moved a wall after being challenged by a tiger-riding yogi and got a buffalo to recite the Vedas have been narrated in most homes in the Marathi-speaking regions for centuries. They are metaphorical – the speaking buffalo indicated that the

Vedas were no one's monopoly and that all life was divine, and the second shows faith can move mountains. Savarkar was dismissive of the tales. If Dnyandeo had moved walls and got a buffalo to recite sacred texts, why hadn't he erected a gigantic wall to block the path of Allauddin Khilji who invaded in the same period and ensured the buffalo sent out timely warnings about the invasion instead, Savarkar asked. As much an admirer of the Bhakti poet-saints as anyone else, Savarkar clarified the point he was trying to make was that it was fine to say the medieval saints had created fertile ground for a societal renaissance but actions to proactively defend oneself and achieve one's goals, not simply noble-sounding words or beliefs, were critical, he said. Tilak too had underlined the primacy of action in his book on the Gita, but he had done so carefully. Savarkar, operating in a largely tradition-bound society, was ruffling feathers by touching upon very important components of religious imagery around him.

~

Savarkar's fervour for Shuddhi, taken from the Arya Samaj, was twice as contentious with its bearing on interfaith relations. He oversaw the reconversion of a Mahar and a Brahman family of eight from Christianity in 1925–26; the Brahman, apparently grateful for the 'ghar wapsi', asked Savarkar to do the kanyadan at his youngest daughter's wedding. The expenses for the girl's wedding, as well as for her older sister's, were borne entirely by Savarkar.

But Savarkar had stirred the proverbial hornet's nest with his zeal for reconversion to fortify the Hindu fold. The Khilafat leader Shaukat Ali met Savarkar in Mumbai, when the latter was on his way to Nasik from plague-hit Ratnagiri in 1924. The result was a bitterly acrimonious exchange which was reported by all the leading papers, the British-owned ones not making an effort to hide their glee. Ali, who complimented the Hindu leader first for his 'heroic sacrifices' for the country, asked him to 'give up Shuddhi and Sangathan'.[10] Savarkar agreed to do it provided Ali abandoned his own Khilafat, Tabligh and Jamiat-ul-Ulema campaigns – the first of which stood for restoration of the Islamic Caliphate, the second for religious proselytization and the third, with the Jamiat as the principal group of India's Muslim ulemas or scholars with knowledge of Islamic laws, for spread of Islamic knowledge. Cut to the quick, Ali launched into a diatribe against Hindus, and Savarkar retaliated with his own charges against Muslims, the two bringing their blow-up to a close at last by swearing to their respective programmes of conversion and reconversion. Elsewhere at that time, Lala Lajpat Rai, presiding over the Hindu Mahasabha's annual conference, said that Shuddhi was a 'purely defensive' movement and that Hindus had no desire to establish their own Raj. He added, 'As long as conversions continue, as long as other religious communities have a right to carry on their propaganda for converting Hindus to their faiths, the Hindus have an equal right to do the same.'[11]

Some of the arguments Savarkar had with Shaukat Ali were elucidated by him in *Hindu Pad-Padashahi*, an appraisal of the Maratha movement from Shivaji's time to the rule of the Peshwas, which he wrote later in 1924. The book, published by B.G. Paul and Co. in Madras, was not written after their conversation, however, but well before it, and it spoke of the

Maratha struggle as a broader Hindu fight against Islamic forces. The *Indian Historical Quarterly* in its review[12] wrote that 'historians of the chronicler type may not see eye to eye with Mr Savarkar in his dramatic way of marshalling the facts of Maratha history' but acknowledged that he had 'added flesh and blood to the dry bones of history' and that 'every page of the book thrills with the noble spirit of patriotism and religious fervour which inspired the writer'. In contrast, the eminent historian Jadunath Sarkar had serious criticism to offer. Apart from faulting Savarkar for not citing sources – which he had done in his 1857 book – Sarkar thought the new work 'the latest example of romantic history writing'[13] and opined that Savarkar could not be placed in the category of, say, V.K. Rajwade or G.S. Sardesai, as an authority on Maratha history. Himself the writer of pathbreaking books on Shivaji and Aurangzeb, Sarkar wrote that the outpouring of sentiment, as demonstrated by Savarkar, was fine for someone speaking from a dais, but a flawed reading of India's past could impede the country's advancement.

The other critical element of Savarkar's drive for Shuddhi was 'purification' of the Marathi language. By this he meant the purging of Urdu words and the process of restoring Marathi to its 'original allegiance' – as Savarkar saw it – to Sanskrit. The idea had originated for Hindi with Dayanand Saraswati and was being carried forward by the Arya Samaj, the Hindu Mahasabha and the Nagari Pracharini Sabha formed in Banaras in 1893 and led by Madan Mohan Malaviya. The Pracharini Sabha was to a great extent responsible for the phenomenal rise of shuddh, or pure, Hindi in north India and especially in the United Provinces, where even Brahmans and Kayasthas had for long been in the habit of employing Urdu owing to its long-time status as official language during the rule of the Mughals. Slowly, the local courts there began to accept pleas and issue summons in Hindi as well as Urdu, bills and acts began to be published in both scripts, and Devanagari took its place on currency notes and coins as well. The initiative created unease among local Muslims, and a near-identical push for the Gurmukhi script in the Punjab led to resistance from Muslim members of the provincial council. Savarkar called upon every Hindu and Sikh youth in that region to 'write in Hindi or Gurmukhi alone' and, controversially, to 'break up the Urdu pen'.[14]

Embracing the idea for Marathi, which is also written in the Devanagari script, he wrote a booklet titled *Bhasha Shuddhi*, in which he articulated the fear that Marathi would wither away if Urdu's intrusions continued unchecked. The preponderance of Arabic and Persian had already wrought havoc in Sindh, Punjab, Agra and other parts of north India, he claimed, and Urdu – which he would not acknowledge as a language in its own right, labelling it as 'nothing more than a distorted form of Hindi'[15] – was in his view the one big contributor to the damage. The way things were going, Marathi would suffer the same fate the other languages had, he said, asking all those who cared for it to be saavdhan (cautious and vigilant) and not khabardar, the latter an Urdu word carrying the same meaning but used more frequently by Marathi speakers.

At the annual Marathi literary meet in 1927, the writer and playwright Shripad Krishna Kolhatkar, who presided over it, appealed to all those who spoke the language to eschew English words and phrases lest they swamp the mother tongue. But in the same speech,[16] he piercingly criticized the campaign for

Bhasha Shuddhi, saying it smacked of prejudice against Islam. So many Urdu words had blended beautifully with Marathi, he pointed out. Besides, they followed all the rules of Marathi grammar and had a certain history, having been coined with considerable effort. A number of other Marathi writers too opposed Savarkar's new clean-up act, saying that words of foreign origin were not likely to impoverish a language but enrich it, as the example of English brilliantly demonstrated.

Savarkar, in his response to the critics,[17] said that the *Bhasha Shuddhi* campaign had been started by Shivaji when he asked the scholar Raghunath Pandit to prepare the *Rajvyavaharkosh*, a dictionary of terms shorn of Islamic influences that the independent Maratha state would use in official communication. He told Kolhatkar that his own arguments in favour of Urdu could easily be marshalled against him. Hadn't English words too blended nicely with local grammar? Didn't they too have a history of careful cultivation? And was Kolhatkar a hater of the English people just because he wanted English words out? Foreign words, Urdu or English, were not anathema to him, Savarkar explained, and said that they could be adopted and retained if there were no local words to replace them. He insisted there were, in most cases, fine old words which had been discarded because the Islamic rulers had forced a new vocabulary on Hindus and Urdu expressions, in turn, had been internalized by a subject population over centuries. Some new Marathi words could be invented, just as the word *duradhvani* had been coined to mean a telephone, quite a few old ones revived, and some others borrowed from 'Indian languages such as Kannada and Telugu'. That, too, was a sensible way of enriching and revitalizing the language, he argued.

But in Savarkar's time, it was not just writers and publications in Marathi that were critical of his 'language purification' programme. The Anglo-Indian *Times of India* took a no-holds-barred swipe at Savarkar at the height of his no-Urdu push. Among the words of Islamic origin Savarkar wanted erased from usage was the extraordinarily common 'saheb'. The *Times* commented:[18]

> Patriot Savarkar . . . wants to drive out of the language every word of foreign, especially Islamic (i.e. Perso-Arabic) origin. Thus he will have no 'Saheb' in the Marathi language – and he has substituted 'rao' for this extremely popular mlechchha (alien, especially Islamic) word in Maratha nomenclature – and thus made [ex-Tilak aide and a popular figure] Mr Kelkar known in private and public life as 'Tatyasaheb' rather ridiculous by renaming him 'Tatya-rao.' We suppose even the highly coveted title 'Raosaheb' comes out of the patriotic crucible transformed into the still more ridiculous 'Raorao.'

In the event, language purification became neither a full-fledged literary nor a mass movement, remaining confined to Savarkar and his band of followers, and after his passing it died altogether. Not that it was not without its positive outcomes. Savarkar invented a host of indigenous terms – for words such as mayor, legislator, legislature, cinema, director, producer, actor, and even the then not-so-common lifts and air conditioners, among others. In doing so he made genuinely original contributions to Marathi vocabulary that have stood the test of time.

During his time in Ratnagiri Savarkar remained a prolific

writer. Either in his own name or under assumed ones, Savarkar wrote tirelessly for the thirteen years he was in the district and added three plays to his oeuvre. The first of these, *Sangeet Usshap*, a warning to lower-caste Hindus against 'conversion traps' allegedly set by Islamic and Christian missionaries, got flak from almost all quarters: the Raj's censors demanded and enforced multiple cuts to rid it of communal overtones, residents of Muslim-majority Malegaon distributed pamphlets denouncing its 'anti-Islam character', and a prestigious Marathi literary magazine, *Mauj*, felt it was sorely lacking in literary merit.[19] The second one, *Sanyasta Khadga*, a musical on the life of the Buddha but intended as a critique of Gandhi's absolutism on non-violence, was moderately successful chiefly on account of the thespian Chintamanrao Kolhatkar's acting prowess and Dinanath Mangeshkar's moving notes. Kolhatkar and Mangeshkar had commissioned the writing of the play by offering Savarkar an advance sum of Rs 1000, unheard of at the time.[20] The third play, *Uttar Kriya*, again an ode to Maratha valour in the face of Islamic aggression, tanked miserably, the critics attributing Savarkar's overall failure in theatre to the propagandist in him forever getting ahead of the playwright.[21]

More people were by now beginning to despair of Savarkar's post-Andamans ideological tilt. Waman Kabadi, a nationalist-minded journalist who had joined the *Chronicle* in 1918 at the age of eighteen and was later associated with the *Indian National Herald* and the *Independent*, was, one day in the early 1930s, on his way from Goa to Mumbai on a boat when, to his surprise, he saw Savarkar hop on at Vengurla. Savarkar was apparently returning to Ratnagiri town after the opening of a temple for untouchables in the neighbouring town in the district. (He was still under 'district arrest'.) Curious, Kabadi headed to the lower deck, where he found the leader helping himself to a bowl of rice and fish curry. Fortunately Savarkar was in a mood to talk, but Kabadi found him 'too bitter' about the non-cooperation movement, in which the young man had taken part, and about Gandhi and Khilafat. 'There is no doubt that he was a great scholar and a great orator, because I could see that his words came to him even before he thought, as it were,' Kabadi recollected later. But he could not help feeling that it was 'a national tragedy' that this 'great anti-imperialist Indian patriot, who suffered so much at the hands of the British', had 'turned his attention away from those oppressors to fight Gandhiji, who was determined to take the country on the road to freedom'.[22]

~

If the revolutionary violence after the partition of Bengal could be seen as the first prominent wave of the ideology's appearance on the Indian national scene, then its second wave came in the second half of the 1920s and the early 1930s, culminating in the Chittagong uprising and the sacrifices of Bhagat Singh, Sukhdev and Rajguru. The Kakori conspiracy case stirred Indian opinion greatly in this period, after the revolutionaries Ramprasad Bismil, Roshan Singh, Ashfaqullah Khan and Rajendra Lahiri were sentenced to death, four others transported for life and several others given prison terms ranging from five to fifteen years for a dacoity on a railway train heading from Kakori to Alamnagar carried out in August 1925 to 'secure' Indian money being transported by the British government.[23] And the Lahore conspiracy case inflamed popular opinion further as Bhagat Singh and other members of the Hindustan Socialist Republican Association (HSRA) were arraigned for the murder of Lahore Assistant Superintendent of Police John Saunders in December 1927, for throwing two bombs inside the Delhi assembly in April 1929 and for having organized a bomb factory in Lahore (discovered soon after Bhagat Singh and Batukeshwar Dutt hurled the bombs) that could produce 7000 bombs. Bhagat Singh, Sukhdev and Rajguru were convicted and hanged in March 1931, seven were transported for life, and many others were awarded lengthy prison terms.[24] What was Savarkar's response to the eruption of violence? Did he not react at all fearing a clampdown on him?

Savarkar and his family, which now included two small children, had just about warded off financial ruin and regained some stability. Half the public purse he was gifted by the Savarkar Purse Fund Committee he had given to Narayan to buy a house in Mumbai's Khar suburb, and Narayan, who worked as a dentist, in turn sent him Rs 75 a month for expenses. Of this Rs 15 went towards paying rent in Ratnagiri. Savarkar was in part also helped by the subsistence allowance of Rs 60 the authorities paid him every month for his exile to a region where gainful employment was hard to find. He had made the pragmatic choice of accepting the conditions imposed on him by the Raj. But he did not quite maintain a sullen silence on the freedom movement.

Two weeklies, first *Shraddhanand* and then *Hutatma Shraddhanand*, had been launched with Narayan as editor in order to enable Vinayak to propagate his political views by using pseudonyms. Both were ordered shut by the authorities, but not before Savarkar had made his opinions public under the cover of a pen name. He wrote a deeply felt piece on Sachindranath Sanyal after the latter – his co-prisoner for five years in the Andamans – was given a life term in the Kakori conspiracy case of 1925 and a poignant one on Sachindranath's mother. She had lost her husband before her sons could start earning, but had still encouraged them to fight the good fight and had died alone, with two of her sons convicted and behind bars. Through his writings Savarkar also urged Bhagat Singh, whom he described as a 'tapasvi' (man with a monkish determination) and 'a jewel', Batukeshwar Dutt and other prisoners in the Lahore conspiracy case to end their hunger strike. The hunger strike had been launched for two reasons: to protest the inhuman treatment meted out in jail to all those accused in the case, and, in Batukeshwar's words, to 'strengthen the forces of direct action against the imperialist government'.[25] The 'direct action' bit was meant as public criticism of Gandhi's strategy at the time. The Congress, with Motilal Nehru as president, had in 1928 declared its aim to be 'Dominion Status', but a radical section within the organization, among whose members were Subhas Bose and Motilal's own son, Jawaharlal, was pushing for complete independence. Gandhi brokered a truce, saying the Congress would demand 'complete independence' in the next session if the Raj did not give India Dominion Status within a year. Bhagat Singh and Batukeshwar did not want the issue of total freedom and 'direct action' temporarily shelved in favour of negotiations with the British.

However, a bigger cause awaited Bhagat Singh and Dutt outside jail, Savarkar said,[26] urging them to call off the hunger strike. He feared if anything untoward happened to them, it would cost India dear.

Savarkar and Bhagat Singh's HSRA had fundamental differences on the nature of revolution, for neither Bhagat Singh nor Sukhdev entertained the idea of Hindu unity – although Rajguru was in favour of it – and were proponents of Marxist ideology. Yet they had not allowed these to diminish their mutual admiration: if Savarkar extolled the HSRA's actions, Bhagat Singh published from Lahore,[27] in two volumes, the English translation of Savarkar's banned work on 1857.

Since all the articles in *Shraddhanand* had appeared under pseudonyms, how do we know Savarkar was indeed the author? Both he and Narayan had owned up to it in subsequent years, and one of Savarkar's aides later gave this bit of information to the British authorities. The head of the Brahman family of eight that Savarkar had reconverted from Christianity and whose daughters' weddings he had funded fell out with him and handed over to officials the records of some of the pieces in Savarkar's own handwriting. What the fallout was over was never known, though the handing over of the pieces written by Savarkar meant the Raj had enough material evidence against the ex-revolutionary both to justify his continued conditional confinement and its extension.[28]

Two things in the aftermath of the Kakori case verdict merit mention. Four of the convicted were ordered to be hanged and others were awarded prison terms. While Savarkar hailed the sentenced patriots and lauded their sacrifices in a tribute, he mentioned only three of the four sent to the gallows by name – Ramprasad Bismil, Roshan Singh and Rajendra Lahiri. He failed to name-check the fourth, Ashfaqullah Khan. By doing so he opened himself up to the charge of clear bias. The second notable thing: the convicted first filed an appeal before the Privy

Council, and when that was rejected – as were pleas made by leading citizens to the governor of the United Provinces and the Viceroy – they sent a petition for mercy to the King-Emperor himself in London.[29] These revolutionaries have fortunately not been branded as 'traitors' or 'British collaborators' – charges that Savarkar has faced from time to time.

Sometimes, Savarkar's support for the revolutionaries went beyond the written word. He penned a panegyric for Bhagat Singh, Sukhdev and Rajguru on the day they were hanged and immediately left for another town in the district for a school's opening; before leaving, he gave his followers the piece of paper on which the tribute was written. Next morning youngsters carried out prabhat pheris, or morning processions, in the heart of Ratnagiri, reciting his poem loudly as they walked past homes. Three days after the hangings, when Savarkar was back, there fluttered atop his small, rented cottage a black flag instead of the saffron one that was the distinguishing feature of his temporary residence.[30]

Through these and other actions Savarkar showed that perhaps he had not fully embraced the 'constitutional' path as he had professed in his mercy petitions. He did not truly believe that there was no space for revolutionary activity. Another example of this was Savarkar's mentorship of an idealistic student of his alma mater, Pune's Fergusson College, V.B. Gogate, who in a show of solidarity with the executed trio of the Lahore conspiracy case was distributing photos of Bhagat Singh and Savarkar among his mates. Gogate soon travelled to Ratnagiri to meet Savarkar and seek his guidance. He seemed to have been contemplating becoming a journalist. It was fine if he wanted to be an editor, Savarkar told Gogate, but stressed that 'whatever political consciousness is created by writing in a newspaper is of much less effect than the political awakening which is created by sacrifice, like that of Bhagat Singh and Rajguru'. Asked by the student if revolutionary methods were justified, Savarkar said, 'So long as India is in bondage, the only way to fight the British will be by revolutionary activities,' and told him that the martyrs' shouts of 'Vande Mataram' just before their execution had 'created greater political awakening than 10 sessions of the Indian National Congress'. Three decades after the interaction, Gogate recalled[31] that he had asked the leader if 'shooting a governor here or there' was of any help. Savarkar, Gogate said, believed that such isolated acts would certainly not bring freedom but they were needed to register protests against atrocities. 'Every British man who is good enough to rule India is bad enough to be killed,' he noted. The conversation seemingly produced an effect: Gogate shot at Ernest Hotson, acting governor of Bombay, when the latter visited Fergusson College that year. Hotson survived with minor injuries, and Gogate was sentenced to eight years in prison.

The British were still wary of Savarkar, and knew that even if Gandhi was the biggest star of the national movement, Savarkar was still revered by revolutionary-minded youth. This is apparent from the account of another young Indian of the time. He was the Congressman and Gandhi follower Indravadan Oza. A resident of Vile Parle in suburban Mumbai, Oza was picked up during Gandhi's 1931 Salt Satyagraha from Shiroda in Ratnagiri district, where a number of salt estates were raided, and packed off to the local prison. When the time came for him to leave prison after a month and a half, the local collector, who had come to witness the proceedings as quite a few agitators were being freed, asked Oza what he would be doing next. The youngster told him, 'Savarkar is here and . . . I must see him first and then proceed to my place.' The collector 'was shocked' at his reply, Oza recounted later,[32] and he was promptly put on a bus, with ten cops around him, and told he better not get off before he had reached Kolhapur, that is, well beyond Ratnagiri district. 'If you leave the bus in between, it will be at your cost and risk,' he was warned.

Savarkar's older brother, who visited Banaras frequently for treatment, was similarly in touch with the revolutionaries there, including Chandrashekhar Azad, and a very noteworthy encounter he had in the year 1929 with the Hindi writer Yashpal, then a sprightly member of the Naujawan Bharat Sabha, in New Delhi has more or less remained securely hidden in the litterateur's memoirs. Yashpal had so much admiration for the Savarkar brothers that he knew by heart entire passages of Vinayak's *Echo from the Andamans*, translated into Hindi as *Andaman Ki Goonj*, and 'didn't want to miss an opportunity to meet them'; for him they were 'not merely leaders of the revolutionary movement but its pioneers'. So when he found out Babarao was in Delhi, he went to meet him along with his group's ideologue Bhagwati Charan Vohra. 'I have generally no desire to touch the feet of great men,' he wrote afterwards. 'Even when I met Gandhiji I didn't feel like it, but I remember the two of us touched Babarao's feet when we met him and, speaking of our work without hesitation, asked him for help with the cause.' Babarao suggested Delhi was not the right place to discuss these things and asked Yashpal to see him in Mumbai. Later that year, Yashpal travelled to Akola in

Vidarbha, where Babarao was temporarily staying in a tiny room with just a mattress for a bed. It was December, and Babarao's clothing, Yashpal recalled, was basic and hardly suited for the weather. The sole blanket he had he handed over to Yashpal to wrap around himself, and despite the youngster's protestations, would not take it for himself. 'You've just completed a long journey,' he said. Yashpal knew the Savarkar brothers had taken up Hindutva but was confident they would assist with revolutionary actions as they shared with the Naujawan Bharat Sabha the goal of driving away the British.

Babarao agreed their common aim was to evict the British. 'But apart from the British,' he said, 'there's another enemy of the nation who's opposed to national unity and is thwarting our attempts at liberation in league with the Raj. That's the separatist feeling among the Muslims.' Since freedom would come 'only if national unity, based on cultural oneness' was achieved, 'it would be futile to think of Swaraj without first freeing ourselves of such adversaries', he told the youth. 'The most dangerous thing for us today is the policy of the Muslims, under Jinnah's leadership, to forge another nation within the nation. Jinnah is the symbol and representative of this policy. If you will take up the responsibility of assassinating Jinnah, the biggest obstacle in the path of freedom would be removed. We could give you Rs 50,000 as monetary help for carrying out the task,' Babarao said.[33] Yashpal politely declined, and Babarao seemed not to mind at all and even gave him some money for his return journey. 'There was no doubting Babarao's dedication and sacrifice, but our group's perspective was different from that of the Savarkar brothers,' Yashpal recorded.

Did Vinayak Savarkar know of Babarao's plan to kill Jinnah?

The older brother had taken up the role of Vinayak's follower and always played second fiddle, so it is unlikely he proposed it without Savarkar knowing. Yashpal feared, on his way back home from meeting Babarao, that the plan, if implemented, could result in a communal bloodbath[34] considering how fragile Hindu–Muslim relations were even in the late 1920s. Jinnah had not called for a separate Muslim nation until then, and his hold over the League too was not as powerful as it would be in later years. However, in 1929, Jinnah had rejected the Nehru Report, a constitutional plan for India put forward by the Congress by getting an all-parties committee headed by Motilal Nehru to draft it. The report called for elections to be held on the basis of joint electorates, while seats could still be reserved for minorities in the central and provincial councils, but in proportion to their population. Jinnah said the Nehru Report was Hindu in character and presented his own 'Fourteen Points', which included the continuation of separate electorates and a quota for Muslims in government jobs, among other things. These 'Fourteen Points' became the basis of his communal agenda, which moved increasingly towards separatism in the next decade and culminated in the Pakistan resolution of 1940.

Interestingly, Chandrashekhar Azad was to soon ask one of the HSRA group members to shoot Yashpal himself as he had got married, an act considered against the interests of revolution, forcing the Hindi writer to go underground for some time. Babarao, like Vinayak Savarkar, was also still a cult hero among revolutionaries. When Durga Devi Vohra, the intrepid wife of Bhagwati Charan, shot at a European couple outside Lamington Road police station in south Mumbai in October 1930, she left her son Sachi in Babarao's home in the city.[35] Six months after that, there were twin bombings inside Mumbai's Imperial theatre, and Babarao was arrested by the police on suspicion. His involvement was never established, but he was kept in lockup for a week and subsequently interned in Nasik, where he had to live under conditions similar to those imposed on Vinayak. As a widower he lived there alone (in Mumbai he had Narayan and his family to look after him), and, with his tuberculosis getting progressively worse, his health suffered greatly.

Around 1927–28, efforts to get the restrictions on Vinayak Savarkar lifted had begun afresh as the end of the initial five-year term drew near. In September 1927 B.R. Ambedkar moved a motion in the Bombay Council saying he should be allowed freedom of movement, and Yusuf Meherally, B.G. Kher and N.M. Choksey of the Bombay Youth League passed a resolution saying the former revolutionary must be released unconditionally and every Indian ought to make this demand regardless of ideological differences.[36] The government nevertheless refused, and by 1931 it had the examples of Bhagat Singh and Surya Sen of the Chittagong uprising to cite as reasons why all the checks needed to still apply. The Raj also suspected that a new book published during this period, a collection of articles on Nepal and its 'Hindu' link with India, was written by Savarkar. The Raj was right. Savarkar was indeed the author, and had made indirect references to Bhagat Singh's father and uncle in the introduction – a point that was not lost on anyone, certainly not on the Raj.

In 1936 Gandhi refused to sign a memorandum calling for the release of the Savarkar brothers. Savarkar's internment in Ratnagiri had been extended for the fourth time at this point, and the older brother was confined to Nasik. When Gandhi was asked about it he explained,[37] 'I had in my own humble way endeavoured to secure full freedom for both [the] Savarkar brothers and no one would be more glad than I to see the restrictions on Savarkar removed. I refused to sign . . . because my way of moving in such matters is different.'

It was finally in 1937, when, following the Congress's refusal to form a ministry in Bombay after provincial elections across India, a non-Congress government was formed by Jamnadas Mehta and D. Kapoor, that the brothers were restored to complete freedom in the month of May. For Vinayak the period from 1910 to 1937 had seemed a lifetime. Now individual freedom had at last come, but the bigger freedom for which he had fought was still a decade away.

11

World war, word wars

The first few months after his release in 1937 were especially intense for Savarkar. He travelled several hundred kilometres for a host of public receptions, addressing packed gatherings. The instinctive reaction of many Indians was summed up by the *Bombay Chronicle*, which, welcoming him back to freedom, wrote, 'Savarkar's is almost a legendary figure to the modern generation. His career reads almost like a romance, and though the struggle for freedom has received a new orientation during the last quarter of a century under the leadership of Mahatma Gandhi, there will not be a true nationalist in India who will not feel happy today.'[1] The paper's editors were still 'not sure that he will not be the object of attention by the all-pervading C.I.D.', but the equally big question was whether, with the movement's 'new orientation', he would be able to push his thoughts to the front of national conversation once again. He was, after all, finally freed from the undertaking he had signed not to get involved in politics.

At the outset it appeared he would still be able to make his voice extremely prominent; there opened up a spectrum of possibilities. The Congress, the Socialists, the Democratic Swaraj Party populated by ex-Tilakites and the Hindu Mahasabha all wanted him on their side. The first public speech he made after his release was at a function in Ratnagiri to welcome the then Bombay Pradesh Congress Committee chief K.F. Nariman. With the Congress's tricolour unfurled in style, Savarkar led the salutation ceremony and reminded locals that it was Madam Cama who had first publicly raised the flag in 1907. 'The flag stands for complete independence and they must keep it forever flying,' he said.[2]

Thirty groups in Bombay, including the city Congress unit, organized an enthusiastic reception, carrying him in a procession along a four-kilometre stretch from Azad Maidan to Girgaum. Jawaharlal Nehru, C. Rajagopalachari and Subhas Bose sent congratulatory messages, Bose saying in a statement from Dalhousie that 'there is no Indian who would not be delighted' at Savarkar's release and poignantly welcoming him 'to what freedom we now enjoy in this unhappy land of ours'.[3] At the Bombay function, M.N. Roy, a young, left-leaning Congress leader who would go on to become a communist icon, said he was one of Savarkar's oldest admirers; as a schoolboy, he had taken inspiration from him when his prosecution had created a global sensation.[4] Referring to Savarkar's new ideological tilt, Roy said that he and his childhood hero were nevertheless united in the cause of freedom and appealed to the freed leader to join the Congress. Soon, Roy himself would leave the Congress, and Savarkar's relations with it would sour even more than during his prison term.

What did Indian politics look like when Savarkar surveyed it on his release? And what of constitutional advances? Had there been any?

The one very significant development since his confinement in Ratnagiri in 1924 was the passing of the Government of India Act of 1935. The 1919 reforms were to have been reviewed after ten years, but the Raj had carried out a review in 1927–28, that is, more than a year in advance, chiefly in order to scuttle Indian aspirations; the then ruling Conservatives in Britain feared that the Labour Party, more sympathetically inclined towards Indians, might come to power soon, and it was in the Empire's best interests that a new constitutional framework be put in place before that. The London government had then set up the all-British Simon Commission which was famously sent 'back' in 1928 by the Indian nationalists, and from 1930 to 1932, there had been roundtable conferences which had been washouts, largely because there was no commitment to giving India Dominion Status as a measure towards the eventual grant of self-government. Propelled by radicals like Bose and Nehru, the Congress had adopted 'Purna Swaraj' as its aim on 31 December 1929, but it wanted Dominion Status immediately as a step that would make the walk to freedom more meaningful and real rather than something simply in the legislative air.

The 1935 Act did not even make a mention of Dominion Status, but notably it granted provincial autonomy which would replace the much-criticized 'dyarchy' of the 1919 reforms at least in the local administrations, at the central level, 'dyarchy' remained, with the critical areas of foreign policy, defence and national security in the hands of the Raj and its top representative, the Viceroy.

The Act envisaged an All-India Federation, where power would be shared between the provinces of British-ruled India or 'British India' and India's 500-plus princely states. The federation was to be 'a perpetual and indissoluble union of the States and the Provinces', and the princely states would have to accede to it by way of an instrument of accession.

Power would be divided between the central and provincial assemblies, for which the electorate was expanded so that nearly 25 per cent Indians became eligible to vote as against just a small fraction of the population in 1909 and 1919, albeit still qualifying only on account of being property-owners and taxpayers. The central and provincial governments would have two chambers, upper and lower, with the lower house having a fixed term of five years and the upper house a permanent body whose members would be changed when their individual terms ended. With three lists of subjects – federal, provincial and concurrent – drawn, the provinces were given plenty of important matters to oversee such as police and land revenue, which had been outside their ambit in the past.

Yet there was massive opposition to the Act because, as Indians of various political hues seeking self-government saw it, the governor general or Viceroy at the centre and the governors in the provinces still had extraordinary discretionary powers and could easily thwart legislation or return it to the legislatures. Further, there was some overlap between the subjects to be decided by the federal and provincial assemblies and those on the concurrent list, so if any confusion arose, the final call would inevitably be taken by the British 'constitutional monarchs' –

the Viceroy and governors – or, if an issue had to be sent for consideration across the oceans, the Secretary of State for India, the British government or 'His Majesty'.

The Congress, the Hindu Mahasabha and the Liberals all felt that the separate electorates provided under the new Act would imperil the unity of India, while Jinnah felt the share the Muslims were being offered was not enough. In August 1932 the then British premier, Ramsay MacDonald, had announced the Communal Award which gave the Muslims, Sikhs, Indian Christians, Anglo-Indians and Europeans, among others, separate electorates and a quota of seats in the provincial legislatures. Gandhi scuppered the separate electorate and reserved seats for the so-called 'Untouchables' by going on a fast which ended in the Poona Pact of 1932 with B.R. Ambedkar, under which the Depressed Classes agreed to give up the separate electorate; the Mahatma's contention was that separate categorization of these deprived sections would take them away from the Hindu fold, and he would have none of that.

But most nationalist Indian leaders opposed the award because of the skewed representation offered to various communities under the 1935 Act. For instance, the breakup of the 156 'British India' seats in the 260-member Council of State or the upper house at the centre would be eighty-one Hindus, including six members of the Scheduled Castes, forty-nine Muslims, seven Europeans, four Sikhs, two Indian Christians and one Anglo-Indian, in addition to six seats set aside for women and six others for the governor's nominees. The 104 seats for the princely states were to be decided according to their 'rank', as indicated by the number of 'salutes' they were entitled to, thus Hyderabad had five seats, Mysore three, Patiala, Udaipur and Bikaner two each, and so on; their representatives would all be nominated by the princes. The central legislature, which was to be called the House of Assembly, would have 375 seats in all, 250 of which would be elected representatives from 'British India'. Of these 250 seats, Hindus would have 105, nineteen within this group reserved for Scheduled Castes, Muslims eighty-two, Europeans and Indian Christians eight each, Sikhs six and Anglo-Indians four.

This meant Hindus had nearly as many seats as all the minorities combined, though the minorities formed about 30 per cent of the Indian population. Muslims, who formed about 25 per cent of the population, had 33.5 per cent of the seats in both houses.

In the event, the Act was implemented only partially. The federation never materialized, because the princes, afraid of compromising on their sovereignty, rejected the idea. The Congress, Muslim League, Hindu Mahasabha and others protested against the nature of provincial autonomy, each for different reasons, but finally agreed to fight the provincial elections scheduled for 1937 under the Act. The Congress won handsome victories in the majority of the eleven big provinces and assumed power, though many of its elected members were confused about whether they were supposed to work the new constitution or wreck the assemblies from within. Both ideas had been discussed by the Congress before the elections, and Gandhi had left the decision for after the poll outcome. The British of course hoped the taste of power would ensure that the Congress accepted the arrangement, which is what happened till war broke out.

Savarkar was bitterly opposed to separate electorates, which offered Muslims seats disproportionate to their numbers in the larger Indian population. This meant, according to Savarkar, that one Hindu vote was less powerful or effective than one Muslim vote, and it was ostensibly intended to make the Muslims feel secure in a Hindu-majority land. Savarkar stood for a one-person one-vote system, and he believed that the Congress was either far too soft in opposing communal representation or open in what he alleged was its appeasement of Muslims.

Though there was near-universal celebration at Savarkar's release, lurking under the surface was hostility within the Congress stemming from Savarkar's aversion to Indian Muslims. In 1936, a fifteen-year-old Hindu girl had been kidnapped by a Muslim in Bannu in the North-West Frontier Province. After the man was convicted and the girl returned to her parents, the Fakir of Ipi, raising the alarm of 'Islam in danger', demanded the girl be sent back to her abductor. The Fakir had brought warring tribes together in a fight for an 'independent Pushtunistan'. When his tribal army attacked roads, bridges and convoys and kidnapped more Hindus, the British launched operations against him. These operations were severely criticized by the Congress. Its president Nehru asked, 'Do you think the British government invaded Waziristan because, say, one or two or some Hindu women had been kidnapped?' Pointing out that there were other ways to get the women back, Nehru said the action was 'in furtherance of imperialist designs' and claimed the Raj had 'no justification whatever for the waste of millions of our money'.[3] In mid-1937 'Frontier Gandhi' Khan Abdul Ghaffar Khan's older brother Abdul Jaffar Khan, commonly known as Dr Khan Sahib, became premier of the province's new Congress-led government and was quoted by the media as echoing the Fakir's view that the girl be handed back to the kidnappers. Reports also stated that his statement, purportedly made in the assembly, was applauded by Congress legislators. Savarkar referred to it in a speech in Miraj in southern Maharashtra and described the applauders as rashtriya hijre (national-level eunuchs).[6]

This caused a public furore, and pro-Congress papers condemned Savarkar's words as unbecoming of a leader of his stature and Congress units in various cities cancelled receptions they had planned in his honour. Congressman N.V. Gadgil resigned in protest as head of a panel formed in Pune to host a reception for Savarkar and told reporters that Dr Khan Sahib had never made the statement attributed to him. Savarkar clarified that nobody would be happier than him to know the reports were unfounded and said he was accepting the veteran Congressman's statement, in which case his own remarks obviously 'were to be dropped'.[7] Fake news was causing havoc even back then!

Savarkar went on to praise Congressmen as 'torch-bearers of freedom' and lauded its past leaders such as Tilak and Naoroji and his own contemporaries like 'Gandhiji, Pandit Nehru, Bose and Nariman'.

The clarification and withdrawal, however, did not help. Savarkar had landed on the Congress's blacklist. Angry Congress activists resolved to greet him with black flags at every reception hosted to honour him.

At this vulnerable moment for Savarkar, the writer, playwright, editor, film-maker and activist P.K. Atre lent him support. One of Maharashtra's leading twentieth-century opinion-makers, the bespectacled Atre, tall, dark and handsome before his paunch and receding hairline became distinguishing features in his later years, had shunned the ivory tower and famously struck a vibe with the people with his powerful oratory, distinguished chiefly by his skill at eliciting laughter and applause. With his humorous, theatrical, passionate and explosive style, he drew huge crowds everywhere and happily fuelled controversies. He was often accused of exaggeration in both praise and criticism. After Independence, he championed the movement for a linguistic Marathi province with Mumbai as its capital and came up with the name 'Shiv Sena' for an organization for the rights of native Maharashtrians that he planned to set up in 1963. His idea of the Sena was different from that of Bal Thackeray, who eventually established it in 1966. Atre had envisioned it as a non-violent group bearing no hostility towards migrants and functioning along constitutional lines. Like M.N. Roy, Atre had grown up absorbing stories of Savarkar's courage and narrating his ballads on Shivaji and Tanaji at public festivals. Now Atre jumped at the idea of meeting him for the first time and organized a reception for him in Pune on behalf of the Balmohan Theatre Group that he ran. The Congress threatened to bring out its black flags and distributed handbills denouncing Savarkar. Still thousands turned up for the reception, where Atre bestowed the title of 'Swatantryaveer' on Savarkar – a title that later contracted to the easier-on-the-tongue 'Veer' (Braveheart) and stuck. At the reception Atre took a dig at the Congress, saying, 'Savarkar was not scared of the dreaded *kaala paani*. Whatever makes these people think he'll be scared of their *kaala nishaan* [black flags]?' Enthused by the 'ringing applause' that followed, Savarkar, running a fever, spoke for one and a half hours without a break and, in Atre's words, 'conquered Pune'.[8] A few days later, Savarkar returned the compliment. He described Atre, at another function in the city, as 'Acharya' or great teacher. And that name too stuck, and both 'Veer' and 'Acharya' are to this day attached as prefixes to their names.

Some days after this, youths belonging to the Congress socialist wing tried to disrupt an anti-caste dinner organized by Atre for Savarkar in a locality of low-caste Mangs. Here, according to Atre, a young man tried to assault Savarkar, forcing the organizers to wind up proceedings. Savarkar was to take a train to Mumbai that evening, and word reached Atre that some protesters would create a ruckus at the Pune railway station. So he drove Savarkar in his own car to the next railway station on the route, Talegaon, and left only after the train had departed safely.

In August 1937 Savarkar announced that he was joining the Democratic Swaraj Party of former Tilakites, and in a reception for him in Solapur, 150 Congress workers wearing Gandhi topees hurled stones, shoes and whole buckets filled with muck, one of these from a terrace. At the head of the procession was a man seated on an elephant. He was pulled down and beaten up; another was hit with a stick, and his shirt torn. The car that was carrying Savarkar suffered some damage, and when he reached the house of his host, the building was surrounded by an irate mob that kept banging at the doors till the cops arrived and forced the crowd to disperse. Twenty Congress workers were booked for rioting.[9]

Though Savarkar maintained that the Democratic Swaraj Party's principles were consistent with those of Hindutva, he concluded that he and the Hindu Mahasabha were far better suited to each other and switched parties soon thereafter, in October 1937. The Mahasabha had been little more than a social group; he sought to refashion it as a political organization.

On a hectic tour of the Central Provinces and Berar, his first as Mahasabha leader, Savarkar drew massive crowds at all places, asking his listeners, among other things, why Indians should at all be sympathetic to the Arabs 'wrongly elbowing out Jews' from Palestine or with the Chinese fighting the Japanese and reminding them that they need not look to Russia for inspiration when it could be had from within. Savarkar was taking aim at the international preoccupations of the Congress leaders, particularly Nehru. But what precisely did Savarkar want? Presiding over the annual Mahasabha session in Ahmedabad in December 1937, he stressed that his group and the Congress had the same goal – Swaraj – and pushed for equal rights for all citizens in a free India. Hindus wanted only their interests safeguarded and no special privileges, he said. Nonetheless, in the same address, he described Hindu–Muslim unity as a 'will-o'-the-wisp' and claimed that 'Islam aimed at domination' and that 'thousands of Muslims could be found conspiring with the Turkish Khilafatists and Afghans' in order to establish Islamic rule in India. One Marathi publication asked him why he had derived inspiration from Mazzini if no inspiration was needed from outside, and an English paper lamented that it was 'tragic to listen to such things' from someone so estimable.[10]

Within days, Savarkar was seeing absolutely no common ground between the Mahasabha and the Congress. The shift seemed to have been brought about by Nehru's assurance in 1938 to Muslim leaders that the Congress's 'declared policy' was 'not only to do full justice to them [Muslims] but also to go even beyond that' and that the Communal Award guaranteeing separate electorates stood 'for the present', with the Congress seeking 'no change except with the concurrence of those concerned'. The Congress had always pronounced itself against the award, Savarkar said. Was it now abandoning its 'saner mood of assuring all communities of just and equal treatment', he wondered. What did 'going beyond' mean, he demanded to know from Nehru and said that Nehru was getting into the habit of using the word 'minorities' deliberately ambiguously. There was, according to Savarkar, no need to implicate India's Christians, Parsis or Jews in a discussion on communalism. They were in his opinion neither fanatical nor troublesome; only the Muslims were, he alleged, and urged the Congress to 'call a spade a spade'. He argued that the Mahasabha was more national than the Congress as it asked for nothing more for Hindus in terms of political franchise or religiously and culturally 'beyond what was due on the principle of equality of treatment' and deplored accusations that it was communal. A group was not communal simply on account of being sectional, he argued, so long as it tried to defend the just rights of the section it represented against the 'unjust aggression' of another and did not impinge on 'the equal and just rights and liberties of others'. Thus, he asserted, anyone who wanted to speak to the Hindus needed to get in touch with the Mahasabha and not the Congress, which had 'no right' to represent the community;

any Hindu–Muslim pact would be meaningless 'unless it was sanctioned by the Mahasabha'.[11]

The Congress's response was to disallow its members from also being members of the 'communal' Mahasabha.

The hostilities continued when in 1938 Bose became Congress president. He was criticized by Savarkar for suggesting that Indian languages be written in the Roman script instead of Devanagari. Savarkar was invited to helm the annual Marathi literary meet held that April in Mumbai; when he accepted, some of his friends suggested he should avoid discussing the divisive issue of 'language purification' in his keynote address. He refused and, speaking to over 3000 delegates, called for the purging of Urdu words once again and re-emphasized his demand for recognizing Sanskrit-based Hindi as the national language. He called for formulating a scientific vocabulary for Indian languages and a sharp focus on translations, but the out-and-out headline-grabber was his plea to Indian youth to 'put aside pens and pick up guns' and 'leave literature, for the time being, to those over 40 years old'. He explained: no literature could survive if the national soul perished. If an analogy could help, he was willing to provide it: 'If, say, art and culture lovers were enjoying a play and the auditorium caught fire, they would run to save themselves. Similarly, if a nation's life were under threat, it had to seek strength in arms and not in the arts.'[12]

The Marathi press mostly agreed with Savarkar that adopting the Roman script was not a great idea but assailed him for suggesting the wiping out of Urdu and Persian terms. About the abandon-your-pens comment, it simply expressed its astonishment. Savarkar was taking an enormous chance by asking for the picking up of guns; the Raj would not appreciate it one bit, especially from someone who, in its view, had a notorious anti-British record. That John Bull did not make a dash for the red rag, probably because the situation in Europe demanded complete attention then, was sheer luck.

With a call to arms in the unlikely setting of a literary fest, it was not surprising that Savarkar cited, immediately after Adolf Hitler's Anschluss in Austria – the annexation of that territory to Nazi Germany – in March 1938, the example of Germany as a nation which had 'achieved the unity . . . to which task she had set her heart'. Similarly, he felt, 'the unity of a Hindu India could be brought about'.[13] Was he in favour of Nazism then? No, he was neutral, he emphasized, and he believed India's foreign policy desperately needed to move away from this or that 'ism' and be guided only by self-interest. As war clouds loomed over Europe, he could not understand why Nehru had thought it fit to go 'out of his way to condemn Germany and Italy'[14] and saw 'no point' in the Congress's attempts to help China or sympathize with Spain when Indians locked away in the Andamans were going daily without food and basic facilities.[15] He described England's professed sympathy for the Czechs after the Munich Pact as a 'stunt' and a 'mere eyewash'[16] and said that if England's cry of democracy in danger was really sincere, she would have left Indians to themselves so they would have their own freedom and democracy.

~

Savarkar's criticism portended the dissension within the Congress itself. As war broke out early in September 1939, the Congress was a house divided. Gandhi could not contemplate the destruction of London and told Viceroy Lord Linlithgow that his sympathies lay with England and that he was not thinking of India's deliverance; Nehru wanted India to offer 'unconditional support' to Britain; Bose, ousted as Congress president in May 1939 by the Mahatma in a coup and in a new avatar as leader of the rebel 'Forward Bloc' within the outfit, felt the moment was ripe for launching a mass movement against the Raj; and C. Rajagopalachari advocated cooperation provided the Congress got Britain to agree to a time frame for the grant of Dominion Status to India. After four days of animated debate, the Congress Working Committee issued a cautiously worded resolution. 'India cannot associate herself with a war said to be for democratic freedom, when that very freedom is denied to her,' it stated. It demanded that Britain declare its 'war aims . . . in regard to democracy and imperialism' and, in particular, 'how those aims are going to apply to India' and 'given effect to in the present'.[17]

With the Congress thus leaving the door open for possible cooperation for the war effort and putting the onus on the Viceroy to respond, Savarkar preferred to wait and watch.

Not all Indian leaders agreed with such an approach. With the Congress taking a semi-combative approach towards the Raj, Jinnah met the Viceroy and, delighted at the importance he was given vis-à-vis the Congress, he got his Muslim League to adopt a resolution that no constitutional steps should be finalized without the League's approval. At this juncture Jinnah did not commit himself this way or that: he merely urged Linlithgow to give him 'something positive to take back' to the League 'to help him rally Muslim support for the war'. On another point he was not quite so vague: he told the Viceroy he now saw 'partition' as the sole political solution for India.[18]

Ambedkar, on the other hand, had spoken out in favour of India staying within the British Commonwealth and was '100 per cent opposed to self-government at the Centre'.[19] The princes were only too happy to back Britain and offered men for the war effort and tremendous amounts of money.

In the first week of October 1939 Savarkar travelled to Simla for a one-on-one meeting with Linlithgow. Just before he entered the Viceroy's palatial summer residence, Linlithgow had interviewed Ismail Khan, president of the Muslim League's United Provinces unit. And among those who had featured in the discussions was Savarkar.

The Cambridge-educated Khan told Linlithgow, while debating the Viceroy's newly floated idea of an all-party conference, that Savarkar and the Mahasabha were 'intensely unpopular with Islam and its followers everywhere' as a result of their 'recent activities in Hyderabad'. They had been part of a civil disobedience campaign to protest against the Nizam's oppression of his people and his denial of civil and religious liberties to Hindus within the province. Savarkar had complained that Muslims 'monopolized' the public services there, controlling all aspects of administration even though Hindus constituted 85 per cent of the population, and had demanded the majority community get at least 75 per cent of the posts, including in the legislature.[20] When the Nizam, under pressure, announced reforms and opened up 50 per cent of the legislative seats for non-Muslims (50 per cent were kept reserved for Muslims), Savarkar welcomed the move and called for an end to the agitation. For this, he was criticized by some who asked why he was okay with a 50 per cent Muslim quota. Savarkar's view was that the reforms were acceptable for two reasons: they constituted 'a substantial advance', and they showed Hindus had finally made 'a constitutional breach in the citadel of fanatical autocracy'.[21]

In the letter Linlithgow sent to the Secretary of State in London, Lord Zetland, after meeting Savarkar he indicated how he had approached the interaction. 'I passed from the Nawab [Ismail Khan],' Linlithgow wrote, 'to the company of Mr Savarkar, whose somewhat lurid record and alleged connection with the murder of Sir Curzon Wyllie will be sufficiently familiar to you.'[22]

The tall, well-built Viceroy found Savarkar 'a not very attractive type of little man' but said 'he was definitely interesting and we had a very friendly talk'.[23] Savarkar took the position of what could be described in foreign policy terms as realism. None of the belligerent powers, he was convinced, was actuated by any moral or human principle like liberty, democracy, political justice or equity. India's task was simply to see what she could gain. For the defence of India during the war the Mahasabha was willing to offer 'responsive cooperation' to Britain, but the British must grant India the status of a self-governing dominion after the war and introduce responsible and popular government at the centre 'as an immediate step'.[24] Was this a climbdown from the independence demand? No. It was rather much like the Congress's demand, even after its push for total freedom in the early 1930s, for Dominion Status as an immediate step so that India would be just one step away from complete Swaraj while negotiations continued.

Savarkar had other demands to place on the table: an end to separate electorates, and if that was not possible, representation to Hindus on the basis of their strength in numbers and reservation only for the Depressed Classes; military training for Hindus and complete Indianization of the Indian army by removal of 'artificial distinctions' of the 'martial and non-martial classes' which, introduced after the 1857 revolt, had barred members of communities seen as more rebellious than others from joining the armed forces; compulsory military training for high school and college students as in England and Germany; and encouragement to Indian firms so that they could manufacture 'aero engines', 'motor engines' and other 'implements of modern warfare' and make the country 'self-sufficient' in terms of protecting itself.[25]

Despite these scheduled meetings with Indian leaders Linlithgow was mostly indifferent to Indian nationalist opinion. He had in any case already declared, at the outset of the conflict, that India, as part of the British Empire, was at war with Germany, before consulting a single Indian, group or individual. These consultations were held after the fact.

After the consultations with Indian leaders, and in a bid to get their support for the war that the Raj had already signed India up for, Linlithgow declared on 17 October 1939 that Dominion Status remained Britain's goal for India. For now the 1935 Act, partly implemented with its grant of provincial autonomy, stood, but once war came to an end 'it would be open to modification' in keeping with Indian views, with 'full weight'[26] given to the views of the minorities.

As an immediate measure, he was proposing the setting up of a consultative group comprising Indians from all major political parties and the princes so that Indian opinion could be considered in the prosecution of war.

Savarkar dubbed the statement disappointing. From 1919 Britain had been talking of Dominion Status and it had not happened. That status, a 'wordy mirage' that India was 'sick of', he said,[27] could not be the final aim anyway but merely a step towards realizing the goal of absolute political independence. A constitution based on that status needed to be granted to India 'at the end of the war at the latest'. But the Viceroy's statement 'studiously omitted' any such time frame, he noted.

But his response was tempered by the message that the Mahasabha was not really shutting the door on cooperation. If 'a definite declaration' were made, he said, Indians could still be part of the war effort.

Savarkar wanted India to take advantage of the war and desired for Indian capital and labour to seize this opportunity, when supplies from Europe would dry up, to start producing the myriad things that were being imported. What twenty years of a Swadeshi agitation could not do, the next two years could, he underlined.[28] He also saw an opportunity for Hindus to join the army, learn how to fight and use modern weapons, so if needed they could later put these skills to use.

Upset with Linlithgow's statement and the lack of a definite timeline for the grant of Dominion Status, the Congress asked its ministries in eight out of eleven provinces to resign, a move welcomed by the Raj as it meant that the Congress could not thwart the war effort and also by Jinnah as it suddenly robbed his adversaries of power. The Congress was being pulled in different directions: the left wing led by Bose's bloc was keen to launch a civil disobedience movement, and Nehru, who along with the new Congress president, Maulana Abul Kalam Azad, desired cooperation, was firm that a protest campaign 'when Britain is engaged in a life and death struggle would be an act derogatory to India's honour'.[29] Nehru and Azad got the Congress Working Committee to pass a resolution at its meeting in Delhi in August 1940 that Britain should make a declaration of complete independence for India and form a provisional national government as an immediate step. This, the resolution stated, 'would enable the Congress to throw in its full weight in the efforts for the effective organisation of the Defence of the country'.[30]

As almost nobody in India had bought Linlithgow's vague talk, the Viceroy offered an olive branch in January 1940. Speaking at the Orient Club in Bombay, he declared, 'I can assure you that His Majesty's Government's concern and mine is to spare no effort to reduce to the minimum the interval between the existing state of things and the achievement of Dominion Status.'[31] Three days later he assured the Congress that 'there was only a difference in name' between Dominion Status of the Westminster variety and complete independence. The 1931 Statute of Westminster had promised autonomous status to dominions, allowing them to manage their own domestic and foreign affairs and have their own diplomatic contingents apart from separate representation in the League of Nations. Any law framed by the British parliament would not extend to a dominion without the request and consent of that dominion, it stated. Savarkar considered this to be no small step forward and welcomed Linlithgow's statement as 'clear and definite'.

Savarkar had a second meeting with the Viceroy in Simla in July 1940. He called the conversation 'frank, considerate and impartial' and said he was opposed to the Congress's proposal for formation of a national government as an immediate step. He had himself asked for a national government, but if it were to be formed, as the Congress had demanded, from among the current members of the Central Assembly, it could not be truly national; all parties needed to be represented in the government, and for that a fresh election was a must.

Recuperating in his new Dadar home after an illness and an operation for sciatic pain in his legs, Savarkar issued a statement on 22 September outlining the Mahasabha's revised 'terms of cooperation'. Earlier, in March 1940, the Muslim League had passed its Pakistan resolution in Lahore. Savarkar wanted the Viceroy to reject any proposal or scheme for partition and also the League's demand for 50 per cent seats on an expanded Executive Council. Jinnah had wanted a virtual veto on any constitutional progress, and reports had said the government had agreed to give the League two seats on the Executive Council and six on a proposed War Advisory Council. The Hindu Mahasabha wanted three times the number of seats – six on the Executive Council and fifteen on the War Advisory Council – on the basis of population. Of the six council seats of the Mahasabha, one each should be given to Sikhs and the Depressed Classes, Savarkar said; the Mahasabha's nominees would keep the other four.

In October, Savarkar took a step back. He was willing to settle for the Viceroy's 'original proposal' of one seat for the Mahasabha and one each for Sikhs, the Depressed Classes, and a Muslim or non-Hindu party. But with the Congress and the League shooting down the Viceroy's plans, and the sole offer of 'unconditional cooperation' coming from Ambedkar's Independent Labour Party, the Council's expansion was shelved for the time being; when it was finally carried out in July 1941, all the Indians included were non-political personalities.

After nearly four months of confinement at home, Savarkar in December 1940 travelled to Madurai in the Madras Presidency for the Mahasabha's annual session. Politically he targeted Nehru and Gandhi in his presidential address, apart from the Muslim League. Starting April 1940, the Nazis had invaded Norway, Denmark, France, Luxembourg, Belgium and the Netherlands, and although Russia and America were still neutral, Stalin having signed a non-aggression pact with Hitler and neatly swallowed Poland along with the Germans, it was anybody's guess how the conflict would further unfold. Gandhi had appealed to Britain to practise non-violence against the Nazis and had later extended the same appeal to the people of Norway and France. Japan's advances in the east and its aggression in China, on the other hand, had convinced Nehru all the more of the need to choose between Britain and the totalitarian regimes which, according to him, placed democracy in peril.

Savarkar said that if Hitler and Mussolini were expansionist, so were Churchill (who had by now taken over as British premier), Stalin and Roosevelt, regardless of the labels such as democracy, Soviet Republic and Empire that they used to mask their real motives. He saw 'no meaning' in all the pleas to Indians that it was their 'duty' to fight Germany because it was autocratic and felt that 'the bogey of the Germans conquering

India' being employed by the British did not have to be taken seriously. According to him, it was 'altogether improbable' that England would be so disastrously defeated in the conflict as to be forced to hand over its Indian Empire, and if it really felt helpless at any point without the help of Indians, it would offer India not only Dominion Status but some of its colonies and possessions too! Japan's advances in the east would similarly compel the British to depend on India for military assistance, so 'pseudo-moral reasons' trotted out for offering unconditional support to the British should not be allowed to dictate Indian policy, Savarkar said.

The British were 'crafty', he told the Mahasabha delegates, yet Indians needed to participate in the war effort – regardless of the fact that their demands over a definite timeline for Dominion Status, among other issues, had not been granted. Not to help Britain but, as a matter of fact, to help themselves. First, Savarkar argued, a 'disarmed, disorganized and disunited' people were in no position to launch an armed revolt against the British. Second, Gandhi's approach of absolute non-violence in the face of armed aggression was sure to bring devastation to India and to Hindus in particular. And third, the Hindus badly needed to bolster their numbers in the armed forces now that recruitment had been thrown open to all castes and creeds; otherwise their 'second enemy', the Muslims, who were also keen to subjugate them, would be 'strengthened' and in a position to hold them hostage. Savarkar reeled off numbers to show that the revised pattern of recruitment had already brought significant benefits for the majority community. In the last one year, one lakh Indians had joined the army, and nearly 60,000 of the new recruits were Hindus. Likewise, the figures had swelled in the navy, the air force and in teams engaged in producing war equipment, with all the new members acquiring actual training on the war front, he said. Indian industry, in addition, had received a fillip, with one of its magnates, Walchand Hirachand, being allowed to open a shipyard in Bezwada near the eastern port of Vizag and an aircraft production factory near Bangalore.[32]

These claims were not without basis. Before 1939, Muslims from the Punjab, NWFP and elsewhere in north India had formed 34 per cent of the army and the non-martial Hindu castes only 3.7 per cent. During the war, 25 per cent of the new recruits were Muslims and nearly 29 per cent were Hindus, and Sikhs made up 4.5 per cent. The other noticeable change was in the zones from which the recruits came. The Punjab, NWFP and north India in general, where classes identified as 'martial' were mainly located, had in the past contributed the most to the armed forces; this time, those from other regions were well represented. For instance, southern India provided nearly 18 per cent of the new recruits and Bengal, which had had zero representation earlier, provided 3.7 per cent.[33] And Walchand Hirachand had made some genuine breakthroughs, though permissions had not been given to the Indian industrialist with alacrity by the government. Soon enough, much to the satisfaction of the British, Japanese air raids frustrated Hirachand's shipbuilding plans in Vizag, and the aircraft factory was taken over by the Raj in 1942.[34]

'The militarisation and industrialisation of the Hindus must constitute our immediate objective,' Savarkar made clear.[35]

In October 1940, Gandhi launched an individual satyagraha whereby people courted arrest to lodge their protest against the war. Despite serious differences with Nehru and Gandhi over the 'individual' satyagraha agitation, Savarkar sharply criticized the British when Nehru was arrested and subsequently sentenced to four years in prison. Savarkar described the sentence as 'vindictive' and 'a painful shock to every Indian patriot'. Differences in principles and policy might have compelled the two of them to work 'under different colours', he said, but he had nothing except 'deep appreciation of the patriotic and even the humanitarian motives which had actuated Pandit Jawaharlalji throughout his public career'. In the same breath he reminded Nehru that unlike the Mahasabha, 'Pandit Jawaharlalji himself maintained a guilty silence and led by Gandhiji did not utter a word of protest or sympathy when patriotic public workers like Senapati Bapat, Babu Subhash Chandra Bose and several other leaders and followers who differed from the Gandhist school in the Congress were being sentenced under the Defence of India Act ever since the war broke out.' Savarkar asked the Raj to ponder over 'why a man like Pandit Jawaharlalji who, as soon as the war broke out, was impulsively carried off his feet as to declare that India should offer unconditional cooperation to the British who were out to fight the cause of world democracy' should now be 'so embittered'. No genuine cooperation was possible if the government employed repressive measures. If, instead, it laid out a timeline for the grant of Dominion Status, 'even men like Nehruji will feel it their duty . . . to ally themselves with the British'.[36]

In January 1941 Subhas Bose, who unlike Savarkar felt the moment was opportune to crush the British, disappeared from his home on Elgin Road, Calcutta. Savarkar was by now confined to bed again. His excruciating sciatic pains had returned. As the British launched a search for Bose, whom they had very reluctantly released from jail a month earlier for health reasons, Savarkar made a statement voicing anxiety over 'Deshpriya' Bose's safety and hoped that 'the gratitude, sympathy and good wishes' of the Indian nation 'would be a source of never-failing solace and inspiration to him'.

Bose, incidentally, had visited Savarkar's house in June 1940. Savarkar later made the claim that he suggested to Bose during this meeting that he should try to escape and plot against the British from outside India and even showed him a letter that another Bose, the revolutionary Rash Behari, had sent him from East Asia to discuss possible action plans. The claim was subsequently reiterated by Savarkar's assistant Bal Savarkar, who added that the Mahasabha leader specifically suggested that Subhas join Rash Behari in Japan.[37] But in a book that Subhas Bose wrote from Germany after his escape, he wrote of the meeting that 'Mr Savarkar seemed to be oblivious of the international situation and was only thinking how Hindus could secure military training by entering Britain's army in India.'[38] Bose was also disappointed with Jinnah, who was 'only thinking of how to realise his plan of Pakistan' and was unreceptive to the idea of putting up a joint fight with the Congress for independence even though Bose suggested that if a united struggle were launched, 'Mr Jinnah would be the first Prime Minister of Free India'.[39] It is not known if Bose told Savarkar about this offer of his to Jinnah, but from a statement that Savarkar had made about 'Boseism' in August 1939, we get an idea of what his response might have been. Criticizing Gandhism, Boseism and Royism (referring to M.N. Roy) at a rally in Pune, Savarkar said the Forward Bloc was unacceptable to him as 'Bose did not differ very much from Mahatma Gandhi, except that he went further to woo the Muslims'.[40]

~

The political deadlock showed no signs of ending in early 1941. For his part, re-emphasizing Jinnah's primacy in the British scheme of things, Leo Amery, the new Secretary of State for India appointed by the new premier Churchill, told non-Congress, non-League Indian leaders that instead of putting forward their own demands, they should focus on getting the Congress and the Muslim League to reach an agreement.[41]

The Congress's continuing indecisiveness and the League's exercise of its veto on everything stymied all constitutional progress in 1941. Jinnah did not explicitly offer cooperation to the war effort but, time and again, kept putting down conditions that would have to be met for him to think of offering cooperation – for instance, he wanted total parity with the Congress in all discussions and in councils, recognition of the League as the only representative of Muslims, and equal partnership with the British in running the Indian government if the Congress would not join such a government. These conditions were not accepted, along with some others, but Jinnah cleverly kept things hanging and pressed forward with more demands and more discussions. As one chronicler put it, 'he never refused cooperation – he simply did not offer it', all the time working to strengthen his bargaining powers.[42]

Meanwhile, Britain found itself in a tight spot as Hitler attacked the Soviet Union, claimed Yugoslavia and Greece and notched up successes in North Africa. The scene in the Middle

East, South-East Asia and East Asia looked just as worrying for the Allies, and America felt, in view of Japan's threat in the east, that India increasingly mattered not merely logistically but strategically.

On 9 August 1941, Churchill and US President Franklin Roosevelt met on a cruiser in Newfoundland and declared a Statement of War Aims that came to be known as the Atlantic Charter. Article 3 of the charter raised eyebrows, and expectations, in India. Both Britain and America, it said, 'respect the right of all peoples to choose the form of government under which they will live and they wish to see sovereign rights and self-government restored to those who have been forcibly deprived of them'.[43]

Savarkar sent a telegram to Roosevelt asking whether the Atlantic Charter 'covers the case of India' and whether America guaranteed Indian freedom within a year of the end of war. If it did not, 'India cannot but construe this declaration as another stunt like the War Aims of the last Anglo-German war'.[44] Many other prominent Indians too raised their voices.

Churchill's clarification was characteristically blunt. He said the Atlantic Charter applied only to European countries under Nazi domination and not to India. This generated tremendous disappointment across the Indian political spectrum, and the Central Legislative Assembly passed a motion saying the charter must apply to India.[45]

Subhas Bose's older brother Sarat, then leader of opposition in the Bengal legislative assembly, commented sarcastically that Savarkar's cable to the US president had made him 'almost breathless by surprise'. It reminded him, Sarat Bose said, of 'by-gone days when Indian political leaders used to look to the Liberals and Radicals of England to make them a gift of independence'. Savarkar was depending on Roosevelt's 'generosity', he pointed out, adding that the Mahasabha leader's 'disillusionment will be complete'. There was no way Savarkar could 'cajole' or 'intimidate' the US president with his telegram, Sarat Bose pointed out.[46] S.A. Brelvi, editor of the *Bombay Chronicle*, quoted from Savarkar's telegram in his editorial and dismissively remarked, 'We are sure there will be no reply from America.'[47]

Savarkar was surprised that 'Babu Sharatchandra' should think he was counting on choices to be made by Roosevelt. He replied that 'there is a difference between demanding an explanation of a diplomatic statement with a view to exposing its underlying casuistry and political hypocrisy and expecting any help'. Reminding him that the Congress had, not very long ago, sent Sarojini Naidu to America to drum up support for India on US soil, Savarkar said the Mahasabha, unlike the Congress, Forward Bloc and the Communists, had never looked at Russia as a symbol of 'anti-imperialistic innocence' but had had a realistic view of every country's motives since the war began.[48] In a separate statement on Churchill's 'clarification', Savarkar said the British prime minister had torn off 'the mask of vague platitudes under which the Anglo-American Announcement of War Aims was deliberately camouflaged' and wondered if Roosevelt would 'speak out now or play second fiddle to the dictates of Mr Churchill'.[49]

Irrespective of Churchill's duplicity and the Raj still not declaring a timeline for Dominion Status, Savarkar continued to exhort, through a Hindu militarization board formed by the Mahasabha, the youths to join the army, navy and air force.

He blocked a resolution passed by the Mahasabha on 'direct action' against the Raj, saying the war was approaching both the western and eastern frontiers of India and 'any foolish jail-seeking programme' ought to be postponed.[50] His opinion on not taking any precipitate action remained firm even after he was arrested in Gaya for attempting to go to Bhagalpur for the annual session of the Mahasabha in December 1941. The Bihar government had banned the session citing law and order concerns, but Savarkar decided to defy orders and was sent to custody along with many other Mahasabha activists and leaders. In his presidential address, read out by G.V. Ketkar at the session that proceeded in spite of more than 300 arrests and a lathi charge, Savarkar asked Hindus to enter military service 'without losing a single minute'. Earlier the same month Japan had entered the war on the Axis side. Savarkar cited that as the reason for urgency, for India now stood exposed 'directly and immediately to attack by Britain's enemies'. 'Whether we like it or not,' he said, 'we shall have to defend our own hearth and home against the ravages of the war, and this can be done only by intensifying the government's war effort to defend India.'[51] Savarkar's arrest was condemned by several, including by the Muslim League's Calcutta organ, *Star of India*, which was upset that British officials had cited Muslim concerns to impose the ban when the League had asked for no such thing. Gandhi was happy because Savarkar and his aides had courted arrest by way of civil disobedience. 'It fills me with delight to find Vir Savarkar, Dr Moonje and others being arrested in their attempt to assert the very primary and very fundamental right of holding an orderly meeting subject to all reasonable restrictions about the preservation of public peace,' he said.[52]

Around the time of his release from prison in January 1942, the Congress Working Committee passed a resolution in Wardha again offering cooperation to the British in the war in return for acceptance of its demand for independence and immediate formation of a national government. The Congress had been totally divided on the issue and had swung this way and that for two years. While in September and October 1939 it had said it could not cooperate in the war effort, the 'Gandhi camp' in the organization, as Subhas Bose called it, led by Nehru and Azad, had got the Congress Working Committee and the All India Congress Committee (AICC) to adopt resolutions offering support in June and July 1940, and the internal struggles continued for a while after that. Nehru favoured cooperation with the British, Bose was totally opposed to it, and Gandhi, though opposed to cooperation simply on grounds of his professed pacifism, had his sympathies with the Allied forces. He half-heartedly launched an individual satyagraha campaign for a brief while in 1941 but withdrew it before the Congress Working Committee's January 1942 resolution making the cooperation offer.

Savarkar wondered why the government was not responding to the Congress's 'overt and covert' overtures. He assured the Raj that it had 'nothing to fear while the Congress was led by men like Gandhiji who have not only been pro-government but sincerely pro-British throughout their life'.[53] That last bit was widely believed to be payback for Gandhi's remark that he was happy about Savarkar having practised civil disobedience in Bhagalpur.

The fall of Singapore in the middle of February at last forced Britain to shun its pointless academic exercises, that too after an unmistakable nudge from Roosevelt to 'settle matters with India'. With the greatest reluctance, Churchill announced on 11 March 1942 – four days after the fall of Rangoon, bringing Japan perilously close to India – that British cabinet minister Stafford Cripps would 'proceed as soon as possible to India' for talks.[54] Apart from his own arch-imperialistic approach and Cripps's relatively liberal one towards India, Churchill had one more reason to hope that his cabinet colleague would not in any way succeed: Cripps was a direct contender for the prime ministerial post. If he solved what Britain referred to as its 'India problem', he would definitely make a pitch for 10 Downing Street.

A day after Rangoon fell, the *Manchester Guardian* reported that Savarkar had sent a cable to Churchill calling for the proclamation of Indian independence with equal partnership in an Indo-British Commonwealth. He had also asked for immediate formation of a national government, the report stated.[55] (While these demands were indeed made, the Mahasabha continued to exhort Hindu youth to join the army.) Asked by an Indian journalist about Cripps's impending visit, Savarkar said he welcomed the member of the British war cabinet but wondered why the cat – the constitutional scheme to be proposed for India – was still in the bag and not quite out of it.[56]

Cripps arrived in Delhi on 23 March 1942 and first called the Congress and the League for discussions. The Congress was to be represented by Azad and Nehru, but the latter was unwell, so Savarkar's one-time London colleague Asaf Ali accompanied Azad instead. After that the Mahasabha leader, Ambedkar, the Sikhs, and members of the Chamber of Princes were invited, among others. When the Mahasabha delegation comprising Savarkar, Moonje, Syama Prasad Mookerjee, Jwala Prasad Srivastava and Ganpat Rai met Cripps in the capital on 28 March, Cripps was left with the feeling that he was not being allowed to talk much. Savarkar, he said afterwards, 'spent most of his time lecturing me upon the principles of majority determination and of fallacies in the document'.[57] Emerging from the meeting, Savarkar was indisputably the one who let the cat out of the bag. 'We will fight Pakistan,' he told the journalists assembled outside Cripps's Queen Victoria Road residence in Delhi. The *New York Times* described his statement as 'virtual confirmation' that Pakistan was on the list of Cripps's proposals, which had still not been made public, and 'the first public intimation of anything other than smooth sailing in Sir Stafford's fulfillment of his mission'.[58] The proposals were eventually rejected by most Indian parties, with the exception of the League, mainly on account of the option given to the provinces to opt out of a united India. Savarkar said the secession proviso had compelled the Mahasabha to reject the scheme.[59]

Savarkar was in 1942 into his fifth consecutive year as Mahasabha president. His health was not holding up for rigorous tours and endless meetings, so he decided to hand over the mantle towards the end of July. But early in August, things came to a head with the launch of Gandhi's Quit India movement, and he was persuaded to withdraw his resignation and remain in charge in a fast-changing, critical situation.

Up until March 1942 the Congress had made offers of cooperation if complete independence were granted and even after Gandhi issued a resolution in April 1942 at the All India

Congress Committee's meeting in Allahabad asking the British to simply withdraw from India, Nehru and Rajaji disagreed vehemently with the Mahatma. When the Quit India resolution was passed in August and all the top Congress leaders were promptly arrested, Nehru, according to his sister, was 'almost thankful' to be behind bars, 'so uncomfortable had he felt opposing the war effort'.[60]

Savarkar considered the timing of the Quit India agitation terribly problematic in view of the war situation: the Japanese had already bombed the ports of Vizianagaram and Kakinada in east India and captured the Andaman Islands. But Savarkar was willing to cooperate with the Congress in the Quit India agitation and withdraw support for the war provided Gandhi withdrew his recent 'offer' to Jinnah to form a government on behalf of the Indian people – which did not happen. For Savarkar 'Quit India' was fine as a slogan, but 'keep your army here' was an unworthy extension to it and incongruous to boot. The resolution passed by the Congress Working Committee in Wardha on 14 July 1942 had, while asking the British to leave at once, invited the Allied forces to remain on Indian soil 'in order to ward off and resist Japanese or other aggression, and to protect and help China'.[61] What was the point if Britain's armed forces were not going anywhere, he wondered.[62] Were the Japanese a better option then? 'They are foreigners and we do not want any foreigners in India,' he told the *New York Times* correspondent.[63] Savarkar then preferred to help the British defend India from another foreign aggressor.

The entire Congress leadership was put behind bars on the morning of 9 August 1942, and many of its workers who were still free went underground to evade arrest. Reports of arson and violence, and the stern crackdown on protesters, began to come in from various parts of India. Savarkar said his deepest sympathies were with the patriots suffering at all levels, 'from detention to death'.[64] Yet sympathy and sentiment could not be allowed to cloud one's judgement, he said; he worried greatly that 'Quit India' might ultimately pave the way for 'Split India'.[65]

The success of the Quit India movement continues to be debated, though it was beyond a shadow of doubt the biggest mass uprising in India since 1857. Michael Brecher wrote in his biography of Nehru that the long-term consequences of the movement were politically significant.

> For almost three years the Congress was outlawed, its leaders in prison, its funds seized and its organization virtually destroyed. In the political vacuum thus created the Muslim League was able to build a mass party, by appealing successfully to religious emotions and genuine Muslim fears. Between 1942 and 1945 the League increased its membership to two million with the result that by the end of the war it was able to put forward a strong claim to Pakistan. The Congress was to pay dearly for its 'Quit India' Resolution. Unwittingly it helped to pave the way for Partition.[66]

The other truth is that the Quit India stir 'evoked a chorus of dissent and alarm' from within, for the Japanese were at the gates. 'No party other than the Congress, no politician outside its ranks, approved of it,' one observer remarked.[67] Savarkar, Ambedkar, Jinnah, the Sikhs, the other smaller minorities, the liberals, the communists, the All India Students' Conference and many of the Nehru-inspired kisan sabhas sternly opposed and even denounced Gandhi's 'Do or Die' call.[68] The sobering reality for all of these opponents, however, was that when it came to influencing popular opinion, it was no one else but the Congress that had the ability to take on Jinnah, a man consciously pushed to the forefront by a powerful Raj at every step.

Savarkar was slammed by most Congress sympathizers for opposing the August 1942 revolt. The story of Aruna Asaf Ali, the plucky nationalist who unfurled the tricolour at Mumbai's Gowalia Tank even as Gandhi and the 7500-odd Congress delegates swore to either free India or perish in the attempt[69] is, however, an intriguing example of how the strands of the Indian national movement were so intricately interwoven that portraying things in black and white would be an egregious error. Aruna Asaf Ali told her biographer that the most important book she was introduced to in her youth was Savarkar's *First War of Independence*. 'I was thrilled by it. It politicized me,' she said. She was first arrested as a Congress worker during Gandhi's Salt Satyagraha and was not released from jail after the Gandhi–Irwin Pact of 1931 because the pact did not cover those who had 'incited violence'. When, in the wake of a sustained campaign by the nationalist papers, she was eventually freed, she went to meet Gandhi in Delhi. He wanted to know if she had really incited people. 'I had to confess to him,' she later said, 'that having recently read Savarkar's book on the Indian struggle for Independence in 1857, I could not help being influenced by it and did refer to it quite often in my speeches.'[70] She also saw 'nothing wrong' with Savarkar's position when he told Muslims, as the leader of the Mahasabha, 'We shall fight for freedom along with you if you join us, without you if you do not, and despite you if you stand in the way.' When her biographer asked her if her husband, Asaf Ali, regarded Savarkar as a Hindu communalist, she replied in the negative and added, 'He only spoke admiringly of Savarkar the revolutionary.'[71]

While cooperating with the British in the war effort, Savarkar also saw an opportunity to push his demands at this point when the Raj had its back against the wall. In the immediate aftermath of the Congress leaders' arrests, Savarkar came up with a five-point plan which, he insisted, the British needed to implement forthwith. He wanted an immediate declaration that India had been raised to the position of a completely free and equal partner, complete Indianization of the Viceroy's Council with its decisions binding on the Viceroy, and a conference at the end of the war 'to frame a national Constitution and to give full effect to the declaration of independence'. If these steps were taken, he said, Britain could still secure India's 'willing cooperation in the war'[72] – which the Mahasabha was counter-intuitively giving the British in any case. The top dailies in the UK – *The Times*, *Manchester Guardian*, *Daily Herald*, *News Chronicle* and *Yorkshire Post* – carried the statement prominently, and the London correspondent of an Indian daily wrote that Savarkar's appeal 'has been the topic of discussion among a section of political leaders here and it is felt that an early initiative on the part of the British government on the lines suggested by Mr Savarkar is well worth making'. The statement also 'came up for informal discussion among the Indian residents in London' who had gathered for 'a public meeting of the Indian League in the Central Hall'.[73]

Churchill, however, appeared to take no notice. In a speech delivered in the House of Commons on 10 September 1942, he said the offer of Dominion Status and other proposals included in the Cripps scheme still stood and, after making condescending remarks about the Congress and highlighting the differences among India's various communities, commented with undisguised pride that 'the numbers of white soldiers now in that country . . . are larger than at any time in the British connection'.[74] The speech was condemned by almost all parties in India for being 'provocative' and 'extremely reactionary', and Churchill was accused of being 'insolent' and 'fond of annexations'. Savarkar believed the speech was 'a sharp reminder that moral obligations have no place in stern politics' and had 'confirmed beyond cavil or criticism how the Hindu Mahasabha was correct in revealing the inner purpose of Britain in entering the war'. Savarkar, though, was increasingly finding himself in an unenviable position. Not only was he attracting considerable flak from Congress-minded Indians, whose numbers were so large as to easily dwarf the Mahasabha's, but many of his own followers too were deeply uncomfortable with his opposition to the Quit India movement and his urging Hindus to join the army. N.C. Chatterjee, one of Savarkar's close colleagues in the Mahasabha and father of India's future communist leader and Lok Sabha speaker Somnath Chatterjee, was so disturbed by his stand on Quit India that he wrote to another colleague, B.S. Moonje, that 'the entire Hindu population is with Gandhiji and his movement and if anybody wants to oppose it, he will be absolutely finished and hounded out of public life. The unfortunate statement issued by Veer Savarkar [opposing Quit India] made our position rather difficult in Bengal.'[75]

But if Savarkar was distressed that many of his own party functionaries were thinking along the same lines as Chatterjee, he was in for something that would upset him much more.

Against all expectations, one of Savarkar's staunchest defenders, the writer and playwright P.K. Atre, turned on him for encouraging Indians to join the British-led Indian army. In 1937, Atre had joined the Congress and had been elected to the Pune civic corporation on a Congress ticket. In January 1940 he started a Marathi weekly, *Navyug*, whose very first issue carried a piece characterizing Savarkar as 'a lion in a glass case'.[76] By Atre's own admission later, the piece, written by his editorial colleague Ramakant Veldey, was 'totally lacking in civility and condescending in its ferocious attack on Savarkar'. The next couple of issues contained similarly personal attacks on Ambedkar and Subhas Bose,[77] and Atre subsequently wrote that these articles, again penned not by him but by his colleagues, made him feel as uneasy as the hatchet job on Savarkar because, whatever their political differences, he had deep respect for all three leaders. Yet Atre was so well known for the sheer pungency of his own prose that the explanations would not easily wash, and definitely not when the weekly's printline carried his name as the chief editor. Moreover, the term Atre himself used for Savarkar soon thereafter left no doubt about what he was really thinking. The man who had bestowed the title 'Swatantryaveer' upon Savarkar now caustically branded him a 'Recruit-Veer' for assisting the British in augmenting the ranks of the armed forces.

In April and May 1940, Atre happened to be in Nagpur for hearings in a court case. One afternoon, some youths approached him asking if he would deliver a lecture on Marathi theatre on the grounds of the local Neel City High School. Atre readily agreed and had a crowd of over 500 waiting to hear him at 5 p.m.

on the scheduled day at the school maidan. But his reputation for rib-tickling humour notwithstanding, he realized during the course of his speech that he was not eliciting any laughter at all, whereas the number of grim-faced listeners in the audience increased gradually. The moment he winded up his speech, still somewhat perplexed at the crowd's indifference, stones and chappals were hurled in his direction, and a section of the mob began aggressively pushing itself towards the dais. Atre was whisked away by some of the organizers into the school building, where the room in which he and his rescuers locked themselves was pummelled. Sticks and fists rained on the room's doors and windows, and those inside had no way of calling up the police as the telephone wires had been snapped from outside. The violent Savarkar supporters left only after they realized that the door and windows would not give way.[78] Atre refused to buckle in the face of such intimidatory tactics and continued to publish articles highly critical of Savarkar, and he was attacked a second time in September 1941, this time in Pune. Invited as the chief guest for a function at the Sir Parshuram Bhau College, he was 'repeatedly heckled'[79] by a group of pro-Savarkar students as he rose to speak, and one hostile student forced his way on to the dais and assaulted him before the principal managed to rush in and fend off further blows. Atre sustained some injuries to his head but fortunately they were not major. Not very long after Savarkar's release from internment in 1937, Atre had faced serious physical assault from Congress activists for hailing and defending Savarkar; the position having been reversed, he was now taking blows from diehard Savarkarites.

Rash Behari Bose, the revolutionary leader of the India Independence League in East Asia, used gentle words in place of Atre's fierce reproach. In a letter addressed to 'Venerable Vinayak Rao Savarkarji' from Tokyo in March 1942 (before the Quit India movement was launched), Rash Behari referred to the Mahasabha leader as 'a senior as well as a comrade in spirit' and said that he represented 'the very spirit of sacrifice'. In an imploring tone, he continued:[80]

> Please do not let your vision be blurred at this critical moment. That England is in extreme difficulties must be known to you. That England's difficulty also offers the golden chance for India's independence must also be known to you . . . I have, therefore, decided to mobilize all my Indian brothers in East Asia in a supreme effort to strike at the fetters that have hitherto reduced our Motherland to a state of national slavery. But, I know that I shall not succeed in my attempt unless yourself and other leaders at home support me at the right time . . . At this stage, Britain may offer all kinds of temptations to Indians – she might even offer independence. But please do not accept even independence if it would involve India in a war with which she has got nothing to do. For, fighting on the side of England in a war in which Britain is sure to lose, would mean for India all that accrues from a military defeat.
>
> . . . Why not side with Japan and destroy the British power which alone is responsible for the present miserable state of India?

Subhas Bose also made an appeal to Savarkar. He made a radio broadcast from Germany at the end of August 1942. In it he spoke chiefly of the spirit of patriotism fuelled among ordinary Indians by the Quit India movement and said the agitation 'was spreading like wild-fire'. He then said:

> I would request Mr Jinnah, Mr Savarkar and all those leaders who still think of a compromise with the British to realize once and for all that in the world of tomorrow there will be no British Empire. All those individuals, groups or parties who now participate in the fight for freedom will have an honoured place in the India of tomorrow. The supporters of British imperialism will naturally become non-entities in a free India . . . I will appeal earnestly to all parties and groups to consider this and to think in terms of nationalism and anti-imperialism, and to come forward and join the epic struggle that is going on.[81]

~

As momentous a question as the war was whether the British would divide India before they quit. Savarkar's reaction to the Muslim League's 1940 Lahore Resolution was strongly negative. For him there was no question of allowing Muslim-majority areas in India's north-west and east to be 'grouped to constitute Independent States' that would be 'autonomous and sovereign'.[82] As the Pakistan proposal was hotly debated, he cited it as another reason for Hindu participation in the war effort. If the British left without any of the Axis powers occupying India and Hindus were faced with 'internal anarchy and a consequent civil war with the Muslims', being in a state of military readiness would help safeguard their interests, he contended.[83]

Days after the League's Lahore Resolution, Savarkar,

addressing Mahasabha activists in Madras, said he wanted 'Hindustan and not Anglostan or Pakistan'. His party 'could not tolerate and would oppose with all its might the Muslim idea of dividing India'. Referring to Gandhi's statement offering Jinnah to form and lead a government of India in which he also said that he would be willing to live in 'Jinnah's Raj' as it would 'still be Indian', Savarkar said the Mahatma should not be encouraging such 'bluffs' on the part of Muslims[84] and warned the Hindus that the Congress was 'bound to betray' their interests.[85]

For all this, Savarkar played entirely into Jinnah's hands during the Mahasabha's twenty-first session in Calcutta held just two months after the start of war in 1939. He elucidated a theory of nationhood that mirrored Jinnah's. Criticizing the Congress for harping on territorialism – in other words, geography – as the basis for national unity, he said nationality was more a cultural, linguistic, racial and historical concept. Thus 'the Hindus were marked out as an abiding nation by themselves', he emphasized. Critics went on the attack vigorously. S.A. Brelvi accused Savarkar of being full of 'historical and political paradoxes' and wrote that, just like Jinnah, he was 'the victim of a psycho-political complex'.[86] The English writer and playwright Beverley Nichols in his book *Verdict on India*, panned by the Indians just as much as Katherine Mayo's *Mother India*, accused Savarkar of harbouring a 'smouldering hatred' and gloated that 'it was something to obtain such a confession from a representative Hindu leader of such wide responsibility'.[87] F.K. Khan Durrani, a propagandist of Pakistan who wanted the re-establishment of an Islamic empire in India, dug up Savarkar's 1937 speech at the Mahasabha's Ahmedabad session, where he had similarly stated that in India 'there are two nations in the main, the Hindus and the Muslims', and described the Calcutta speech as further elaboration of the thesis. Durrani had no quarrel with the theory at all. 'The quarrel,' he stated, 'arises when he [Savarkar] becomes inconsistent with his own thesis.' While accepting Muslims as a nation, Savarkar did not accept their right to a separate national existence but claimed 'the whole of India as the undivided holy land of the Hindus', Durrani pointed out. In such an India, 'Hindus will be the ruling race' and 'Muslims a subject people', Durrani believed.[88] Two leaders of the Congress socialist wing, Asoka Mehta and Achyut Patwardhan, felt that Savarkar's perspective was 'warped by its communal bias' but added that 'if India is a land of many nationalities it does not follow that each such nationality must enjoy the luxury of a separate sovereign state'.[89]

In the same speech, Savarkar had enunciated the principle of 'one man one vote' across India and said the Mahasabha guaranteed the legitimate rights of minorities with regard to religion, culture and language.[90] But there would be no separate electorates and no special weightage for minorities in seats in the regional and national legislatures. If Muslims rejected the idea of joint electorates, seats would be in proportion to the populations of the communities, he said. To assuage concerns a bit more, he said the Hindu flag was not against 'the flags of other races in India but would remain allied to them'.[91] He still insisted that Hindus and Muslims were separate nations, but he was making a distinction between a 'nation' and a 'state'. Hindus, he declared, 'do not advance any special claims, privileges or rights . . . over and above the non-Hindu sections of Hindustan. Let the Indian state be purely Indian. Let it not recognize any invidious distinctions whatsoever as regards the franchise, public services, offices, taxation, on grounds of religion and race.'[92]

Ambedkar saw this attitude as 'illogical, if not queer'. In his tract on Pakistan, he remarked that 'Mr Savarkar admits that the Muslims are a separate nation. He concedes that they have a right to cultural autonomy. He allows them to have a national flag. Yet he opposes the demand of the Muslim nation for a separate national home. If he claims a national home for the Hindu nation, how can he refuse the claim of the Muslim nation for a national home?'[93] Ambedkar was not batting for Pakistan, but he was convinced the creation of Pakistan with peaceful transfer of populations was the best way out in the circumstances. The major thrust of his argument was that there was no unity between Hindus and Muslims, and the tenets of Islam were such that 'if this spiritual Pan-Islamism seeks to issue forth in political Pan-Islamism, it cannot be said to be unnatural'.[94] It was this Pan-Islamism that 'leads every Musalman in India to say that he is a Muslim first and Indian afterwards', Ambedkar wrote.[95]

In Savarkar's case, the critics had yet another paradox to talk about. After the resignations of Congress members from the provincial legislatures in October 1939, legislators belonging to the Hindu Mahasabha joined the 'Muslim ministries' – so named because of the statutory or legally sanctioned majority guaranteed to the community in Muslim-majority areas – in Sindh, Bengal and the North-West Frontier Province. The Bengal ministry was headed by A.K. Fazlul Haq of the Krishak Praja, the one in Sindh by G.H. Hidayatullah of the Muslim

League, and the NWFP government was led by Aurangzeb Khan, also of the League.

By no means was the League the only Muslim party in India, or even the most successful. Apart from Haq's Krishak Praja, other parties like the Unionist Party in Punjab had done very well, and the League had won only about 25 per cent of the total Muslim seats in the 1937 elections. But after 1940, all the Muslim ministries were either heavily influenced by Jinnah and his ideology or were constituted or reshaped 'with either Muslim Leaguers as Premiers or with the Premiers baptized in League waters'.[96]

In spite of this, Savarkar gave his sanction for the formation of coalition ministries. 'In the Hindu-minority provinces whenever a Muslim Ministry seemed inevitable – whether it was sponsored by the Muslim League or otherwise – and Hindu interests could be better served by joining it, the Hindusabhaites should try as a matter of right to capture as many seats as possible in the Ministry and do the best they could to safeguard the interests of the Hindu minority,' he said. Boycotting a ministry, in his opinion, could be 'more often than not highly detrimental to Hindu interests', and participation would mean an assertion of Hindu rights.[97] Savarkar even sent a telegram to the Akali leader Tara Singh saying 'Hindus and Sikhs should join' the League ministry in Punjab 'and transform it into a coalition ministry'.[98]

Savarkar issued instructions to the Mahasabha's ministers to 'oppose publicly every attempt on the part of the Muslim Ministry to support Pakistan or the treacherous principle of self-determination to secede'. The provincial party units were free to agitate against 'any anti-Hindu' steps taken by these ministries; so long as the Hindu ministers recorded their protests against such steps, they 'should not be asked to resign from the Ministries'.

The Congress leader Pattabhi Sitaramayya described these developments as a case of the Mahasabha being 'frankly out for the crumbs'. He added, uncharitably, that joining the League ministries was Savarkar's 'return gift to the nation which had presented to him a purse of about three lakhs of rupees'.[99] Some other Congress leaders called the Mahasabha legislators 'job-hunters'.[100]

Savarkar's defang-the-League-by-joining-a-ministry policy was not entirely without effect. Stanley Wolpert says in his biography of Jinnah that as long as Fazlul Haq 'continued presiding over a non-League coalition in that Muslim majority province [Bengal], he appeared to belie the basic premise of Pakistan'.[101] But sixteen months was all that Haq could endure outside the League. (He had earlier left the League to form his own party.) After that he dissolved his own party and went back over to Jinnah's side, preferring to sacrifice his position as Bengal premier in the process.[102]

Just as disconcerting for Mahasabha sympathizers was the Sindh assembly's resolution in favour of Pakistan, passed in March 1943. The Hindu ministers 'recorded their protests' but did not hand in their resignations, prompting criticism of their, and their leader's, stand.

Interestingly, during this progressively tense five-year period (1939 to 1943), the idea of a Savarkar–Jinnah dialogue was mooted twice. First, early in 1940, reports emerged that Jinnah, who'd had a meeting with Ambedkar in Mumbai, was slated to meet Savarkar as well. Gandhi welcomed the prospect and lauded Jinnah for his intent to 'amalgamate all the parties opposed to the Congress' so that India could have 'mainly two parties – Congress and anti-Congress'.[103] That meeting never fructified, nor did another one, sought by Jinnah in 1943. According to M.S.M. Sharma, a veteran journalist of the time who had worked with the Associated Press and *The Hindu* and was subsequently editor of Bihar's leading daily, *The Searchlight*, Jinnah decided that if he could not see eye to eye with Gandhi, he could at least try to get in touch with Savarkar and see if a pact could be made. One day in Karachi, Jinnah 'quietly broached the subject' to Hemanandas Wadhwani, the Mahasabha member in the Sindh coalition cabinet. A doctor by profession who was then holding the public health portfolio, Wadhwani rushed to Mumbai and, after discussions with Savarkar, 'told Jinnah that as soon as he returned to Bombay [from Karachi], the two leaders could meet'.[104] At a tea party organized around this time in honour of Jinnah in Karachi, M.S.M. Sharma, who was on familiar terms with Jinnah, went up to him and asked him when he would be meeting Savarkar. According to the journalist, Jinnah was stumped and 'for once, betrayed his uneasiness'. He initially dismissed the idea as 'nonsense', but when the journalist told him he had definite information in this regard from Mumbai, he asked the journalist indirectly if Wadhwani was his source. When Sharma told him it was not Wadhwani, Jinnah said, 'Please do not publish the news. But you are at liberty to suggest that it would be good for the country if I and Savarkar – not Savarkar and I – could meet and review the situation in the interests of the country's peace.'[105]

The journalist heard immediately afterwards that Jinnah's

proposal was that since he was the 'senior' of the two, Savarkar should call on him at his Malabar Hill bungalow. Savarkar, on the other hand, insisted that Jinnah come to his Shivaji Park residence. Much time was spent discussing who should call on whom, and with no agreement being reached the idea of a face-to-face dialogue was abandoned.

Savarkar continued to criticize the Pakistan project, using for it the epithet Paap-astan to suggest that, contrary to the word 'Pak' that was meant to stand for 'holy', the proposed state was akin to a sinful enterprise.

From mid-1940 Savarkar said repeatedly that the Congress would eventually concede Pakistan, regardless of the anti-League stand it had taken. One way the Hindus could solidify their case, he said, was through enthusiastic participation in the 1941 census. The Congress had boycotted the national census in 1921 and 1931. Terming its fresh boycott call in 1941 as bogus in view of its unquestioning reliance on census numbers for determining religion-based electorates and for contesting polls and apprehending that these figures would be decisive in the final reckoning in determining the partition issue, he urged the animists, the Bhils, the Santhals and other tribes to get themselves 'correctly enumerated' and appealed to the Arya Samajists, Jains, Sikhs and Lingayats that even if they preferred to write Vedic, Jain, Sikh or Lingayat in the religion box, they ought to say 'Hindu' in brackets alongside to indicate that their religions were of Indian origin and that India was their 'holy land' and 'fatherland'.[106]

~

In July 1942 Savarkar extensively toured Jammu and Kashmir despite not being in the best of health. In Hindu-majority Jammu, the response to his arrival was mammoth, with 40,000 people taking part in a procession in his honour, and in Muslim-majority Srinagar too several delegations called on him, a public rally witnessed a significant turnout, notably of local women, and he was led in a procession to the banks of the Jhelum. He even took a brief detour to Rawalpindi for a party organized in his honour.

But the stay was not without its verbal jousting. Barely had the Kashmir tour begun, with excited garlanding and welcome chants at Amritsar, Lahore and Wazirabad railway stations, when the pro-partition group J&K Conference gave him a memorandum asking him to specify whether his principle of 'majority rule' applied to Kashmir – where the ruler was Hindu while the majority of the subjects were Muslim. Savarkar's response was that he was still waiting for the Valley's Muslim majority to back the same principle in Bhopal and Hyderabad, states with a Hindu majority and Muslim rulers.[107]

Along with the Muslim-ruled princely states, a prominent Muslim official in a Hindu principality became the focus of fierce criticism. Savarkar voiced his stiff opposition to the appointment of Mirza Ismail, earlier dewan of Mysore, as the dewan of Jaipur in 1942. Ismail did not favour partition, but he told Jinnah in 1941 that the 'main difference' between their viewpoints was that Jinnah 'wanted only Pakistan for the Muslims, while I wanted for them both Pakistan and India!' He thought provincial autonomy was a far better idea than separation as 'the Muslims would be in virtual control' of five provinces and 'have a fairly effective voice in the other provinces as well and especially at the Centre'; with partition, Jinnah 'would have perhaps one-third of India, with little or no voice in the rest of the sub-continent'.[108] Ismail also rejected Jinnah's offer to him to join the League, saying 'my life-long association with a Hindu maharaja and my long service in a Hindu state where I have received the most loyal co-operation from my Hindu fellow-citizens . . . prevent me from identifying myself with a political organization which is avowedly anti-Hindu'.[109] For him, his record was one of creating 'communal concord' but Savarkar laid at his door the charge of being communal by quietly filling up public service posts with Muslims. Ismail cried 'vilification', but the Mahasabha kept at it, and also accused him of promoting the use of Urdu in government offices.[110]

Savarkar's opponents, however, complained that he sprang too quickly to the defence of the Hindu princely states even if the princelings were not exactly ideal rulers. Savarkar also harboured the unrealistic notion that in the event of a civil conflict over the partition row, the Hindu states, and even neighbouring Nepal, would come to the rescue of the Hindu community, whereas Jinnah had 'only Nizam's Hyderabad and the border tribes' to rely on.

The big worry he had was about Hindu-majority Assam. He perceived a demographic threat there as a result of what he termed the 'massive influx of Muslims' from other, mostly eastern, provinces, and asked local Hindus to be on the alert and thwart its 'deliberate Islamisation'.[111]

Some critics, like the Marathi scholar-editor Govind Talwalkar, were of the view that Savarkar's failure to promote reform in the Hindu princely states, and his advocacy of the princes' cause despite his avowedly pro-reform stance in most social matters, affected his party's prospects; Gandhi, on the other hand, although not pro-reform, maintained a studied silence on the matter and did not antagonize a change-seeking local populace.[112]

Savarkar's focus throughout was to portray himself as a powerful antagonist of Jinnah. By December 1941 he could justifiably say that he had riled Jinnah enough to get him to respond to some of the chief points he was raising. On Savarkar's militarization and industrialization idea, Jinnah commented at a gathering of the All-India Muslim Students Federation in Nagpur, 'Militarise what? Industrialise what? The Hindu nation. I ask Mr Savarkar and Field Marshal Moonje: Do you think that everybody in this country is a fool? . . . Why this lip-loyalty of co-operation [with the British] with an ulterior motive?' Once the Hindus had filled the ranks of the armed forces, Jinnah said, Savarkar and his aides would help crush the notion of Pakistan, and the British would go home. 'What is Mr Savarkar's scheme?' he asked his young listeners, and proceeded to give them an answer. 'His scheme is that when he gets 75 per cent of the Hindus' in the armed forces and in the administration, 'he will see then that Hindu Raj is established!'[113] This 'sinister and insidious motive', Jinnah remarked, was accompanied by the demand for Dominion Status at the end of the war. 'Who is to give it? The British Government? . . . Even if they do it, do you expect the British Government to put Savarkar on the *gaddi* and do the policing of the Raj?' he asked.[114] No, that was not going to happen, thus there was 'something else' behind the demand. A promise of Dominion Status would mean 'the constitution will no longer be framed with the consent of the major parties; in other words, the consent of the Muslims is not necessary', only that of 'the Congress and the Hindu Mahasabha', Jinnah said.[115]

Yet, much against his own wishes, Savarkar was finding it increasingly challenging to de-hyphenate his name from that of Jinnah. Ambedkar, for one, referring to a series of Savarkar's statements, laid stress on the fact that 'strange as it may appear, Mr Savarkar and Mr Jinnah instead of being opposed to each other on the one nation versus two nations issue are in complete agreement about it'.[116] Tom Treanor, a correspondent for the *Los Angeles Times* who interviewed Savarkar at his Mumbai residence in 1942, concluded in American idiom that 'if Savarkar has his way, the Mohammedans will get what is known in the trade as sweet damn-all. It's the sort of attitude which makes Mr Jinnah argue for Pakistan.'[117] And a political commentator for the journal *Indian Review* stated that 'Savarkar is to the Mahasabha what Jinnah is to the Muslim League' and that 'Savarkar has made the Mahasabha as aggressively Hindu as Jinnah has made the Muslim League aggressively Muslim'.[118]

~

If being equated thus with Jinnah was hardly flattering for Savarkar, who would rather have preferred parallels with Gandhi, Nehru, Patel and Bose, the gradual souring of ties with his deputy-in-chief, Syama Prasad Mookerjee, and quite a few other Mahasabha activists was just as disturbing.

Mookerjee had a reputation of being an overachiever. Son of an illustrious judge of the Calcutta High Court and former vice chancellor of Calcutta University, he topped his varsity exams, earned his spurs as a lawyer from Lincoln's Inn, entered the

Bengal Legislative Council from the University constituency in his twenties and, like his father Ashutosh, became vice chancellor of Calcutta University, at the age of thirty-three. After he was re-elected to the Bengal Legislative Council in 1937, he felt the Congress in his province was giving in easily to the Muslim League's demands. In February 1939, Savarkar was on a Bengal tour, and N.C. Chatterjee, his host in Calcutta, invited Mookerjee and some other prominent faces from the city for a conversation with the famous ex-revolutionary. Mookerjee left the meeting 'deeply impressed'[119] with Savarkar's worldview and joined the Hindu Mahasabha. The same year, he became party vice president and, with Savarkar's health showing signs of growing fragility from 1940, was appointed acting president. In December 1943, when Savarkar was indisposed on account of a fresh bout of illness, Mookerjee stepped into his shoes for the first time, delivering the presidential address at the party's annual convention in Amritsar.[120] He concurred with Savarkar's stand that joining the Fazlul Haq ministry in Bengal was necessary and, while serving as the finance minister in that ministry, he truly believed that the Hindu–Muslim arrangement gave the lie to the British line that 'India's future political advancement was being retarded because of the failure of the leaders of Hindus and Moslems to work together in the sphere of State Administration'.[121] He was similarly one with his leader on the Quit India movement.

When Savarkar said he wanted to quit as Mahasabha head just ahead of the launch of the Quit India movement, Mookerjee had dispatched to him a telegram saying his leadership was sorely needed at a crucial hour.[122]

After the Cripps Mission's failure, the Mahasabha formed

a committee of its own to initiate talks with various parties on three of its demands: total independence, formation of a national coalition government, and the setting up of a constituent assembly after the war. Mookerjee here led from the front, attracting much public attention, and reached an agreement with some non-League Muslim groups, some Christian organizations, the Liberals and the premiers of Sindh, Bengal and Orissa (two of these Muslims, as Savarkar emphasized[123] while lauding the Bengali leader's efforts). Mookerjee was somehow keen to engage Jinnah too. On learning of this, Savarkar promptly sent him a telegram with the 'instruction' that Jinnah 'must not be interviewed or negotiated with on behalf of the Hindu Mahasabha unless he invites' the Hindu party's leaders himself. Mookerjee worked his way around this diktat: he met the League president 'in his personal capacity'[124] at Jinnah's New Delhi residence. This marked the first breach in the relationship. A month later, some diehard Savarkarites in the Mahasabha voiced the suspicion that the Congress, and Rajaji in particular, had begun to exert a lot of influence on Mookerjee and were keen to see him elected as Mahasabha president. Savarkar was persuaded by some of these distrustful followers to contest the election for party president, for the first time. He won the poll, unopposed, at the Kanpur session in December 1942, where he got the Mahasabha to pass a resolution against the Pakistan scheme. Was the seed of doubt planted in the minds of Savarkar's followers, if not Savarkar himself, well before Mookerjee's meeting with Jinnah? Although there is no way of knowing, the record of Mookerjee's meeting with Gandhi almost immediately after he had joined the Mahasabha provides some room for speculation. Gandhi was on a visit to riot-hit Bengal in February 1940 when he met the genial scholar and told him, 'Patel is a Congressman with a Hindu mind, you be a Hindu Sabhaite with a Congress mind.'[125] Perhaps this statement stuck, making Savarkar believe, finally after the Mookerjee–Jinnah talks, that his deputy appeared to be going through the motions of following his policy but was quietly taking a different line.

The extent of damage caused to their ties became evident in the way Savarkar requested that he be relieved of the Mahasabha's presidency late in 1944. He had withdrawn his resignation earlier on more than one occasion after Mahasabhaites had pleaded with him, but now his health was far too precarious, and the time had come for Mookerjee to take over. In December 1944, Savarkar formally passed on the mantle to his successor at the Mahasabha's annual session in Bilaspur. But just as Mookerjee was presiding over the session in a pandal, Savarkar addressed a big crowd outside, parallelly and without any prior notice.[126]

Raja Maheshwar Dayal, the other 'suspect' in the eyes of Savarkar's followers, was often at the receiving end because he headed a faction in the UP Mahasabha unit that 'favoured a rapprochement with the Congress', and Savarkar, with his 'anti-Gandhian proclivities', would not allow it.[127]

With the Mahatma himself, a never-to-be-healed rupture took place after Kasturba Gandhi's death early in 1944. A few historians have claimed that Savarkar did not send any message to the Mahatma after his wife's passing in Yerwada prison. That is untrue. In a telegram sent to Gandhi, Savarkar paid his homage to the woman popularly known as 'Ba'. 'With a heavy heart I mourn the death of Kasturba. A faithful wife and an affectionate mother, she died a noble death in the service of God and man. Your grief is shared by the whole nation,' he stated.[128]

Some of Gandhi's followers had started the Kasturba Gandhi Memorial Trust after her death. Congress activists were clear that the money collected by it should be handed over to the Mahatma so that it could be used for the benefit of society and especially for Indian women, and Gandhi himself, on his release from jail, said the money should go for the education of women and children in villages.[129] As millions of rupees poured in, and not just from Congress loyalists, Savarkar issued a statement angrily denouncing the 'Congressite fund' and asked 'Hindu Sangathanists all over India not to contribute a pie' to it. He laid out seven arguments in all. First, Kasturba had been 'universally mourned' by Hindu Sangathanists, and 'this national honour done to her memory did in fact pay the debt of gratitude we owed to her'. Second, if Kasturba were to be thus honoured, what about the women whose husbands had been hanged or transported for life? Many of them had not even had the chance to meet their husbands in prison before they had died. So many of the women had 'silently and unknown . . . died a martyr's death', and so many had suffered lifelong imprisonment and 'even faced death'. The suffering of 'Shrimati Kasturba' was 'insignificant relatively', Savarkar maintained, but had the Congress kept 'even a list of addresses' of martyrs' wives? Third, if a fund were to be set up at all, it would have to be for all these sacrificing women, and its distribution overseen by an all-party committee so that the money was handed out 'with no party bias'. But then, he noted caustically, the Congress and 'Gandhiji in particular' had 'condemned vociferously' the martyred husbands, sons and brothers of these women, simply because they were revolutionaries, as 'murderers, anarchists, as a curse, as a blot on "Indian" culture and Ahimsa-Charkha politics'. The women sufferers were 'consequently not thought worthy of even grateful recognition'. This list of women certainly included, for Savarkar, his older brother's wife, who had died when he and Babarao were in the Cellular Jail, though he did not name her in his statement. But she was not the only 'mother figure' for him on that hallowed list. He said, advancing his fourth argument, 'Has the Congress said a single word in commemoration of the heroic Madam Cama who championed the cause of Indian independence publicly, when the Congress could not dare even to claim home rule and Gandhiji was dancing to the tune of the British Imperial Anthem and prided himself on his hearty loyalty to the chains that bound Mother India!' Five, he was convinced the Kasturba fund would be misused by the Congress, just as the one-time Tilak–Swaraj fund, collected after Tilak's death, had been 'spent in vilifying and exterminating the Tilakite principles and parties'. Half of that sum, Savarkar alleged, had gone 'to enrich the Moslem purse and drive the propaganda for Khilafat', and – so his sixth point went – the new fund too would 'flow under-channel into Moslem pockets', considering that 'Ahimsa, Charkha, Hindu–Moslem unity and vote for the Congress cannot but be the chief planks on which he [Gandhiji] wants women to work organisedly'. Point number seven was that 'crores of rupees' were needed at that moment 'to save our people', 'especially in these days of famine' and other calamities, and any money better be sent out there.[130] In Bengal, where the famine would eventually result in three million deaths, and in similarly afflicted Orissa,

Muslim groups were aggressively engaged in proselytization in the midst of death and devastation, he claimed, and urged the Hindus to channel any money they wished to give for relief either through Hindu groups or 'secular' ones such as the Ramakrishna Mission.[131]

If Gandhi's followers scented bitterness and a lack of generosity in Savarkar's words and the pro-Congress papers went all out against him, many of the ex-revolutionary's backers too were left with the feeling that the timing of the statement was grossly wrong. Even so sympathetic a biographer as Dhananjay Keer, who had several interactions with Savarkar in the course of writing about his life, felt he 'should not have ungenerously raised a discordant note' and instead 'should have started a separate fund for the memorial of the patriotic and self-sacrificing women'.[132]

Savarkar's apparent lack of a spirit of generosity also hurt his close associates. When Savarkar turned sixty in 1943, a purse of Rs 3 lakh had been gifted to him by his well-wishers who had sought contributions across the board. At that time Gajanan V. Damle worked with Savarkar as his personal assistant, A.S. Bhide as office assistant, and Apparao Kasar was employed as his sole security help. According to more than one chronicler,[133] Bhide was not being paid even a junior clerk's salary but, like the other two, had stuck to the job out of his commitment to the Mahasabha leader. He made a request for a reasonable pay hike, but it was turned down. Disappointed, Bhide put in his papers and ran his own weekly magazine for a year. Damle and Kasar also 'suffered silently', wrote Keer, adding that Savarkar, perhaps as a result of the suffering he had undergone, 'was always afraid that his family would come to want'.[134] Not that he was hoarding money. He was extremely frugal, in the manner of so many people of that period. A significant percentage of the amount gifted to him he gave away to various Hindu nationalist groups at once, and the first thing he did on receiving the sum was to ask three of his regular patrons – the prince Narayanlal Bansilal, the Hindu Rashtriya Nidhi and the Kesari Trust – to stop their contributions. This salutary step was indeed praised, but most people who knew of the work put in by the three personal assistants also despaired of their sorry situation.

If Savarkar's relationships with colleagues and foes were slightly brittle then his family was a source of comfort and support. But in March 1945 Savarkar lost his brother Babarao, who had moved to Sangli some years ago where Narayan had set up home. Gandhi sent 'Bhai Savarkar' a telegram, saying, 'I had done a little bit for his [Babarao's] release and ever since I had been taking an interest in him. Where is the need to condole with you? We are ourselves in the jaws of death. I hope his family are all right.'[135] The formal communication thus continued on occasions sad and happy, with both men attempting to show some warmth, but both were acutely aware that their dialogue could not really go beyond that any more.

Even so, for M.N. Roy, and for two other leaders, Ambedkar and Sarat Bose, Savarkar continued to have a genuine conviviality despite sharp political differences. He described Ambedkar, on the latter's fiftieth birthday in 1941, as 'an outstanding asset to our nation' who had rendered 'inestimable service' with his attempts 'to stamp out untouchability'.[136] And when Congress leaders lodged in prison were released in 1944 and 1945, he wondered why an 'influential leader' like Sarat Bose was still languishing behind bars.[137]

~

Savarkar was more than ever convinced of the irreparable rift with Gandhi when the Mahatma, in September 1944, conducted marathon talks with Jinnah at the latter's Malabar Hill bungalow. Savarkar was incensed that Rajaji's proposals on self-determination – in 1942 Rajaji had appealed to the Congress to 'acknowledge' the Muslim League's 'claim for separation'[138] and work towards forming a national government with the League and also a provincial coalition one in Madras – had formed the basis of these talks, and believed that Gandhi had, with that single move, ended up giving 'parity' to Jinnah, and said the Congress was now ready to concede 'Pakistan, Nizamistan and even a Moplahstan'.[139]

But the Central Assembly and provincial elections held in 1945–46 after the war ended showed that Savarkar's appeal to the electorate to defeat the Congress notwithstanding, the Grand Old Party continued to hold sway over the general constituency seats, where Hindu voters were in an overwhelming majority. So long as the Congress had been out in the cold and its leaders in prison after the Quit India agitation, the Mahasabha had, under Savarkar's leadership, registered its best performance in polls and in overall political participation, getting its members elected to several civic bodies and some of its members installed in key ministries in the provinces. Now things turned out disastrously for it.

In polls to the Central Assembly held in November

1945, the Mahasabha did not win a single seat. Of the five seats in Bombay Province and the Central Provinces that it contested, four of its candidates had their deposit forfeited. Similarly, in Bengal, all six seats were lost, and the party's president Mookerjee lost to a novice Congress candidate. Some Mahasabha leaders from the Punjab and other regions, sensing the groundswell of support for the Congress, in fact had jumped ship before the elections. Though Mookerjee was now leading the Mahasabha, the blow to Savarkar was equally big, for he was still the group's lodestar, and if the electability of Mahasabha nominees had suffered grievously, there was no way the man who had built the party into a mid-sized political force could escape responsibility and even blame. Gandhi and Nehru were undisputed favourites among the masses, and it was the Congress that was perceived by the Hindu majority of India as its real representative, as it also was by minorities such as the Parsis and Christians and by the Depressed Classes. Savarkar had provided leadership, but he did not get too much into the nitty-gritty of daily party functioning; in terms of organizational strength, the Congress, with those like Patel at the heart of it, was tremendously robust. And for all of Savarkar's championing of Hindutva, it was Gandhi who was seen as the devout Hindu who worshipped the cow, spoke of Ram Rajya and at the same time extolled the virtues of Hindu–Muslim unity. As the Mahasabha's rout in the provincial elections of early 1946 turned out to be equally spectacular, Savarkar attracted greater criticism for his relative aloofness from the party cadre and for not nurturing a culture of entertaining visitors at his home with generous cups of tea. Besides, according to Keer, Savarkar 'failed in his promise to resort to direct action at the opportune time',[140] leading to disillusionment among many followers and potential voters.

Notably, in the elections of 1945–46, Mahasabha candidates across the country were explicitly branded by their Congress rivals, in their speeches and writings, as 'British agents', 'anti-nationals' and 'traitors', as P.K. Atre, one of the Congress's key campaigners, confessed in his tell-all autobiography.[141] The slur of being 'deshdrohi' (traitorous) and 'rashtra-drohi' (anti-national) thus had its origin in pre-Independence India. On his part Savarkar, during this period, made it a habit of dubbing Congressmen and women as 'pseudo-nationalists'.

The RSS, founded by Hedgewar, might have provided a volunteer corps for the Hindu Mahasabha in the elections. But Hedgewar had decided to keep his group away from politics. Nevertheless, RSS members were regulars at many of Savarkar's public rallies while Hedgewar, who looked up to the Savarkar brothers, was around. His death in 1940 brought an unexpected change of guard in the form of M.S. Golwalkar, with whom the reformist radical in Savarkar never really got along, though both publicly praised one another from time to time and Golwalkar's essay 'We or Our Nationhood Defined' was in reality an abridged version of Babarao Savarkar's essay 'Rashtra Mimansa'. Savarkar did not like Golwalkar's posturing as a bearded ascetic wearing a garb much resembling that of a renunciate; he was all for temporal stuff, with temporal concerns obtaining such urgency, and believed that the truly spiritual greatness of India lay in the past and it could not be assumed as genuine in any individual simply on the basis of outward appearances. Another reason for the dislike we can only speculate: Savarkar might have felt that Golwalkar had appropriated his own brother Babarao's theories and was passing them off as his own. The 'swayamsevaks' took their cue from their 'Guruji' and kept a distance. And Savarkar contributed to widening that distance by stating bluntly that 'the epitaph for the RSS volunteer will be that he was born, he joined the RSS and he died without accomplishing anything'.[142] As if to eliminate all doubt about where he stood, Savarkar got his office to put out a statement immediately after Golwalkar took over as Sangh chief that wherever RSS cadres seemed to be campaigning against the local Sabhas, the Hindu Sabhaites must leave the RSS at once.[143]

~

With the emergence of top Congress leaders from prison, the end of the world war and the ousting of the Churchill regime in Britain, Archibald Wavell, the new Viceroy appointed by the new Labour prime minister, Clement Attlee, began efforts to end the Indian constitutional crisis. At a conference of Indian leaders he organized at his summer home in Simla in June 1945, he did not extend an invite to the Mahasabha. Savarkar claimed they were left out because of their staunch opposition to Pakistan, but the truth lay elsewhere. Regardless of the whitewashing of Indian history in the post-Independence years, the fact was the Congress was seen by the Indian people as representing Hindu interests. Wavell therefore questioned the Mahasabha's locus standi to be invited to the meeting. But by seeing the Congress as the voice of the Hindus Wavell also reinforced Jinnah's assertion that he was the sole spokesperson for the Muslims. Jinnah was getting much more than parity in this plan. According to Wavell's plan, the central cabinet in an 'interim government' to be formed on the basis of the 1945 election was to have fourteen members, five each from the Congress and the League, and four – two Harijans, one Sikh and one member of the Unionist Party in Punjab – would be nominated by the Viceroy. The Congress decided to have two Hindu nominees and one Muslim, one Parsi and one Christian. Thus, with Jinnah nominating only Muslims, India's largest minority community would have the highest number in the cabinet. In spite of this, Jinnah rejected the plan, and the official version put out by Wavell was that Jinnah had insisted no one but the League could appoint Muslim nominees. The Congress would not accept such a condition as it wanted to highlight its own all-India character. Jinnah then told the *Hindustan Times* correspondent Durga Das, off the record, that British officials had promised him that if he shot down the Wavell plan, he would get the real deal: Pakistan. 'Am I a fool to accept this when I am offered Pakistan on a platter?' he told the 'stunned' journalist.[144]

Gandhi himself told Durga Das that 'most of his colleagues had come out of jail tired and dispirited, and without the heart to carry on the struggle. They wanted a settlement with Britain and what is more, hungered for power.'[145] Thus the Congress formed a coalition cabinet with the Muslim League in Assam, making Savarkar wonder why there had been such a fuss over the Mahasabha–League ministries and the Congress's 'principled resignations and boycott of legislatures'. The working of the interim national government after the League eventually came on board from 1946, with Nehru as its head and a League member holding the critical finance portfolio, heightened

Savarkar's concerns. The League's deliberate intransigence in that cabinet, and escalating Hindu–Muslim violence across the country on Jinnah's instigation, made the top Congress leadership feel that partition, though they did not want it at all, was unavoidable.

Unwilling still in this riot-ridden phase to accede to the Pakistan demand, Savarkar himself was tired and dispirited, and he was, besides, seriously unwell. He had formally entered national-level politics again in 1937, when he was fifty-four years old, and worked as Mahasabha president for seven straight years, criss-crossing the length and breadth of the land, delivering impassioned speeches at political gatherings and literary and drama festivals, carrying out political negotiations with contemporaries, Indian, British and American, interacting with political, social and diplomatic delegations and press representatives, chairing and attending meetings, issuing statements on crucial issues and, through it all, trying to run his own home. Fever was a constant companion, as was exhaustion, aided not a little by exasperation at the way things were unfolding politically. After he had all his teeth removed in 1945, he stopped most of his tours and public speeches. In a letter to N.C. Chatterjee in late 1945 he wrote, 'My nerve system has been literally shattered for the last two years. It has now collapsed.'[146] The nervous exhaustion was additionally causing occasional memory lapses and nightmares of crowds banging at his door or attempting to break open the walls of his home with iron implements.[147] On doctors' advice, he moved to Walchandnagar in the Pune region for rest and recuperation at the start of 1946. Here, in January, he suffered two heart attacks in quick succession and was saved by the timely intervention of doctors and the care given him by his wife, son Vishwas and personal assistant Damle. After three months of convalescence, he moved to the industrialist Walchand Hirachand's brother Gulabchand's residence in Pune, where the problems of vomiting and his shattered intestines persisted, requiring admission for a while to Sassoon Hospital in that city. From there he moved to his friend Nana Jog's house for a month and returned to his own Mumbai residence only in August 1946, after a gap of eight months.

To his continuing dismay, he realized the vivisection of India was imminent. Calcutta had seen 5000 killings in August 1946, Noakhali in East Bengal was up in flames in October, as were many other areas such as Mumbai and Ahmedabad. When there was, in the scribe Durga Das's words, 'a chain reaction'[148] in Bihar and other places, and the bloodshed got worse in June 1947, when all but the formalities of partition remained to be completed, Gandhi told the Hindus of Bihar that they should provide food and shelter to Muslim families. Savarkar said scores of Hindu refugees were pouring in, and the Hindus needed to accommodate them first. Still a member of the Mahasabha's executive committee, he issued a statement instructing all Hindu nationalists to observe 23 July as 'a day of mourning' as the motherland was, the following month, to be split up into two. He sought to assure the Hindus that this was not the end of the matter for them, and there was no reason to take a defeatist approach. If only they looked at the India map in the year 1600, he said, they would see that the Muslims ruled all of India. 'The whole of it was Pakistan,' he remarked. But barely 150 years later, between 1750 and 1798, Hindu forces had succeeded all across the subcontinent. The Marathas had reached Delhi; the Sikhs and Hindus had won Punjab and Kashmir and were ruling from Kabul to Tibet; in Nepal the Gurkhas had assumed control, and 'down south, right up to Rameshwar, the saffron flag of the Marathas had risen triumphant'. In the same way, the Hindu people would overcome the current crisis and emerge revitalized and rejuvenated in the future 'if only they did not betray themselves'.[149] Closer to 15 August, when freedom was welcomed at midnight inside parliament with the blowing of conch shells, Savarkar pushed for the adoption of the saffron flag as the national flag, which did not happen as neither the overwhelming Congress majority in the Constituent Assembly nor the flag committee of the assembly agreed to it. His second request, for replacing the charkha on the flag by the 'chakra' etched on the columns of Sarnath, was accepted, however.[150] And though Savarkar did not quite celebrate on 15 August, there fluttered atop his residence that morning two flags, side by side: the saffron and the Indian tricolour. He would not say, like some others of the Hindu nationalist variety did, that this was not freedom. Of course it was, he said, and it had come about because of the struggle and sacrifices of armed revolutionaries and not because of non-violence, he insisted.[151] He had never really captured the popular vote, but at this moment, he seemed to reflect a very powerful public sentiment. A *Hindustan Times* correspondent reported that when Nehru, anointed as the first prime minister of free India, unfurled the tricolour at Red Fort on the morning of Independence Day with 'nearly a million people' in attendance, 'they reserved their loudest cheers for a reference to Subhas Bose, who Nehru said, had raised the flag of independence abroad'.[152]

12

New prisons and a final release

'The War, the Viceroyalty were jokes' compared to the communal madness that had consumed India, Louis Mountbatten told his daughter Patricia in September 1947. India had become free in August that year, but this self-government was that of a dominion; 'Purna Swaraj' would come when it became a republic in 1950. Mountbatten had stayed on as Dominion Governor General on Nehru's request and was heading the emergency committee formed by the government to resolve issues arising out of the humanitarian crisis that had developed. Brutal massacres had begun in Punjab and Bengal in the lead-up to Partition, and apart from grisly stabbings, shootings and hackings, entire homes, localities and railway carriages were burned, properties taken over or destroyed and women raped to wreak vengeance on the 'other' community, depending on who the unfortunate 'other' was on either side of the border. Nearly 15 million people were displaced and, having lost their all, became refugees across the subcontinent, and the dead numbered over a million.

Appalled by the bestiality, Gandhi began a fast unto death on 12 January 1948, at Birla House in New Delhi, where he was a guest of the industrialist G.D. Birla and where the rioting had spread, with refugees huddled in Purana Qila. This fast – the fifteenth and last in the Mahatma's life – was to call for an end to the insanity, and built into it was the demand for the release of Rs 55 crore to newly created Pakistan. On 14–15 August 1947 the cash reserves with the central bank of India came to Rs 220 crore, and out of it India had agreed to give Rs 55 crore to Pakistan as part of the spoils of division. But early in October, Pathan tribesmen commanded by Pakistani forces infiltrated into Jammu and Kashmir, a state whose Hindu ruler still had not decided on acceding to India or Pakistan, and Nehru and his deputy and home minister, Sardar Patel, decided to withhold payment. Until mid-January 1948, by which time Kashmir's Hindu maharaja had acceded to India, the money had not been released, but Gandhi's fast impelled the cabinet to give in. Nehru accepted it was a volte-face but felt it would work, as a 'goodwill gesture',[1] to ease tensions with Pakistan, India having recently sought UN intervention on Kashmir, and burnish India's image abroad. On 18 January Gandhi ended his fast, with fruit juice fed to him by Nehru and Azad.

Patel was less amenable than Nehru to releasing the money, but that was the least of their differences. Other sharp divisions had arisen, and Gandhi was requested to play the role of reconciler. The critical difference was over Hindu–Muslim relations. Nehru was incensed over violence against Muslims by the Hindus in India, and in a secret note to his cabinet asked irately if India wanted to 'make secure and absorb as full citizens the Muslims who remain in India' or 'do we wish to make it, as certain elements appear to desire, definitely a Hindu or a non-Muslim state?'[2] Patel and some other close Congress colleagues such as Purushottam Das Tandon and J.B. Kripalani faulted Nehru for not recognizing the reasons behind Hindu fears and believed that the prime minister was unfairly singling out Hindus as the aggressors when fanatical hordes were running riot on both sides. They blamed Nehru for what they saw as his ignorance of the plight of the Hindu refugees who were the victims of much violence, and for erroneously dismissing their concerns as 'communal'.[3] Nehru swore by what he called the country's 'composite culture', while Patel, by no means communal, had a certain faith in the Hindu underpinnings of Indian culture.[4]

There were other contrasts and differences too, which built up quickly once they began work as prime minister and deputy prime minister amid the mayhem unfolding all around. Among other matters the two leaders had differing economic visions and Patel disagreed with Nehru's style of functioning and leadership within the cabinet. Naturally, the warring twins turned to Gandhi to try to find a way out. Gandhi did not take sides immediately, but it was decided that he would see Nehru and Patel together so that issues could be thrashed out face-to-face.[5]

On 30 January 1948, minutes after one such meeting with Patel in Birla House to try to effect a workable peace between his two illustrious disciples, Gandhi stepped out on to the garden lawns on the premises for his evening prayer meeting. He had hardly reached the lawns, with arms around his grandnieces Manu and Abha, when a man in the crowd bent down to touch his feet and rose up in a flash and pumped three bullets into the Mahatma at point-blank range.

It soon emerged that the man who carried out the assassination that shocked the world was a Marathi-speaking Brahman from Pune. His name was Nathuram Godse, he was thirty-seven years old and he was the editor of *Dainik Hindu Rashtra*, on whose masthead he carried a picture of Vinayak Damodar Savarkar.[6] As Gandhi was cremated amid colossal public grief, more facts came to light from the assassin's interrogation by the Delhi police, who had taken him into custody from the murder scene after he had made no attempt to escape. Godse, born in 1910, hailed from a modest middle-class household; his father Vinayak, from Kamshet near Pune, was a postmaster with a transferable job, so Godse had done his primary schooling in Marathi in schools spread across the Bombay Presidency. For his secondary school the family had shifted him to Pune. He had failed his matriculation exams but had later studied history and sociology, among other subjects, and had first met Savarkar when he was nineteen, when the Godse family had travelled in 1929 to Ratnagiri, where Savarkar was then interned. This was a defining moment for Godse, who would be a lifelong follower of Savarkar and his ideology. In the early 1930s Godse, who started out working as a tailor, became one of the early recruits to the RSS, but once Savarkar rejoined politics in 1937, he joined the Hindu Mahasabha.[7] When Savarkar launched his civil resistance campaign against the Nizam of Hyderabad in 1938, Godse led the inaugural group of protesters, courted arrest and spent a year in prison.[8]

Another man who joined the Mahasabha around the same

time was Narayan Apte. A year younger than Godse, Narayan was the son of Dattatray Apte, a Sanskrit and history scholar based in Pune. After acquiring a bachelor's degree in science, Narayan moved to Ahmednagar, about 110 kilometres from his home town, to take up a job as a teacher in a missionary school. Here he joined the local Mahasabha unit headed by one Vishnu Karkare. Having lost his parents early in childhood and pushed into penury, Karkare, of about the same age as Godse and Apte, had studied at an orphanage in Mumbai before he moved to Ahmednagar to open a tea and puri shop. Gradually the small shop was converted into a smallish hotel and then into a sizeable one, where needy students were often given rooms either free or at nominal rates. In 1943 Karkare was elected civic councillor on a Mahasabha ticket. Through him Godse, who was living in Pune, got to know Apte, and when Apte moved back to Pune, having obtained a job as an assistant recruiting officer in the army, the two became good friends.[9] Their common love for detective fiction might have helped strengthen their bond, for Godse swore by Erle Stanley Gardner and Perry Mason and Apte by the brilliant Agatha Christie and her Miss Marple and 'Belgian, not French' Hercule Poirot.[10]

All the three Mahasabha men were, like their hero Savarkar, Chitpavan Brahmans, and all three were implicated in the murder plot. Apte and Karkare had mixed in with the crowds on the lawns of Birla House when Godse pulled the trigger. Godse had made it clear to them that he wanted to do the deed himself and they should not directly participate, because Apte had a wife and child to look after, and Karkare had the resources that would help run their paper.

Savarkar had given Godse a loan of Rs 15,000 in 1944 to

start a newspaper called *Agrani* (Forerunner). With his friend Godse as editor, Apte had agreed to be the paper's manager. That year the *Agrani* ran, with evident pride, a story on its front page with a picture of Apte, saying he had led a group of nationalist youths who had heckled Gandhi when he was visiting the hill station of Panchgani, eighty kilometres away from Pune. As the communal temperature soared from 1945 onwards, the *Agrani* was accused by the Raj of violating the Press Act with its inflammatory writings that incited communal hatred.

In letters written to him, both Godse and Apte implored Savarkar to write for their daily, from its first issue onwards. But Savarkar did not contribute, except for allowing them to carry all his public statements, issued from time to time. When the government asked Godse and Apte to shell out Rs 6000 as a security deposit in 1946 to stop them from putting out any more incendiary writings, Savarkar made a public appeal to every family that believed in Hindutva to contribute one rupee to show solidarity with a paper that was 'truly the forerunner of the ideology of Hindutva'.[11] That deposit was forfeited as the paper refused to mend its ways, and it was quickly thereafter renamed *Dainik Hindu Rashtra*.[12] Karkare, meanwhile, was doing what he thought was his bit for the ideology: in 1946, he went to Noakhali as part of a group to provide relief to the riot-hit Hindus.[13]

The morning after Gandhi's assassination, anger against the Brahman community took the form of violence in many parts of the Bombay Presidency. In the afternoon, a tall and handsome police officer raided Savarkar's Shivaji Park residence. He was Jamshed Dorab Nagarvala, the Parsi head of the Bombay police's Intelligence Branch. Nagarvala's team searched the place and seized all of Savarkar's papers, 143 files and some 10,000 letters. Savarkar was not apprehended that day. Five days later, another police team sent by Nagarvala knocked on Savarkar's doors, and when he went forward to meet them, told him he would have to go along with them. 'So you've come to arrest me for Gandhi's murder?' he asked.[14] The cops nodded.

Police had no material to produce in the magistrate's court for his arrest and remand. Among the letters they had seized were almost twenty from Godse and a dozen from Apte, but none that contained anything that directly implicated him in Gandhi's murder. But there was the indisputable fact that Savarkar knew Godse, Apte and Karkare well, he had corresponded with them closely, and funded their extremely provocative newspaper, and they looked up to him as their icon. Indeed, the three men were not merely Hindu Sangathanists or Mahasabha members; they could truly be described as Savarkarites, so totally did they echo his word, his ideology, his philosophy and intense dislike for Gandhi. They were also pretty convinced that Gandhi's alleged pandering to and humouring of Jinnah was responsible for India's partition.

So Savarkar was arrested and booked under the Preventive Detention Act, a draconian colonial legislation. The law had existed under different names – the Defence of India Act, Rowlatt Act and Defence of India Rules, for instance – from the nineteenth century onward, allowing the Raj to detain anyone without trial, with no offence established or charge formulated.[15] No matter what their political persuasion, Indian luminaries had repeatedly called for quashing the legislation, but Savarkar became one of the first Indians to be held under it just months after the country gained freedom. Thus made a 'detenu', he was taken to Arthur Road Jail in central Mumbai. Over a month later, he was arrested by the Delhi police for being part of the conspiracy – though he was already under arrest under the Preventive Detention Act and already in Arthur Road Jail, where he remained even after his arrest by the Delhi police. His wife and son were allowed to see him in jail only after one and a half months.

In mid-May the government issued a notification naming nine persons, including Savarkar, as accused and declared that the trial in the assassination case would be held in the Red Fort in Delhi, with special judge Atma Ram presiding. The same month, Savarkar was flown to Delhi, with two doctors in attendance carrying oxygen and other equipment should the heart patient, now sixty-four years old, need it. The other accused were taken by train.[16]

Only the most important trials were held on the upper floor of a colonial building constructed inside the Red Fort. The last Mughal emperor, Bahadur Shah Zafar, had faced charges there earlier, and two years before Gandhi's killing the famous Indian National Army trials, in which Nehru defended Subhas Chandra Bose's comrades, who were the accused in the case, had taken place in the same building. The prison was on the same premises but in another structure, nearly half a kilometre away, and once the trial began the accused were taken for every hearing from jail to court and back in a police van.

The day the court proceedings began, the full charges were read out to all the accused: murder, conspiracy and offences under the Arms Act and Explosive Substances Act. The prosecution claimed Savarkar was the mastermind of the murder plot, a mentor and guide to Godse and the other accused. Savarkar was number 8 on the list of accused, but as soon as the trial started he moved up to number 7. This was because one of the accused, Digambar Badge, had turned approver.

Badge was an arms dealer who ran a shastra bhandar, or storehouse of weapons, in Pune's Narayan Peth. A short, thickset man with a flowing beard and long hair, and one eye smaller than the other as a result of a childhood injury, he was a compulsive name-dropper and lover of disguise. Karkare had taken protective chain-mail jackets from him for his trip to Noakhali in 1946, and Badge visited the *Dainik Hindu Rashtra* office occasionally for a chat with its editor Godse and manager Apte and spoke highly of Savarkar.[17] Badge's servant Shankar Kistaya, twenty years old, was also named as an accused. Manohar Malgonkar's acclaimed account of the conspiracy behind the Mahatma's assassination, for which he spoke extensively to Badge in his native Marathi, throws light on their relationship. On a trip to Solapur for 'business', Badge had met Kistaya, who worked as a trainee carpenter, and impressed with his skills, had offered him a job in his storehouse and home for Rs 20 a month. But once Kistaya started working for Badge he was paid hardly Rs 2 a week and made to work non-stop; additionally, he faced abuses from Badge and his sister at their residence. Fed up, he ran away to the Solapur home where his mother lived. Badge then lodged a complaint with the police saying the servant had escaped with Rs 20 in cash, and Kistaya was arrested and thrashed by the cops in the lockup. Badge did not pursue the case in court and the magistrate dropped the charges eventually, but Kistaya was back with Badge as a servant, this time for good and for as pathetic a monthly sum – Rs 8.[18]

The entire case against Savarkar hinged on Badge's version of events. The approver told the court he had, along with Godse and Apte, gone to Savarkar's Dadar residence on 14 January with a bunch of weapons. Godse and Apte asked him to wait in the compound, took the bag inside, and came out with the bag about ten minutes later. On 17 January, he said, the three of them visited Savarkar's house again. He was made to wait on the ground floor inside the house while the other two went up to Savarkar's study for a darshan of their guru and for obtaining his final instructions, he said. When Godse and Apte were on their way downstairs along with Savarkar, he heard Savarkar telling them, '*Yashaswi houn ya*,' which meant 'Come back with success.'[19] Afterwards, in the cab, Apte told Badge, 'Savarkar predicted that Gandhi's hundred years are over. There is therefore no doubt that our mission will be successfully accomplished.'[20]

Savarkar refuted all the charges laid against him, saying he was not part of any conspiracy to assassinate Gandhi, had no knowledge of any such 'criminal design' and had no reason to commit any of the offences either. He knew Godse and Apte, but as the letters seized by the police made clear, all the correspondence between them was related to the work of the Mahasabha, the Hindu Sangathanist movement or their paper, which he saw as an organ of the Mahasabha but for which he wrote nothing at all. As to the picture on its masthead, it was wholly Godse and Apte's choice; there were other papers too which carried his picture. So many publications carried Gandhi's picture too, and *Kesari* still had Tilak's picture on its front page. Surely, the late Tilak was not being held responsible for the paper's policy any more but the editor, as it ought to be, he said, bringing his customary satirical touch to his statement in court.

Savarkar said that Badge had got in touch with him via a letter some years ago in which he said he was a Hindu Sangathanist and sold arms. But this was many years before Gandhi's murder. The 'Badge and the bag' story was of no evidentiary value at all, Savarkar pointed out. If Godse and Apte had indeed visited Savarkar Sadan with a bag on the morning of 14 January, when Badge was asked to wait outside in the compound, it could not be assumed that they had gone to meet him. His secretary Damle and ex-secretary Bhide had rooms on the ground floor, and his security assistant Appa Kasar too usually spent time on the same floor, so they might have gone to see any one of them, or someone else as well, as the ground floor also had a room dedicated to the Mahasabha and its work and a reading room besides, and hundreds of people came in every day. Both Godse and Apte had in any case denied they had gone to Savarkar Sadan with the bag.

The second incident of 17 January narrated by Badge was similarly fictitious, Savarkar said. Neither Godse nor Apte had seen him that morning, nor had he given them his blessings. And he had 'never predicted that Gandhiji's hundred years were over', not to Apte and not to anyone else, he said. Drawing on his Gray's Inn days, he said that even if it were assumed that Godse and Apte had visited his residence, Badge, who admitted to having waited on the ground floor, would have no idea whom they met on the first floor; it could have been a member of his family, or a tenant who lived on the first floor, or anyone else. If the assumption were carried further to include a possible conversation between him and the two other Mahasabhaites, Badge just could not have known what they had discussed, being unmistakably out of earshot; it could have been a conversation about the civil resistance in Hyderabad, the newspaper or Mahasabha work, or they may have simply made inquiries about his health. To forestall any other legal complications, he said that even if it were thought that he had uttered the line '*Yashaswi houn ya*' it could have been a reference to anything. Godse and Apte had also categorically denied the entire incident and the boast about 'Gandhi's hundred days'.

Yet there were certain things that did not appear to be going in favour of Savarkar. While all the accused (except Badge) denied that Apte and Godse had gone to Savarkar Sadan on 14 and 17 January, there were eyewitnesses who claimed they had visited Savarkar Sadan on those dates. On 14 January 1948, Nathuram Godse and Apte had got into a second-class compartment of the Deccan Express to travel from Pune to Mumbai. Seated on window seats facing one another, Apte and Godse noticed a remarkably good-looking woman walking up and down the compartment's corridor, obviously in an attempt to find a window seat for herself. Apte decided to be chivalrous and offered his own seat to her, and shifted to the seat next to Godse on the opposite bench. The woman's face appeared familiar and Apte asked her if she was the well-known actress Bimba, and she confirmed that yes, that was her stage name. They exchanged pleasantries, during which the actress revealed that she lived in Dadar's famous Shivaji Park locality, where Apte and Godse were themselves headed. As her brother was going to arrive at Dadar railway station to pick her up, she offered to drop the two men as she lived very close to Savarkar Sadan. Bimba later deposed in court confirming that she had dropped the two men just outside Savarkar's home that evening.[21]

Three days later, on 17 January, Godse, Apte, Badge and Kistaya hired a taxi for the entire day and went around Mumbai apparently meeting donors who would contribute to the 'Hindu cause'. They kept the taxi driver, one Aitappa Kotian, waiting near Savarkar Sadan while they went inside for some time in the afternoon. The taxi driver easily recollected their day-long trip later for three reasons: he had earned much more that day because of his customers than he did on a normal day, Badge was dressed in the garb of a sadhu and therefore stood out, and while finally dismissing the taximan, Badge, unlike the norm for Mumbai's kaali–peeli cabs, had asked him for a receipt, which Kotian had provided, a sort of kuchcha (informal) receipt.[22]

In statements recorded by the Mumbai police on 4 March 1948, Savarkar's secretary Damle and bodyguard Appa Kasar also stated that Godse and Apte had met him in the middle of January. Damle did not remember the exact date but recalled that they came to Savarkar's house late at night, while Kasar thought that it must have been on 15 or 16 January, and that 'they had an interview with Savarkar at 9.30 p.m.'

Kasar said Godse and Apte came a second time in January, on the 23rd or 24th, and had a half-hour meeting with Savarkar in the morning.

Damle said that two of the other accused, Vishnu Karkare and 'a Punjabi refugee boy' (a reference to Madanlal Pahwa who made the first attempt to assassinate Gandhi at Birla House in Delhi on 20 January) had come to see Savarkar in the first week of January 1948 and had an interview with him 'for about half an hour or 45 minutes'. Kasar too remembered this meeting, though he placed the date as 13 or 14 January and said the meeting lasted 'about 15 or 20 minutes'.

The Kapur Commission, which looked afresh into the Gandhi assassination case in the late 1960s, remarked in its report that 'people who were subsequently involved in the murder of Mahatma Gandhi were all congregating sometime or the other at Savarkar Sadan and sometimes had long interviews with Savarkar'. That all the main accused in Gandhi's assassination had visited Savarkar shortly before the attempts on his life, that it was Savarkar's virulent criticism of Gandhi that was at the heart of the assassins' hatred of the Mahatma, that Savarkar had in the past probably contemplated assassinating Jinnah, added up to a troubling grouping of circumstantial evidence against Savarkar.

~

But an intriguing aspect was added much later to the history of the case. The legal expert L.B. Bhopatkar of Pune had reached Delhi to be Savarkar's counsel in 1948. He thought that the charges against Savarkar were somewhat vague while those against the others were specific. Put up at the Mahasabha's Delhi office, Bhopatkar apparently one day got a phone call there. According to Manohar Malgonkar, who quoted extensively from a 16 June 1983 report in the Pune newspaper *Kaal* on the subject,[23] the caller identified himself as Dr Bhimrao Ambedkar. After confirming that it was indeed Bhopatkar on the line, Ambedkar purportedly said, 'Please meet me this evening at the sixth milestone on Mathura Road.' He would not say more than that over the phone. When Bhopatkar reached the spot in the evening, Ambedkar was waiting, in the driver's seat in his own car. He asked the lawyer to get in next to him and told him, 'There is no real charge against your client; quite worthless evidence has been concocted. Several members of the cabinet were strongly against it, but to no avail. Even Sardar Patel could not go against these orders. But, take it from me, there just is no case. You will win.'

This incident was purportedly narrated by Bhopatkar to some of his friends after his return from Delhi to Pune in January 1949, and *Kaal* wrote about it more than three decades thereafter. Whether such a conversation happened between Ambedkar and Bhopatkar in the first place, and whether, if it happened, Ambedkar uttered those exact lines we will never know for sure, as neither of them ever made any public statements in this regard or wrote about it. But the hint in the *Kaal* piece, which Savarkar's followers swore by – the newspaper's report was reproduced in a centenary volume brought out by the Savarkar Memorial Committee in 1989 – but many people dismiss as a fabrication, was without the slightest doubt about Nehru, as Ambedkar had been quoted as saying that even the Sardar, who was deputy prime minister, could not stop the prosecution.

Nehru's position on the matter was transparent. He had never had any sympathy for the Mahasabha and had, instantly after Gandhi's death, written to Syama Prasad Mookerjee, who had joined his cabinet following consultations with Savarkar as industries and supplies minister – one of the non-Congress members along with Ambedkar, the economist John Mathai and the finance expert S. Chetty – that he ought to 'sever' his 'connection with the Hindu Mahasabha' as it was 'associated in people's minds in some way with this tragedy'.[24] It would be 'difficult and embarrassing for all concerned for a Minister of the Central Government to be personally associated with a communal organization like the Hindu Mahasabha', Nehru wrote. Days later, the prime minister wrote to another colleague, 'I have learnt that in Jammu there was a hartal because of Savarkar's arrest. I am sorry to learn this as it denotes a certain sympathy with those who are supposed to be associated with Gandhiji's assassination.'[25]

What had been Patel's approach to the case, considering he also held the all-important home portfolio? Nehru had in a letter to Patel expressed his concern about 'a certain lack of real effort in tracing the larger conspiracy'. The government had banned the RSS, and Patel said in his reply all the accused had given long and detailed statements, and 'it clearly emerges from these statements that the RSS was not involved in it at all. It was a fanatical wing of the Hindu Mahasabha directly under Savarkar that [hatched] the conspiracy.'[26] (Patel made clear the RSS had 'other sins to answer for, but not this one'.)

A little before the Red Fort trial started, Mookerjee wrote to Patel voicing his apprehensions about Savarkar getting dragged into the case. 'I do not know,' he stated, 'what evidence has been found against him [Savarkar]. I have not the least doubt that you will satisfy yourself that nothing is done which may give rise to the suggestion later on that he was being prosecuted on account of his political convictions. I hope the records will be placed before you before any decision is taken. His sacrifices and suffering in the past have been considerable and unless there is some positive proof against him, he should not, at this age, be subjected to a charge of conspiracy to commit murder.'[27] To this, Patel responded that he had spoken to the prosecutors, the legal advisers and investigating officers: 'I told them, quite clearly, that the question of inclusion of Savarkar must be approached purely from a legal and judicial standpoint and political considerations should not be imported into the matter.' He added, 'I have also told them that, if they come to the view that Savarkar should be included, the papers should be placed before me before action is taken.' Then came the parting shot: 'This is, of course, in so far as the question of guilt is concerned from the point of view of law and justice. Morally, it is possible that one's conviction may be the other way about.'[28]

What Patel was saying, in effect, was that criminal culpability as established with solid legal proof was one thing, and Savarkar's ethical responsibility was another. The Kapur Commission report of 1969, described by Savarkar's followers as a posthumous hit job against their hero, was to put it much more bluntly: it recorded that Savarkar's staunch admirers such as Godse, Apte and others were believers in political assassination, that 'the Savarkar school of thought' considered Gandhi's activities to be 'pro-Muslim and anti-Hindu', that 'the murderers of Mahatma Gandhi were Savarkarites . . . who were blind followers of Savarkar whom they treated as the Fuhrer' and that 'the bundle of facts . . . were destructive of any theory, but the theory of conspiracy to murder Mahatma Gandhi by Savarkarites'.[29]

Savarkar, then, had been charged presumably after Vallabhbhai appeared convinced that there was a case to pursue. So were Patel's hands really tied? Had Ambedkar really said that 'even Sardar Patel could not go against these orders'? The evidence for Ambedkar having said this is thin and the jury still remains out on this one.

~

The one backstory of Madanal Pahwa, of course, had enough drama to add to the overall puzzle. His was the first attempt to assassinate Gandhi, just ten days before the actual killing. A Punjabi youngster, Pahwa had on 20 January exploded a guncotton bomb on a wall seventy-five feet away from where Gandhi was in the Birla House lawns and had been arrested.[30] Patel's ministry had upped the security there, as a result: in place of one head constable and four other constables earlier, about fifty policemen were placed on guard. Pahwa had come to Pune from a small town in Punjab to join the army during the war. Back home in 1947, he witnessed his father and aunt being killed by a Muslim mob and escaped and entered a refugee camp in Ahmednagar, where he first met Vishnu Karkare and then Godse and Apte and became part of their plot.[31] Visits to Mumbai became regular, and during one such visit he met Dr Jagdish Chandra Jain, a professor at Ruia College in Matunga. Pahwa developed trust in the professor and one day blurted out the whole conspiracy to him. But Jain thought he was just angry and blabbering and told him to put an end to such ideas. When Pahwa vowed to heed his suggestion, the professor felt reassured.[32]

Jain was startled to see, in the morning paper of 21 January, that Pahwa had exploded a bomb in Delhi. A man of some connections, he promptly obtained an appointment with the

Bombay premier, B.G. Kher, for the same afternoon. He told Kher the story, along with the names of the other conspirators that Pahwa had told him, and Kher put him in touch with the home minister in the province, Morarji Desai. An austere Gandhian, Desai demonstrated absolute disbelief in the theory of a plot, subjected the professor to intense questioning and then said, 'Then you must be one of the conspirators!' Stunned, Jain suggested the minister send him to Delhi as Pahwa would speak to him freely and the government would then get all information. Desai would not allow that. But he did summon a police officer and asked him to take down Jain's statement. The same evening, he briefed Deputy Commissioner Nagarvala, who decided to keep an eye on Savarkar's residence as all the so-called conspirators were linked to the Mahasabha. Nagarvala is said to have claimed on receiving the information that the cops had a biggish file on Savarkar – which, in fact, was courtesy the Raj and not the Indian police.

Godse, Apte, Badge and Kistaya were all in Delhi with Pahwa on 20 January, when the failed attempt was made on the Mahatma's life, but even after they returned by train to Mumbai and Pune after the incident, nothing was done.[33] The home ministry, senior police officers, everyone had the names of the plotters. Gandhi's assassination was then a gigantic and scandalous intelligence failure, brought about by a horrible indifference and the criminal neglect of plenty of information acquired beforehand.

Did the government then want to net a 'big catch' like Savarkar to camouflage its own mess-up? Savarkar's followers certainly believed so though the circumstantial evidence against Savarkar seemed to have been building up. Still, Savarkar's followers also smelt an attempt to further marginalize and discredit the Hindu Mahasabha and, by extension, Hindu nationalism; Savarkar may well have retired as its president, but he still decided practically every move of the Mahasabha, in much the same way Gandhi took the final call in the Congress without holding any official post or even its ordinary membership.

~

What the principal characters said at the trial split, and continues to split, opinions even more on this highly contentious topic. Most important is a key flip-flop in the prosecution's case against Savarkar. More than three weeks after Gandhi's assassination, Professor Jain recorded his statement. In it there was no mention of Savarkar as a conspirator, though he had been sent to Arthur Road Jail already, and his was the biggest name linked to the case. At the trial, when he was cross-examined, Jain said, 'I did not state that Madanlal [Pahwa] told me that Veer Savarkar had sent for him.' Jain included Savarkar's name only in his subsequent statements (which among other things led the Kapur Commission to cast blame on Savarkar), leaving unanswered the question of how he had missed giving the authorities the most crucial name earlier.[34]

Madanlal Pahwa himself told the judge, 'I had never been sent for by Savarkar' and 'had never had any talk at any time about Savarkar with Jain'.

The cops tried to tell the court that a trunk call made from the Mahasabha's Delhi office to Savarkar Sadan a couple of days before Pahwa's bomb attack was by Godse, but it was never established that the call was either from Godse or meant to discuss the plot. Moreover, the caller had asked for Damle or Kasar, Savarkar's assistants, and not for Savarkar.

Godse's younger brother Gopal, also an accused, alleged that he ended up with bruises all over his body when he told the police the truth during the questioning that he had not visited Savarkar en route to Delhi.

After Savarkar's death, Malgonkar, doing interviews for his book, also met Karkare, Pahwa and Gopal Godse, who had served life terms in the case (a life term was fourteen years then). All three told him that Savarkar had nothing to do with the conspiracy.[35] The fourth person who told Malgonkar the same thing was Badge himself. 'Of course, Badge, on his track record is a slippery character and not to be relied upon, but he was most insistent to me,' wrote Malgonkar, 'that he had been forced to tell lies, and that his pardon and future stipend by the police department in Bombay depended upon his backing the official version of the case.' Badge especially insisted that 'he never saw Savarkar talking to Apte, and never heard him telling them: "*Yashaswi houn ya*"'.[36] Godse himself, of course, told the court that he alone was responsible for the killing and was seeking no pardon.

Thus, of the two statements made against Savarkar which went beyond just the fact that the accused had met him in the days before Gandhi's assassination, one – by Badge – was eventually retracted, and the other – by Jain – was inconsistent.

~

The trial went on for several months, and Savarkar had a hard time as he was not keeping well. The prison had individual cells, and Savarkar's was at the far end of the corridor, just as it had been in the Andamans. Next to his cell was Apte's, followed by those of Karkare, Dattatray Sadashiv Parchure (a medical practitioner and Mahasabha secretary in the princely state of Gwalior who had provided Nathuram the 9 mm Beretta pistol with which he shot Gandhi), Nathuram and Gopal; and then, after a small door leading into a passage, were the cells of Kistaya and Badge. Jail regimen had to be followed, easier – or less tough – in one's twenties than at the age of sixty-five. The prisoners had to wake up around dawn, got some milk and tea, were given lunch at 9.30 a.m. before heading to court, had milk after they got back at 5 or 5.30 p.m., and dinner followed at 6 p.m. In between, if there was no court hearing, they could get more milk if they paid for it. There was a table fan outside each of the cells, as Delhi's summers were harsh, and there were blankets in the winter, which was as bad, if not worse.

Gopal Godse wrote in his memoirs that Savarkar told him, when they were sent to the prison, that not for nothing had he recently been getting nightmares about the Cellular Jail. 'I could see heavy rain carried by the wind sweep inside my cell, flooding the floor completely, and me standing in a corner, feet drenched and frightfully cold,' he told the younger Godse. Savarkar found it impossible to sleep without taking a sedative, as prescribed by his doctors. He was not allowed to keep the bottle; it stayed in the jail office, and a warder passed on the required quantity to him every evening in a glass, after dinner. One evening he forgot to take it and woke up with a start at 10 p.m. Every Monday, a jail officer carried out a check on the prison floor, during which the prisoners had to stand upright with the jail ticket around their necks. The officer told Savarkar one day that the others did not quite stand the way he did. 'They're new boys. *Main toh dobara hoon* [For me it's the second time],' he replied. Yet his physical weakness was tremendous. One morning the police van that took the prisoners to court was delayed, and the warder suggested they walk instead. The younger ones felt relieved, as they would get a much-needed small walk, but they soon realized they had not thought of the eldest among them. Savarkar said he would wait for the vehicle, and if walking was going to be made mandatory, he would prefer the chain-fetters as punishment. Fortunately for him, the van came in soon.[37]

Badge's statement fell through. An approver's testimony in court has value but requires corroboration; if there is none, it cannot be seen as constituting sound proof against an accused (his retraction, to the writer Malgonkar, came long after the case had concluded). Savarkar was acquitted as no one corroborated Badge's version, and there was no other evidence on record. In fact, he was the only one acquitted. Nathuram and Apte had to face the gallows, and the others were sentenced to life imprisonment.

The damage was, however, done as far as Savarkar was concerned. Taken into custody on 5 February 1948, he was cleared of the charges by special court judge Atma Ram on 10 February 1949; he had spent a year and five days behind bars. Moreover, his political career – and that of the Mahasabha – had been destroyed, for being associated with the worst possible conspiracy on Indian soil was incredibly damaging, and there was no guarantee of it being wiped out even in the future.

Nathuram challenged the verdict in the Punjab High Court, but his appeal was not against his own death sentence but against the charge of conspiracy made out against the others; the government did not challenge Savarkar's acquittal. Justice G.D. Khosla of the high court acquitted Parchure and Kistaya but confirmed the others' sentences on 21 June 1949.

As things have turned out, the case has haunted Savarkar in death as well, with publications and websites regularly, and especially after the BJP's and RSS's rise since the mid-1980s, putting out their own theories of how he was very much at the core of the murder conspiracy. Their reliance is almost wholly on the aforementioned report of the commission of inquiry set up in 1966, that is, after Savarkar had died. After Karkare and others had served their life terms, Tilak's grandson G.V. Ketkar claimed at a function in Pune that he had been aware of the plot to kill Gandhi well before the Mahatma was killed. That led to a fresh burst of speculation about whether it was a bigger plot than previously thought, and the government of the day formed the judicial commission under Jeevan Lal Kapur. As mentioned earlier, the retired judge concluded that the 'facts', as he saw them, 'taken together were destructive of any theory other than the conspiracy to murder by Savarkar and his group'. With a flurry of articles in the media referring to the Kapur panel's report, in particular after Narendra Modi came to power in 2014, a follower of Savarkar moved India's highest court asking it to make things absolutely clear. The court in May 2018 said 'there is no doubt that this [Kapur's] finding does not in any way interfere with the acquittal and is a general observation probably made since Godse and others were found to have been associated with Savarkar. It cannot have the effect of overturning the finding of the criminal court which acquitted Savarkar.'[38] But as Sardar Patel noted to Mookerjee, Savarkar's moral culpability (as opposed to his criminal culpability) is a different matter.

~

The relief provided by the acquittal proved short-lived. The year after Savarkar's release, the refugee crisis in Bengal intensified, and Nehru decided to sign a pact with his Pakistani counterpart, Liaqat Ali Khan, to ensure safety of minorities on both sides. While negotiations were on in New Delhi, Savarkar was arrested from his Mumbai residence on 4 April 1950, again under the Preventive Detention Act, to ward off any potential trouble, and he and his sympathizers Bhopatkar and Ketkar were dispatched to Belgaum jail. On a habeas corpus plea the Bombay High Court suggested he be released, provided he gave an undertaking to stay off politics and stay within the confines of his home for a year or until the next general elections or outbreak of war, whichever happened first, and this the government obtained from him.

Most newspapers criticized the government for loosely applying the detention law in this regard. However, Nehru noted that since Section 3 of the Preventive Detention Act 'specially mentions foreign powers', 'there is justification in our laws to keep in detention people who create trouble with foreign powers. The speeches of the Hindu Mahasabha leaders demand the liquidation of Pakistan. I can imagine no greater offence to a foreign power than to make such a suggestion.'[39] His views on Savarkar's book on 1857, which he had praised in his youth in a letter to his father from England, also appeared to have been drastically revised. In a letter to chief ministers, Nehru wrote, on the centenary of the revolt, 'On the Indian side, so far as I know, the first book on the subject was Savarkar's. As a history this was very inadequate and was tilted to the other side. It could not be considered an objective account and it was inaccurate in many parts.'[40]

Savarkar's followers alleged that their leader's detention was a direct fallout of his attacks on Nehru's policies. India's prime minister had described the demand to declare India a 'Hindu state' as 'communal and medieval' and warned that those making it would face the fate of Hitler and Mussolini. To this, Savarkar said that Nehru had not bothered to find out what a Hindu state would be like but had, incongruously, conceded the demand for the 'genuinely communal and medieval' Islamic state of Pakistan. As to his 'fate', Savarkar said that when India's armed revolutionaries had mounted a fight against the British Raj in the first decade of the twentieth century, 'Gandhiji was, politically speaking, in the cradle, and Nehru was not even politically born'. The revolutionaries had faced bullets and embraced the noose, and their struggles and sacrifices 'were worth more than the sum of the Gandhians' sacrifices', he declared, adding that such people could not possibly be scared of 'Pandit Nehru's paper raj'.[41] When Gopal Godse, in the Red Fort prison, asked Savarkar about Nehru donning the lawyer's garb to defend Subhas Bose's aides in the Indian National Army trials, Savarkar told the youngster that Nehru had done that because of the extraordinary outpouring of public sentiment over the issue just before the 1946 elections, in which the Congress was seeking the votes of nationalist

Indians. 'How could he have lost the chance to show that the slogan "Jai Hind" was actually his own, and that Bose's efforts to free India were in fact under his leadership! If the wind is in favour of the revolutionaries, these hypocrites will also claim Bhagat Singh's plans against the British as their own,' Savarkar said.[42] Savarkar sounded bitter, and his intense dislike of Nehru was transparent.

Such defiant comments might well have gone down well with his diehard supporters, but the Hindu Mahasabha was in a bad way, having stopped its political work for the time being. Scores had deserted it after it came under a cloud in the Gandhi assassination case, Mookerjee too had left, and other senior leaders like Moonje and Bhai Parmanand had recently passed away. In addition, Savarkar himself had exonerated the Nehru regime as well as the local Bombay government in the matter of his implication in the Gandhi killing. After his acquittal, Bhopatkar had pushed for an official inquiry to identify those who had 'framed' Savarkar. But Savarkar had quickly asked his counsel to retract the statement, saying he saw no 'vindictive act' nor any 'deliberate malice' in his prosecution, which may have been the result of hurried legal advice given to the government 'under the shock of a great tragedy'.[43] More supporters quit the Mahasabha when he refused to accede to the inclusion in it of 'non-Hindus' or to transform it into a 'sociocultural organization', an idea mooted by ex-aides such as Mookerjee. In the early 1950s Savarkar himself gave up his membership of the Mahasabha, saying it was time for him to go into semi-retirement considering his age and his health. The party rejoined politics in that decade but won nothing but a handful of seats in parliament and in state assemblies in the next twenty years, with right-wing activists moving steadily to the RSS and its new political offshoot, the Bharatiya Jana Sangh, founded by Mookerjee after his resignation from the Nehru cabinet in 1951.

Just how much Savarkar could be perceived as being beyond the pale even after his acquittal in the Gandhi murder case could be seen from an experience music composer Hridaynath Mangeshkar had in 1955. Only eighteen years old then, Hridaynath had joined Akashwani or All India Radio and composed three songs in his first fortnight into the job; his bosses, and the listeners, had liked them all. According to Hridaynath, for the fourth song he approached Savarkar, whom his family knew well. 'Why do you want my poem for a song? Do you want to go to prison?' Savarkar asked. Finally he agreed, handing Hridaynath the poem he had written in 1909 on the shores of Brighton, with his friend B.C. Pal's son Niranjan by his side. It was an ode to the motherland, 'Saagara pran talamalala', and it was duly recorded. Before it could be broadcast, Hridaynath's bosses issued him a show-cause notice asking him why he had chosen Savarkar's poem. The composer cited two reasons: 'excellent poem, excellent poet'. He was sacked immediately.[44]

Hridaynath had not thought of the possible repercussions beforehand, but those in the political sphere on the Hindu right did. So the Jan Sangh or the RSS in the 1950s and 1960s hardly ever, or rarely and hesitantly, raised a toast to Savarkar's name, though he had been responsible for the codification of Hindutva and his contribution as a freedom fighter was undeniable. Both the Jan Sangh and the RSS focused on the Sangh veteran Deendayal Upadhyaya and RSS icons Hedgewar and Golwalkar as their ideologues. (Until, of course, the mid-

1980s, by which time a new generation had come up, Savarkar was no longer so much of a persona non grata for government and opposition, and even Nehru's daughter, Indira Gandhi, had, as prime minister, extolled him on his passing 'as a great figure of contemporary India' and 'a byword for daring and patriotism' from whom 'countless people drew inspiration'.)[45]

One by one, Savarkar's close ones and aides seemed to be going away. His brother Narayan, who had moved his residence again to Mumbai, was grievously assaulted by a violent mob protesting Gandhi's assassination. He never really recovered and died after a paralytic attack in October 1949. The following year Vallabhbhai Patel, whom Savarkar had praised for his work of getting states such as Hyderabad to fall in line and join the Indian Union, passed on, and two years after that the sudden death of Syama Prasad Mookerjee came as a complete shock. Mookerjee was in Kashmir to agitate for its total integration into India, which meant abrogation of Article 370 and the abolition of the 'two prime ministers and two constitutions in one nation' principle as Jammu and Kashmir had its own premier and its own constitution, when he was arrested and died in the lockup. Savarkar 'could not believe' the news until it was 'thrice confirmed' and called it not just a national loss but 'a personal one'.[46] In the next few years, three of his London and Paris colleagues, Niranjan Pal, M.P.T. Acharya and Sardarsingh Rana, passed away, the first two in Mumbai and Rana in his native Saurashtra.

Savarkar's health was either indifferent or bad right through the 1950s and got progressively worse in the first half of the 1960s, though he continued to issue political statements every now and then, assailing Nehru for abandoning Tibet and embracing the Chinese premier Chou En-Lai, demanding that Hindi be declared the national language and 'Nagari' the national script, formally dissolving his one-time secret group Abhinav Bharat as the new, independent Bharat was now the realization of Abhinav Bharat, calling for the liberation of Goa from Portuguese rule, supporting the demand for the unified regions of Maharashtra and Gujarat but warning all regions to put nation over province, complaining about alleged proselytization in the North-East and especially in Nagaland, asserting that the question much discussed in the early 1960s – 'What after Nehru?' – was meaningless as 'no one was indispensable', saying as India stood on the verge of conflicts with Pakistan and China that his 'last wish' was to lay down his life 'fighting for India', blaming Nehru's ignorance of China's military buildup on the border for India's defeat in the 1962 war, and encouraging the new prime minister, Lal Bahadur Shastri, for his leadership during the 1965 India–Pakistan war but urging him not to go to Tashkent for any truce. He even raised the slogan of '*Ek dhakka aur do, Pakistan tod do*' (which in later decades was slightly modified by Hindu nationalists seeking a temple on the spot the Babri Masjid stood in Ayodhya, with the word 'Pakistan' being replaced by 'Babri') and said the dream of a 'united Hindustan' was bound to come true. He was upset over Partition and over voters' rejection of Hindu nationalism, but he was clear that the day India gained freedom had been the greatest of his life, for so many of his contemporaries who had fought for that goal had not been fortunate enough to see that day, having died before the fulfilment of their long-cherished dream; he was one of the lucky ones. The Hindus need not feel demoralized either, no matter what the state of the country and its tensions with Pakistan, because few countries had obtained complete independence all at once. They at least had three-fourths of their land to themselves after August 1947, and the other parts too would be back over time, he said.[47]

In his own way, even as he mourned the passing of his comrades and peers – except Nehru, after whose death no statement was issued in May 1964, although Savarkar did not celebrate his own birthday the next day – he continued to alienate people. When his daughter, Prabhat, wished to see him in 1948 at the Red Fort prison, he declined to meet her, saying he wanted nothing from her. Some sympathizers said he may have not wanted his daughter to see him as a prisoner. But with the others, there was no such reason that could be offered. Here the brittle aspect of his personality, which could at times be mistaken for a degree of misanthropy, came forth. This one-time revolutionary who had spent years in the most trying of prisons for a people's cause could turn his back on the same people. If Nehru had his infamous temper, Gandhi a whole series of idiosyncrasies and Bose his 'ekla chalo re' (go it alone) single-mindedness which could drive him away from his ideological co-travellers in politics, then Savarkar had the ability to shut people out altogether. People were, according to Keer, regularly turned back from his residence, and definitely so if they came without prior appointment. Even the celebrated K.M. Cariappa, the first Indian commander-in-chief of the Indian army, was thus snubbed, as was, bafflingly, one of the doctors who routinely attended on him. The orthodox among the Hindus were miffed because while he chatted a great deal with the left icon M.N. Roy, he showed very little patience with holy men who claimed special powers and even advised them to stop collecting money for religious rituals and give it to India's poor millions instead. He riled several self-styled spiritual gurus and champions of no-fish-no-meat by saying that the country, in the grip of serious famine in the mid-1950s, could overcome its shortage of food and other stuff if the Brahmans, Buddhists, Jains and other vegetarians took to eating fish and eggs and stopped judging people on the basis of what they ate. People must be allowed to eat what they liked and what they could afford, he declared. Publicly there was praise for the 'saintly' Golwalkar too, but privately his opinion of the Sangh chief was known to be not exactly salutary. As for janeudhari Hindus, he had demonstrated what he thought about the subject by not carrying out the so-called sacred thread ceremony for his son Vishwas.

On the other hand, there was much innuendo, right from his years of internment in Ratnagiri, and also during his years of retirement, about his long conversations with women. He had never appreciated prudery, had undisguised contempt for notions of abstention from sex, especially since Gandhi appeared to have tried to cultivate it into a virtue, and was said by some to have been in love with an English girl, Margaret Lawrence, during his years in London. He believed that armed revolutionaries ought to get into the act of reproduction and not swear, as many of them did during his youth, that they would avoid the coils of 'sansar'. Reproduction, though, was not the sole motive, for pleasure had its own place in life. Referring to 'rati' or passion in one of his poems, he said its fulfilment brought happiness to everybody, and the 'real dharma' was one that brought happiness to human beings.[48] Thus sexual passion was legitimate and there was nothing wrong with giving full expression to it, a view like many other social views of his that did not go down well with a mostly conservative society.

Atre writes in his autobiography[49] that Ram Tatnis, the well-known Mumbai editor who brought out the Marathi weekly *Vividhvrutta*, wrote a piece casting aspersions on Savarkar's character; Atre, of course, thought the article was full of rubbish. After Independence, as Savarkar remained increasingly confined to his home in Dadar, some aides and visitors complained – if Keer, Gokhale and some other chroniclers close to him are to be believed – that some women comrades had rather lengthy conversations with him and did not need much of an advance notice to secure an appointment.

Many felt that his long-suffering wife, Yamuna, was getting neglected. She had sacrificed enormously, having run the household on her own for many years while he was away in prison or, later, carrying out social and political work. They'd had four children in all: a boy, Prabhakar (who died when Savarkar was in England), the daughter Prabhat in 1924, another girl, Shalini, in 1927 (she too died early, like Prabhakar), and son Vishwas in 1928. Prabhat and Vishwas were well-set and married, and both later had daughters. Yet, according to those who knew him intimately, Savarkar hardly ever took his wife along with him when he was touring various parts of India as Mahasabha chief. She remained confined to her household, like so many Indian women of the time,[50] and Savarkar, who was loath to socialize by going for dinners and parties, never took her out much.

All these allusions were later at the heart of a short story, 'Sati', written by the Marathi author Vidyadhar Pundalik for the literary magazine *Satyakatha* in 1974. Savarkar had been dead for eight years then, and the story, without naming him, depicted subtle tensions in his married life after his return from the Andamans.[51] The portrayal of Savarkar and Yamuna was a sensitive one, yet it created a stir in Pune, where Pundalik lived, with some Savarkar supporters marching to his residence and demanding an apology, which the writer, himself a Savarkar admirer and a liberal right-winger, did not offer. (An even more celebrated Marathi writer, Pu. La. Deshpande, was resolutely left-wing and anti-Hindutva, yet it is a pointer to the kind of cross-ideological consensus Savarkar could sometimes create, especially in his native region, that Pu. La. saw the one-time revolutionary, all the controversies around him notwithstanding, as a figure of titanic proportions against whom 'no amount of vicious attacks or propaganda' would work.)[52]

Sometime in March 1963 Savarkar slipped and fell in his house and broke his left thigh bone. He underwent a surgery at a clinic in Dadar and was bedridden for three months. He spent his eightieth birthday thus, with three full-time nurses in attendance at Savarkar Sadan. Just days after he had returned home from his operation, after rubbing astrologers the wrong way and ridiculing their advice of leaving the clinic only on a full-moon night, his wife fell gravely ill. She had been hit by bone tuberculosis in the mid-1950s and had turned considerably weak; now, as she too lay in bed, the residence was converted into a virtual nursing home. In October she was admitted to a local hospital, and there were soon indications that she would not survive for long. She longed to go home so that she could die in peace there, but Savarkar told his aides to let her stay where she was. He had started taking small steps with the aid of a walking stick and said he would visit her at the hospital.

But he never did, and when Yamuna died, he said, 'Don't bring the body home. Take her straight to the electric crematorium at Chandanwadi [near Marine Lines]. There must be no display of public mourning. Ever since I came back from Port Blair, she's had a happy family life. She's played with her grandchildren too. Her life was truly turned into gold.' We do not know if he himself went for the cremation. He was firm, despite requests from many of his relatives and friends, that no post-death rituals be conducted, but his son Vishwas quietly did some rites on his own accord, which Savarkar perhaps got to know of and did not complain about, saying it was an individual's choice.[53]

Such a tough embrace of rationalism, in the last few years of his life, seemed to many to have got the better of his softer instincts. In many respects he had been pretty hard – on his wife, his daughter when he would not allow her to see him in the Red Fort prison, his personal staffers when he would not hike their meagre salaries. The poetry, so essential to his being, had been replaced by hard prose. The last bit of prose he wrote was decried as completely merciless.

In his solitude, he wrote in the early 1960s, mostly on his bed, from which he hardly moved now owing to excessive frailty, *Saha Soneri Paney* or 'Six Glorious Epochs of Indian History'. It depicted the battles and wars that the Hindus had had to fight across eras and drew certain conclusions, some of which were 'shocking' even to its English translator S.T. Godbole,[54] who helped the aged writer gather and cite sources for the text. Savarkar's tit-for-tat policy was well known, but now he extended it to religious shrines, mass slaughter and to women. So many temples had been destroyed by the rampaging Muslim forces, but the Hindus had not touched a single masjid even after they had reconquered their lost territories. That, in his view, was a mistake. When Muslim invaders went about 'slaughtering wholesale the Hindu population' in a region, the Hindus, 'whenever they gained an upper hand, could have retaliated'[55] the same way, but they had not. That was also, according to him, a wrong conception of a virtue. Most controversially, Savarkar suggested that the Hindus should have avenged the humiliations repeatedly heaped on Hindu women by Muslim forces by similarly targeting Muslim women. The Hindus did not even capture women in war but only the men, he said, whereas Islamic armies not only 'polluted and molested' Hindu women but captured them, converted them and, through them, worked to increase the numbers of the local Muslim population. If only the Hindus would 'pay back in the same coin', he claimed, the Muslim conquerors, 'once they are haunted with this dreadful apprehension that the Muslim women, too, stand in the same predicament in case the Hindus win', would never dare to think of such molestation of Hindu women.[56] The theory of such revenge militated against the 'basic Hindu inclination for reconciliation', his sympathetic biographer Gokhale wrote, and was heavily criticized; it continues to be assailed to this day for being, as Gokhale called it, a negation of values such as 'forgiveness, respect for women, and an essential human large-heartedness so dearly prized by the Hindu faith'.[57]

From his eightieth birthday onward Savarkar's health took a turn for the worse. With his health failing rapidly, he had told many of his friends, including the Mangeshkar family, that he now wished to spend his time alone. The Mangeshkars – Lata, Hridaynath and their mother, Mai – used to be regulars at Savarkar Sadan, and Savarkar loved speaking to them on a number of subjects ranging from politics to the arts and culture. Mai invariably took for him the pulao made by her that he so loved, and according to Lata she was once so moved by his thinking during a conversation that she voiced her desire to give up singing altogether and work along with him for the nation's well-being. He dissuaded her, however, saying that giving full expression to her talent as a singer was also a way of serving India, and she ought to continue doing that.

Savarkar had suffered from piles a little earlier, and some time after his wife's death, there was 'prolapsus of the rectum'[58] and swelling in the stomach. The condition became acute in 1965 as he turned eighty-two, forcing doctors to put him on a liquid diet for a short while, and the pain was quite unbearable at times. Fever too was intermittent, and he had become skeletal.[59]

Shortly after his birthday in 1964, Savarkar, his cheeks looking more hollowed out than ever before, had handed an article he had written for a Marathi magazine to his young doctor, Arvind Godbole, who had come to see him for a customary check-up. The headline for the piece was 'Atmahatya ki Atmarpan?', meaning 'Suicide or Self-sacrifice?', and as the doctor, his curiosity piqued, cast a glance over its contents, he saw that it spoke in glowing terms of several Hindu spiritual and philosophical giants such as Shankara, Chaitanya, Tukaram and Dnyaneshwar who, thinking their life's mission over after years of prayer, meditation, introspection – and in the case of Shankara the sheer physical effort of walking from Kerala to Kashmir to preach the faith – had decided they did not want to extend their earthly existence any further. They had locked themselves up in a cave or a mud hut without food or water or chosen death by drowning. The physician feared Savarkar would attempt something similar, but he did not say a word about it to his patient and instead carried on with his work.[60]

By the end of 1965, Savarkar could not even sit up on his bed without support, leave alone walk on his own. Early in February 1966 he told his team of doctors led by Subhash Purandare and comprising Godbole, among others, that they should simply let him be; he'd had enough of life, and it was time to go. He wished to embrace the end by giving up food, water and of course medicine. Would they please not give him intravenous infusions when things got really bad, he said; he did not want to get poked.[61]

They could not do so, as Indian law did not allow passive euthanasia, at least not officially. For some time they had even given him medicines in his daily cup of tea to beat back his resistance, but, protesting that he wanted to die with dignity, he stopped taking tea altogether from 3 February, sticking just to water. After a couple of days that intake was also drastically reduced, there was some swelling in the throat, and in another twenty-four hours he could barely speak. The doctors too seemed to have decided, finally and reluctantly, to respect the patient's decision, though they did slip in some medicine whenever they could and kept up checks on all vital parameters. An irreversible decline set in gradually, and on the morning of 26 February 1966, when the doctors had difficulty in detecting a pulse or getting any figure registered on the blood pressure meter, they did their best to revive him, without success.[62]

The man who spoke of 'complete independence for India' at least twenty years before the Congress, which was the chief organizer of the freedom movement, who formulated the political ideology of Hindutva and who was linked to Gandhi's assassination died at the age of eighty-three. He had spent almost thirty years in prison and raked up one controversy or the other through a dramatic career filled with astonishing ups and downs. His body was not placed on a wooden pyre, and no mantras were chanted; in keeping with his wishes, it was lowered, gently, into an incinerator. The crows in the skies near Savarkar's home, also, were not fed.

Notes

1. The eye of the empire

1. Bose, *Indian Revolutionaries Abroad, 1905–1922*, p. 20.
2. Savarkar, *Londonchi Batmipatre*, p. 122.
3. *Statesman*, Calcutta, 4 July 1909.
4. *New York Times*, 3 July 1909.
5. *Daily Mail*, 2 July 1909.
6. From the proceedings of the Old Bailey, Central Criminal Court, for July 1909, p. 463.
7. *The Times*, London, 6 July 1909.
8. Ibid.
9. *Times of India*, 17 July 1909.
10. *The Times*, London, 6 July 1909.
11. *New York Times*, 3 July 1909.
12. *Guardian*, London, 13 July 1909.
13. The *Chronicle* and the *Daily Express* of UK quoted in the *New York Times*, 3 July 1909.
14. *Times of India*, 8 July 1909.
15. Banerjea, *The Trumpet Voice of India*, pp. 88–93.
16. *The Times*, London, 6 July 1909.
17. Ibid.
18. Ibid.
19. Ibid.

20. Savarkar, *Londonchi Batmipatre*, p. 125.
21. *The Times*, London, 6 July 1909.
22. Ibid.
23. Chirol, *Indian Unrest*, p. 148.
24. *The Times*, London, 6 July 1909.
25. Ibid., 11 July 1909.
26. Leaming, *A Philadelphia Lawyer*, pp. 153–55, 163.
27. *The Times*, London, 20 August 1909.

2. In the land of the Ramayana

1. Savarkar, *Majhya Athvani*, p. 2 (accessed on savarkarsmarak.com); also, Keer, *Veer Savarkar*, p. 2.
2. Savarkar, *Majhya Athvani*, p. 4.
3. Ibid., p. 10; also, Karandikar, *Swatantryaveer Savarkar Charitra*, p. 37.
4. Savarkar, *Majhya Athvani*, pp. 22, 28.
5. Ibid., pp. 25–26.
6. Ibid., p17; and Karandikar, *Swatantryaveer Savarkar Charitra*, p. 49.
7. Savarkar, *Majhya Athvani*, p. 30.
8. Ibid., p. 18.
9. Ibid., pp. 12–13.
10. Ibid., p. 38.
11. Ibid., p. 33.
12. Cashman, *Myth of the Lokamanya*, p. 40.
13. Savarkar, *Majhya Athvani*, pp. 34–35.
14. Ibid., p. 55.
15. Read and Fischer, *The Proudest Day*, pp. 81–82.
16. Savarkar, *Majhya Athvani*, pp. 92–94.
17. Ibid., p. 93.
18. Ibid., pp. 56–57.

3. Turbulence at home

1. The East India Company 'was wound up by the Government of India Act, passed in London on 2 August 1858', as recorded in Read and Fischer, *The Proudest Day*, p. 55. Also see Wilson, *India Conquered*, pp. 262, 286.

2. Read and Fischer, *The Proudest Day*, p. 61.
3. Ibid., p. 56.
4. Wilson, *India Conquered*, pp. 301–02, 310; Read and Fischer, *The Proudest Day*, pp. 63–64, 69–70.
5. Read and Fischer, *The Proudest Day*, pp. 69–70.
6. Cashman, *Myth of the Lokamanya*, p. 23.
7. Read and Fischer, *The Proudest Day*, p. 81.
8. Savarkar, *Majhya Athvani*, pp. 74, 84.
9. Ibid., 112–13.
10. Ibid., p. 78.
11. Ibid., p. 105.
12. Yeshwantrao Mukne's daughter Asharaje Rane, who lives in Mumbai, spoke to the author in July 2019.
13. Savarkar, *Majhya Athvani*, pp. 152–53.

4. Matchsticks for a bonfire

1. Savarkar, *Majhya Athvani*, p. 126.
2. Ibid., p.148.
3. Joglekar, Veer Savarkar, pp. 37–38.
4. Sedition Committee Report, 1918, p. 5.
5. Read and Fischer, *The Proudest Day*, p. 84.
6. Shewalkar, *Lokmanya Tilakanche Nibandha*, p. 44 (excerpts cited translated by Vaibhav Purandare, henceforth VP).
7. Read and Fischer, *The Proudest Day*, p. 89.
8. Bhagwat and Pradhan, *Lokmanya Tilak*, p. 277.
9. Bombay Police intelligence report from 1905 (p. 322) quoted in *Source Material for a History of the Freedom Movement in India*, Vol. 2, pp. 608–09.
10. Cashman, *The Myth of the Lokamanya*, p. 174.
11. *Source Material for a History of the Freedom Movement in India*, Vol. 2, p. 610.
12. For details of the episode, this writer has drawn on Cashman, *The Myth of the Lokamanya*, p. 174 and Joglekar, *Veer Savarkar*, p. 41.
13. Keer, *Veer Savarkar*, p. 20.
14. Gokhale, *Speeches*, pp. 690–91, 964.
15. *Indian Opinion*, 4 November 1905, in Gandhi, *Collected Works*, Vol. 4, pp. 477–78.

16. *Kesari* editorial of 24 October 1905 in Shewalkar, *Lokmanya Tilakanche Nibandha*, pp. 91–92 (excerpts cited translated by VP).
17. Quoted in Guha, *Gandhi Before India*, pp. 217–18.
18. Savarkar, *Shatruchya Shibirat* (Inside the Enemy Camp), p. 2 (accessed on the Savarkar Smarak website; excerpts cited translated by VP).
19. Savarkar's poem quoted in Karandikar, *Swatantryaveer Savarkar Charitra*, p. 259.
20. Karandikar, *Swatantryaveer Savarkar Charitra*, p. 259.
21. Ibid., p. 260.
22. Savarkar quoted in Karandikar, *Swatantryaveer Savarkar Charitra*, p. 82.
23. Bapat quoted in Karandikar, *Swatantryaveer Savarkar Charitra*, pp. 82–83.
24. Savarkar, *Shatruchya Shibirat*, pp. 1–14.
25. Ibid., pp. 26–28.

5. Tumult in London

1. Bose, *Indian Revolutionaries Abroad*, p. 16.
2. Quoted by Savarkar in *Shatruchya Shibirat*, pp. 54–60.
3. Savarkar, *Londonchi Batmipatre*, pp. 5–136.
4. *The Times*, London, 17 June 1908.
5. Ali, *Memoirs*, pp. 69–70.
6. Savarkar, *Londonchi Batmipatre*, pp. 140–41.
7. *The Times*, London, 10 August 1910.
8. Nehru, *Selected Works*, Vol. 3, pp. 39–95.
9. Savarkar, *Londonchi Batmipatre*, p. 114.
10. Quoted in Bose, *Indian Revolutionaries Abroad*, p. 25.
11. Savarkar, *Londonchi Batmipatre*, p. 126.
12. Gandhi, *Collected Works*, Vol. 9, pp. 302–03, 310.
13. *The Times*, London, 19 August 1910.
14. Ibid., 15 July 1909.
15. Garnett, *The Golden Echo*, Vol. 1, pp. 151–62.
16. Payne, *The Life and Death of Mahatma Gandhi*, pp. 205–06.
17. Ali, *Memoirs*, p. 70.
18. Savarkar, *Londonchi Batmipatre*, p. 143.
19. Ali, *Memoirs*, pp. 72–73.

20. Bombay High Court records, 1910.
21. *The Times*, London, 23 December 1909.
22. *Observer*, London, 26 December 1909.
23. *Source Material for a History of the Freedom Movement*, pp. 400–01, 507–11.
24. Chattopadhyaya, *Life and Myself*, Vol. 1, p. 201.
25. Ibid.
26. Chitragupta, *The Life of Swatantra Veer Savarkar*, pp. 157–58.

6. The escape and the global trial

1. *Observer*, 1 May 1910; and *The Times*, London, 25 April 1910.
2. *Source Material for a History of the Freedom Movement*, pp. 445–46; and *The Times*, London, 22 June 1910.
3. *Buffalo Enquirer*, New York, 14 March 1910.
4. *The Times*, London, 22 June 1910.
5. Quoted in Padmanabhan, *V.V.S. Aiyar*, pp. 76–79.
6. Ibid.
7. *Observer*, London, 24 April 1910; and *The Times*, London, 3 June 1910.
8. *The Times*, London, 21 June 1910.
9. Garnett, *The Golden Echo*, Vol. 1, pp. 151–62.
10. *L'Humanite*, 10 July 1910.
11. *Gazette*, Montreal, Canada, 9 August 1910.
12. *Observer*, London, 9 October 1910.
13. *The Times*, London, 20 July 1910.
14. Quoted in the *Manchester Guardian*, 25 July 1910.
15. Quoted in the *Manchester Guardian*, 16 September 1910.
16. *St Louis Post Despatch*, Missouri, 25 September 1910.
17. Sydenham, *My Working Life*, p. 247.
18. Quoted in Bruckenhaus, *Policing Transnational Protest*, 2017.
19. 'Report of the Proceedings of the International Socialist Congress at Copenhagen, 1910', p. 15.
20. Hyndman, *The Emancipation of India*, p. 14.
21. *Manchester Guardian*, 21 July 1910.
22. Chirol, *Indian Unrest*, pp. 347–48.
23. *Times of India*, 25 July 1910.

24. *Manchester Guardian*, 29 October 1910.
25. *L'Humanite*, 28 September 1910.
26. *Times of India*, 16 September 1910.
27. Text of the agreement published in the *Manchester Guardian*, 12 November 1910.
28. Award of the tribunal, 24 February 1911, accessed on www.haguejusticeportal.net
29. Quoted in the *Manchester Guardian*, 27 February 1911.
30. *Manchester Guardian* and *The Times*, 27 February 1911.
31. *Manchester Guardian*, 28 February 1911.
32. Sethna, *Madam Bhikaiji Rustom Cama*, pp. 85–87.
33. Ali, *Memoirs*, p. 75.
34. Savarkar, *Majhi Janmathep*, p. 13. A detailed account of the wife's visit from pages 12 to 14.

7. Kaala Paani

1. Savarkar, *Majhi Janmathep*, p. 2 (excerpts cited translated by VP).
2. Ibid., pp. 43–45.
3. Ghose, *The Tale of My Exile*, pp. 51–52.
4. British Home Department directive quoted in Mathur, *History of the Andaman and Nicobar Islands*, p. 198.
5. Savarkar, *Majhi Janmathep*, pp. 65–67 (excerpts cited translated by VP).
6. Mathur, *History of the Andaman and Nicobar Islands*, p. 202.
7. Ghose, *The Tale of My Exile*, p. 86.
8. Savarkar, *My Transportation for Life*, p. 102.
9. Ghose, *The Tale of My Exile*, p. 86.
10. Ibid., p. 50.
11. Savarkar, *My Transportation for Life*, pp. 103–04.
12. Ghose, *The Tale of My Exile*, pp. 60–61.
13. Details of the brothers' meeting in jail and exchange of letters in Savarkar, *Majhi Janmathep*, pp. 110–13.
14. Savarkar, *An Echo from Andamans*, p. 20.
15. Ibid., p. 18.
16. Rejali, *Torture and Democracy*, p. 300 (accessed on Google Books).
17. Dutt, *Twelve Years of Prison Life*, pp. 63–65.

18. Cathy Scott-Clark and Adrian Levy, 'Survivors of Our Hell', *Guardian*, 23 June 2001, accessed online (www.theguardian.com/lifeandstyle/2001/jun/23/weekend.adrianlevy).
19. *Guardian*, 23 June 2001.
20. Savarkar, *My Transportation for Life*, pp. 163–64.
21. Ibid., p. 177.
22. Savarkar, *Majhi Janmathep*, p. 203.
23. Mathur, *History of the Andaman and Nicobar Islands (1756-1966)*, pp. 204–05.
24. Ibid., pp. 205–06.
25. Choudhary, *Growth of Nationalism in India (1919–1929)*, Vol. 2, pp. 270–71.
26. *Bombay Chronicle*, 12 May 1915.

8. A conditional release

1. *Source Material for a History of the Freedom Movement in India*, p. 478.
2. Savarkar, *An Echo from Andamans*, p. 28.
3. Quoted in Phadke, *Shodh Savarkarancha*, p. 60.
4. Savarkar, *An Echo from Andamans*, p. 40.
5. Quoted in Phadke, *Shodh Savarkarancha*, pp. 60–61.
6. Savarkar, *An Echo from Andamans*, pp. 70–72.
7. Ibid., pp. 62–63.
8. *Bombay Chronicle*, 14 November 1918.
9. Savarkar, *An Echo from Andamans*, pp. 73–76.
10. Ibid., pp. 78–79.
11. Khaparde, *Source Material for a History of the Freedom Movement in India*, Vol. 7, pp. 485–86.
12. Savarkar, *An Echo from Andamans*, pp. 57–58.
13. Ibid., pp. 41–44, 51–52, 85.
14. Ibid., pp. 32–33, 40–41, 84–85, 107–08, 114–15.
15. Ibid., pp. 107–08.
16. *Bombay Chronicle*, 15 March 1920.
17. Ibid., 14 July 1919.
18. Ibid., 13 January 1920.
19. Ibid., 19 January 1920.

20. Ibid., 1 March 1920.
21. *Source Material for a History of the Freedom Movement in India*, Vol. 2, pp. 463–71.
22. Savarkar, *My Transportation for Life* (excerpt here from the original English translation), p. 318.
23. *Bombay Chronicle*, 14 April 1920.
24. *Source Material for a History of the Freedom Movement in India*, Vol. 2, p. 477.
25. *Bombay Chronicle*, 1 March 1920.
26 Ibid., 25 February 1920.
27. Ibid., 5 April 1920.
28. Ibid., 17 May 1920.
29. Ibid., 8 December 1920.
30. Ibid., 5 January 1921.
31. Also among those who spoke up for the Savarkar brothers' release in public meetings at the time was the nationalist M.B. Velkar.
32. Phadke, *Shodh Savarkarancha*, pp. 64–65.
33. *Bombay Chronicle*, 16 October 1920.
34. Ibid., 23 January 1920.
35. *Young India*, 26 May 1920, in Gandhi, *Collected Works*, Vol. 20, pp. 368–71.
36. *Bombay Chronicle*, 31 January 1921.
37. Ibid., 8 February 1921.
38. Ibid., 9 February 1921.
39. Gandhi, *Collected Works*, Vol. 20, pp. 104–05.
40. Savarkar, *An Echo from Andamans*, p. 38.
41. Quoted in Phadke, *Shodh Savarkarancha*, p. 67.
42. Quoted in Phadke, *Shodh Savarkarancha*, p. 68.
43. *Bombay Chronicle*, 11 October and 23 October 1923.
44. Ibid., 8 January 1924.
45. Ibid., 21 February 1924.
46 Ibid., 8 January 1924.
47. Phadke, *Shodh Savarkarancha*, p. 74; and *Bombay Chronicle*, 2 February 1924.
48. Phadke, *Shodh Savarkarancha*, p. 75.
49. Article in *Shraddhanand*, 3 August 1928, quoted in Savarkar, *Garmagaram Chivda*, p. 71.

50. Article in *Shraddhanand*, 3 August 1928, quoted in Savarkar, *Garmagaram Chivda*, pp. 71–75.
51. *Loksatta*, 27 May 2018.

9. The new credo of Hindutva

1. Savarkar, *Majhi Janmathep*, pp. 70–72.
2. Ghose, *The Tale of My Exile*, p. 73.
3. Ibid., p. 78.
4. Details taken from Savarkar, *Majhi Janmathep*, pp. 228–71.
5. Savarkar, *Hindutva*, p. 63.
6. Majumdar, *History of the Freedom Movement in India*, pp. 247–48.
7. Read and Fischer, *The Proudest Day*, p. 78; and Majumdar, *History of the Freedom Movement in India*, pp. 424–25.
8. Majumdar, *History of the Freedom Movement in India*, p. 421.
9. Read and Fischer, *The Proudest Day*, p. 77; and Majumdar, *History of the Freedom Movement in India*, p. 431.
10. Read and Fischer, *The Proudest Day*, p. 79; and Majumdar, *History of the Freedom Movement in India*, Vol. 1, pp. 438–39.
11. Ibid., Vol. 2, pp. 211–18.
12. Read and Fischer, *The Proudest Day*, pp. 107–08; *Keeping the Jewel in the Crown*, pp. 18–21; and the UK Parliament website, www.parliament.uk
13. Read and Fischer, *The Proudest Day*, p. 93.
14. Adams, *Gandhi*, p. 144.
15. Bhagwat and Pradhan, *Lokmanya Tilak*, pp. 481–82.
16. Cashman, *The Myth of the Lokamanya*, p. 214.
17. Read and Fischer, *The Proudest Day*, pp. 130–31; and Cashman, *The Myth of the Lokamanya*, p. 214.
18. Read and Fischer, *The Proudest Day*, pp. 136–38.
19. *Bombay Chronicle*, 25 November 1920.
20. Adams, *Gandhi*, p. 164.
21. Ibid., pp. 163–65.
22. Savarkar, *Majhi Janmathep*, p. 440.
23. Lelyveld, *Great Soul*, p. 161.
24. Ibid., p. 157.
25. Ibid., p. 162.

26. Majumdar, *History of the Freedom Movement in India*, Vol. 3, pp. 192–94.
27. Phadke, *Shodh Savarkarancha*, p. 160.
28. Quoted in Maclean, *A Revolutionary History of Interwar India*, pp. 4–5, 126–27.
29. Tendulkar, *Mahatma*, Vol. 2, p. 307; Savarkar, *Gandhi Gondhal*, p. 14 (accessed on www.savarkarsmarak.com); and *Samagra Savarkar Sahitya*, Vol. 4, p. 151.
30. Tendulkar, *Mahatma*, Vol. 2, p. 346.
31. Gandhi, *Collected Works*, Vol. 33, pp. 133–36; and Tendulkar, *Mahatma*, Vol. 2, p. 348.
32. Savarkar, *Vidnyan-nishta Nibandh*, pp. 55–67 (accessed online on www.savarkarsmarkar.org). Parts of the article were translated, reproduced and quoted by this writer first in an article for the *Times of India*, 'The Cow and Savarkar', published on 9 June 2017.

10. Reconverting the converted, 'purifying the polluted'

1. *Bombay Chronicle*, 1 August and 6 August 1924.
2. Ibid., 2 August 1924.
3. Ibid., 30 August 1924.
4. Lata Mangeshkar, in an interview with this author in March 2018.
5. Keer, *Dr Babasaheb Ambedkar*, pp. 230–31.
6. Ibid., 253–56.
7. *Times of India*, 15 December 1931.
8. Phadke, *Shodh Savarkarancha*, p. 141.
9. Savarkar, *Ksha-Kirney*, pp. 10–13.
10. *Times of India*, 2 May 1925.
11. *Bombay Chronicle*, 13 April 1925.
12. Review by K.K. Banerji in the *Historical Quarterly*, Vol. 2, 1926, p. 432.
13. Sarkar's review for the *Modern Review*, April–May 1926, quoted in Phadke, *Shodh Savarkarancha*, pp. 100–01.
14. *Times of India*, 30 July 1925.
15. Savarkar, *Bhasha Shuddhi*, pp. 7–60.
16. Quoted in Savarkar, *Bhasha Shuddhi*, pp. 69–78.
17. Savarkar, *Bhasha Shuddhi*, pp. 69–78.

18. *Times of India*, 25 June 1928.
19. Phadke, *Shodh Savarkarancha*, pp. 108–18.
20. Ibid., pp. 129–30.
21. Deshpande, *Savarkar*, p. 42.
22. Kabadi quoted in interview given to Uma Shanker in 1970, which is part of the audio archive of Cambridge University's Centre of South Asian Studies; transcript available in both text and audio format at www.s-asian.cam.ac.uk/archive/audio/collection/w-kabadi
23. Majumdar, *History of the Freedom Movement in India*, Vol. 3, pp. 493–94.
24. Ibid., pp. 512–20.
25. Ibid., p. 525.
26. All of Savarkar's essays on the revolutionaries are published in *Tejaswi Taare*.
27. Phadke, *Shodh Savarkarancha*, p. 130.
28. Ibid., p. 145.
29. Majumdar, *History of the Freedom Movement in India*, Vol. 3, pp. 494–95.
30. Phadke, *Shodh Savarkarancha*, p. 143.
31. Gogate quoted in interview which is part of the audio archive of Cambridge University's Centre of South Asian Studies; transcript available at www.s-asian.cam.ac.uk/archive/audio/collection
32. Oza quoted in interview which is part of the audio archive of Cambridge University's Centre of South Asian Studies; transcript available at www.s-asian.cam.ac.uk/archive/audio/collection
33. Yashpal, *Sinhavalokan*, Vol. 2, pp. 110–18 (translation of the relevant passages by VP).
34. Ibid., p. 114.
35. Maclean, *A Revolutionary History of Interwar India*, pp. 70–76; and Phadke, *Shodh Savarkarancha*, pp. 163–64.
36. *Times of India*, 15 September 1928; and Phadke, *Shodh Savarkarancha*, p. 84.
37. *Times of India*, 14 December 1936.

11. World war, word wars

1. *Bombay Chronicle*, 12 May 1937.
2. Ibid., 16 May 1937.

3. Ibid., 20 July 1937.
4. Ibid., 28 June 1937.
5. Tendulkar, *Abdul Ghaffar Khan*, p. 227.
6. *Bombay Chronicle*, 26 June 1937.
7. Ibid.
8. Atre, *Karheche Paani*, Vol. 2, pp. 315–16.
9. *Times of India*, 19 November 1937.
10. *Bombay Chronicle*, 30 and 31 December 1937, and 1 and 2 January 1938.
11. Ibid., 8 January 1938; and *Times of India*, 31 December 1937.
12. Savarkar, *Vividh Lekh*, pp. 80–91.
13. Savarkar, *Whirlwind Propaganda*, pp. 50–51.
14. Ibid., p. 51.
15. *Bombay Chronicle*, 22 February 1939.
16. Savarkar, *Whirlwind Propaganda*, pp. 52–53.
17. Majumdar, *History of the Freedom Movement in India*, Vol. 3, p. 598.
18. *Jinnah of Pakistan*, p. 171.
19. Quoted in Raghavan, *India's War*, p. 15.
20. Savarkar, *Whirlwind Propaganda*, pp. 45–50.
21. Ibid., pp. 111–12.
22. *Towards Freedom* (Part 2), p. 1804.
23. Ibid.
24. Savarkar, *Whirlwind Propaganda*, pp. 147–48.
25. Ibid.
26. Majumdar, *History of the Freedom Movement in India*, Vol. 3, p. 599.
27. Savarkar, *Whirlwind Propaganda*, p. 157.
28. Ibid., pp. 157–68.
29. Majumdar, *History of the Freedom Movement in India*, Vol. 3, p. 601.
30. CWC resolution of 7 August 1940, reproduced in full in Gandhi, *Collected Works*, Appendix 4, Vol. 72, p. 467.
31. *A Centenary History of the Indian National Congress*, Vol. 3, p. 314.
32. Savarkar, *Hindu Rashtra Darshan*, pp. 98–117.
33. Raghavan, *India's War*, pp. 73–74.
34. Ibid., pp. 92–94.

35. Savarkar, *Hindu Rashtra Darshan*, p. 113.
36 `Savarkar, *Whirlwind Propaganda*, pp. 262–66.
37. Letter from Bal Savarkar to K.C. Das quoted in Ohsawa, *Two Great Indians in Japan*, Vol. 1, pp. 94–95.
38. Bose, *The Indian Struggle*, p. 34.
39. Ibid.
40. *Bombay Chronicle*, 4 August 1939.
41. Read and Fischer, *The Proudest Day*, p. 306.
42. Ibid., p. 301.
43. Ibid., p. 308.
44. Savarkar, *Whirlwind Propaganda*, pp. 461–62.
45. Read and Fischer, *The Proudest Day*, p. 308.
46. *Bombay Chronicle*, 24 August 1941.
47. Ibid., 22 August 1941.
48. Savarkar, *Whirlwind Propaganda*, pp. 462–66.
49. *Bombay Chronicle*, 12 September 1941.
50. Ibid., 15 June 1941.
51. Ibid., 25 December 1941.
52. Ibid., 29 December 1941.
53. Ibid., 22 January 1941.
54. Majumdar, *History of the Freedom Movement in India*, Vol. 3, pp. 616–17.
55. *Manchester Guardian*, 9 March 1942.
56. *Bombay Chronicle*, 12 March 1942.
57. Quoted in Read and Fischer, *The Proudest Day*, p. 317.
58. *New York Times*, 29 March 1942.
59. Ibid., 8 April 1942.
60. Vijaya Lakshmi Pandit quoted in *Indian Summer*, p. 107.
61. Read and Fischer, *The Proudest Day*, p. 327.
62. Savarkar, *Hindu Rashtra Darshan*, pp. 144–45; and *Krantighosh*, p. 135.
63. *New York Times*, 2 September 1942.
64. Savarkar, *Hindu Rashtra Darshan*, p. 145.
65. *Krantighosh*, p. 137.
66. Brecher, *Nehru*, pp. 143–44.
67. Coupland, *India*, p. 222.
68. Read and Fischer, *The Proudest Day*, p. 328.

69. Ibid.
70. Raghavan, *Aruna Asaf Ali*, p. 36.
71. Ibid., pp. 25–26.
72. *Manchester Guardian*, 19 August 1942.
73. *Bombay Chronicle*, 28 August 1942.
74. Churchill's speech of 10 September 1942, accessed on the Historic Hansard website.
75. Quoted in Guha, *Gandhi*, pp. 684–85.
76. Atre, *Karheche Paani*, Vol. 3, p. 12.
77. Ibid., pp. 12–13.
78. Ibid., pp. 20–21.
79. *Bombay Chronicle*, 21 September 1941.
80. Rath and Chatterjee, *Rash Behari Basu*, pp. 171–74.
81. Bose, *Testament of Subhas Bose*, pp. 21–24.
82. Excerpts from the Lahore resolution quoted in Read and Fischer, *The Proudest Day*, p. 295.
83. Savarkar, *Hindu Rashtra Darshan*, p. 82.
84. *Bombay Chronicle*, 26 March 1940.
85. *Times of India*, 29 December 1939.
86. *Bombay Chronicle*, 29 December 1939.
87. Nichols, *Verdict on India*, pp. 184–85.
88. Durrani, *The Meaning of Pakistan*, pp. 101–07.
89. Mehta and Patwardhan, *The Communal Triangle in India*, p. 178.
90. *Bombay Chronicle*, 29 December 1939.
91. Ibid., 28 December 1939.
92. Gokhale, *Swatantryaveer Savarkar*, p. 86.
93. Ambedkar, *Pakistan*, p. 143.
94. Ibid., pp. 292–98.
95. Ibid., p. 297.
96. Sitaramayya, *History of the Indian National Congress*, Vol. 3, pp. 541–42.
97. Ibid., pp. 542–43.
98. Ibid., p. 529.
99. Ibid., p. 542.
100. Savarkar, *Hindu Rashtra Darshan*, p. 147.
101. Wolpert, *Jinnah of Pakistan*, p. 216.
102. Ibid., pp. 216–17.

103. Guha, *Gandhi*, pp. 593–94.
104. Sharma, *Peeps into Pakistan*, pp. 109–10.
105. Ibid., p. 110.
106. Keer, *Veer Savarkar*, pp. 292–93.
107. Ibid., pp. 316–19.
108. Ismail, *My Public Life*, p. 31.
109. Ibid., pp. 73–74.
110. Ibid., pp. 90–91.
111. Savarkar, *Aitihasik Nivedaney*, pp. 78–81.
112. Talwalkar, *Naoroji Te Nehru*, p. 203.
113. Jinnah, *Some Recent Speeches and Writings*, pp. 308–09.
114. Ibid., p. 310.
115. Ibid., pp. 310–11.
116. Ambedkar, *Pakistan*, p. 142.
117. Treanor, *One Damn Thing After Another*, p. 84.
118. *Indian Review*, August 1941 issue, p. 373.
119. Madhok, *Portrait of a Martyr*, p. 25.
120. Ibid., pp. 50–51.
121. Mookerjee, *A Phase of the Indian Struggle*, pp. 11–12.
122. Keer, *Veer Savarkar*, p. 320.
123. Savarkar, *Historic Statements*, p. 65.
124. Ibid., p. 59.
125. Madhok, *Portrait of a Martyr*, p. 26.
126. Keer, *Veer Savarkar*, p. 360.
127. Gould, *Hindu Nationalism*, p.246.
128. Bright, *The Woman Behind Gandhi*, p. 107.
129. Guha, *Gandhi*, p. 745.
130. Savarkar, *Historic Statements*, pp. 80–83.
131. Ibid., pp. 70–71.
132. Keer, *Veer Savarkar*, p. 347.
133. Ibid., pp. 350–51; and Gokhale, *Swatantryaveer Savarkar*, pp. 53–54.
134. Keer, *Veer Savarkar*, pp. 350–51.
135. Gandhi, *Collected Works*, Vol. 79, p. 287.
136. Savarkar, *Historic Statements*, p. 37.
137. Ibid., p. 114.
138. Wolpert, *Jinnah of Pakistan*, p. 205.
139. Savarkar, *Historic Statements*, p. 121.

140. Keer, *Veer Savarkar*, p. 366
141. Atre, *Karheche Paani*, Vol. 3, pp. 296–300.
142. *The Brotherhood in Saffron*, p. 36.
143. Ibid., p. 40.
144. Das, *India*, pp. 215–16.
145. Ibid., p. 217.
146. Keer, *Veer Savarkar*, p. 371; and Gokhale, *Swatantryaveer Savarkar*, p. 56.
147. Keer, *Veer Savarkar*, p. 371; and Gokhale, *Swatantryaveer Savarkar*, pp. 56–57.
148. Das, *India*, pp. 232–33.
149. Savarkar, *Aitihasik Nivedaney*, pp. 161–63.
150. Ibid., pp. 164–65.
151. Ibid., pp. 167–68.
152. Das, *India*, p. 256.

12. New prisons and a final release

1. Brown, *Nehru*, pp. 177–80.
2. Ibid., p. 176.
3. Ibid., pp. 193–94.
4. Ibid., pp. 176, 189–96.
5. Ibid., p. 180.
6. Malgonkar, *Men Who Killed Gandhi*, pp. 78–79.
7. Ibid., pp. 43–46.
8. Ibid., p. 59.
9. Ibid., pp. 81–82.
10. Ibid., p. 143.
11. Savarkar, *Aitihasik Nivedaney*, pp. 147–48.
12. Malgonkar, *Men Who Killed Gandhi*, p. 76.
13. Ibid., pp. 82–83.
14. Ibid., 281.
15. Derek P. Links, 'The Anatomy of an Institutionalized Emergency: Preventive Detention and Personal Liberty in India', *Michigan Journal of International Law*, 22(2): 323–324; accessed online at https://repository.law.umich.edu/cgi/viewcontent.cgi?article=1374&context=mjil

16. Keer, *Veer Savarkar*, pp. 405–07.
17. Malgonkar, *Men Who Killed Gandhi*, pp. 82, 92–94.
18. Ibid., pp. 94–95.
19. Payne, *Life and Death of Mahatma Gandhi*, pp. 616–17; and Malgonkar, *Men Who Killed Gandhi*, p. 333.
20. Payne, *Life and Death of Mahatma Gandhi*, pp. 616–17.
21. Malgonkar, *Men Who Killed Gandhi*, pp. 125–26.
22. Ibid., pp. 143–45.
23. Ibid., pp. 281–84.
24. Nehru, *Selected Works*, Second Series, Vol. 5, pp. 46–47.
25. Ibid., p. 52.
26. Both Nehru's letter and Patel's reply quoted in Patel, *Correspondence*, pp. 55–56.
27. Ibid., pp. 63–65.
28. Ibid., p. 65.
29. Kapur Commission Report, Vol. 2, Part D, pp. 301, 331–34.
30. Payne, *Life and Death of Mahatma Gandhi*, pp. 570–71.
31. Ibid., p. 614.
32. Ibid., pp. 620–21.
33. Jain's account narrated in Payne, *Life and Death of Mahatma Gandhi*, pp. 628–30.
34. Malgonkar, *Men Who Killed Gandhi*, p. 279.
35. Ibid.
36. Ibid., p. 281.
37. This account of episodes from the Red Fort prison is derived from Godse, *Lal Killyatil Aathvani*, pp. 22–51.
38. Press Trust of India, 'Plea made to PM to protect under law Savarkar's name from being misused', *Business* Standard, 28 May 2018, accessed online: www.business-standard.com/article/pti-stories/plea-made-to-pm-to-protect-under-law-savarkar-s-name-from-being-misused-118052801160_1.html
39. Nehru, *Selected Works*, Second Series, Vol. 15 (Part I), pp. 159–60.
40. Ibid., Vol. 39, pp. 796–97.
41. Savarkar, *Aitihasik Nivedaney*, p. 172.
42. Godse, *Lal Killyatil Aathvani*, pp. 30–31.
43. Keer, *Veer Savarkar*, p. 418.
44. Account of this episode narrated by Hridaynath Mangeshkar in an

interview with the Marathi news channel ABP Majha on 13 January 2018.

45. *New York Times*, 27 February 1966.
46. Keer, *Veer Savarkar*, pp. 455–56.
47. Quotes from Keer, *Veer Savarkar*, pp. 418–533.
48. Gokhale, *Swatantryaveer Savarkar*, pp. 47–48; and Keer, *Veer Savarkar*, pp. 477–78.
49. Atre, *Karheche Paani*, Vol. 3, pp. 329–37.
50. Gokhale, *Swatantryaveer Savarkar*, p. 49; and Keer, *Veer Savarkar*, p. 436.
51. 'Sati' is part of *Devchaafa*, a collection of short stories by Vidyadhar Pundalik, published by Mauj Prakashan, 2010, pp. 24–57.
52. Pu. La. Deshpande's speech in Port Blair, 1983.
53. Keer, *Veer Savarkar*, pp. 529–30; and Gokhale, *Swatantryaveer Savarkar*, pp. 50–51.
54. Savarkar, *Six Glorious Epochs of History*, p. 4.
55. Ibid., p. 185.
56. Ibid., pp. 175–80.
57. Gokhale, *Swatantryaveer Savarkar*, pp. 115–18.
58. Keer, *Veer Savarkar*, p. 535.
59. Ibid., pp. 534–44.
60. Godbole, *Mala Umajlele Swatantryaveer Savarkar*, pp. 162–67.
61. Ibid., pp. 162–67.
62. Keer, *Veer Savarkar*, pp. 534–44.

Bibliography

Adams, Jad. *Gandhi: Naked Ambition*. London: Quercus, 2010.

Ali, M. Asaf (with G.N.S. Raghavan). *M. Asaf Ali's Memoirs: The Emergence of Modern India*. Delhi: Ajanta Publications, n.d.

Ambedkar, B.R. *Pakistan or The Partition of India*. Vol. 8 of *Ambedkar's Writings and Speeches*. Mumbai: Government of Maharashtra, 1990. First published 1946.

Andersen, Walter K., and Shridhar D. Damle. *The Brotherhood in Saffron*. New Delhi: Penguin Books India, 1987.

Atre, Acharya. *Karheche Paani*, 5 volumes. Mumbai: Parchure Prakashan Mandir, 2012.

Banerjea, Babu Surendranath. *The Trumpet Voice of India: Speeches of Babu Surendranath Banerjea*. Madras: Ganesh & Co., 1909.

Bhagwat, A.K., and G.P. Pradhan. *Lokmanya Tilak: A Biography*. Mumbai: Jaico, 2016.

Bose, Arun Coomer. *Indian Revolutionaries Abroad, 1905–1922*. Patna: Bharati Bhawan, 1971.

Bose, Subhas Chandra. *The Indian Struggle, 1935–1942*. Kolkata: Chuckervertty Chatterjee & Co. Ltd, 1952.

——. *Testament of Subhas Bose, 1942–1945*. Compiled and edited by 'Arun'. Delhi: Rajkamal Publications, 1946.

Brecher, Michael. *Nehru: A Political Biography*. London: Oxford University Press, 1961.

Bright, J.S. *The Woman Behind Gandhi*. Lahore: Paramount Publications, n.d.

Brown, Judith. *Nehru: A Political Life*. New Haven, Connecticut: Yale University Press, 2003.

Bruckenhaus, Daniel. *Policing Transnational Protest: Liberal Imperialism and the Surveillance of Anticolonialists in Europe,1905–1945*. Oxford: Oxford University Press, 2017.

Cashman, Richard. *The Myth of the Lokamanya: Tilak and Mass Politics in Maharashtra*. Oakland, California: University of California Press, 1975.

Chattopadhyaya, Harindranath. *Life and Myself*, Vol. 1. Baroda: Nalanda, 1948.

Chirol, Valentine. *Indian Unrest*. London: Macmillan & Co., 1910.

'Chitragupta'. *The Life of Swatantra Veer Savarkar*. 1926.

Choudhary, Sukhbir. *Growth of Nationalism in India (1919–1929)*, Vol. 2. Delhi: Trimurti Publications, 1973.

Coupland, Reginald. *India: A Re-Statement*. London: Oxford University Press, 1945.

Das, Durga. *India: From Curzon to Nehru and After*. Delhi: Rupa Publications, 2015. First published 1969.

Deshpande, Sudhakar. *Savarkar*. Makers of Indian Literature series. Delhi: Sahitya Akademi, 2010.

Durrani, F.K. Khan. *The Meaning of Pakistan*. Lahore: Shri Mohammad Ashraf, 1944.

Dutt, Ullaskar. *Twelve Years of Prison Life*. Kolkata: The Arya Publishing House, 1924.

Gandhi, M.K. *Collected Works of Mahatma Gandhi*, Vol. 4. Delhi: Government of India Publications Division, 1960.

Garnett, David. *The Golden Echo*, Vol. 1. London: Chatto & Windus, 1953.

Ghose, Barindra Kumar. *The Tale of My Exile*. Pondicherry: Arya Office, 1922.

Godbole, Arvind Sadashiv. *Mala Umajlele Swatantryaveer Savarkar*. Pune: Bharatiya Vichar Sadhana Pune Prakashan, n.d.

Godse, Gopal. *Lal Killyatil Aathvani* (Red Fort Reminiscences). Kolhapur: Riya Publications, 2012. First published 1981.

Gokhale, D.N. *Swatantryaveer Savarkar: Ek Rahasya*. Mumbai: Mouj Prakashan, 2010.

Gokhale, Gopal Krishna. *Speeches of Gopal Krishna Gokhale*. Madras: G. Natesan and Co., 1920.

Gould, William. *Hindu Nationalism and the Language of Politics in Late Colonial India*. Cambridge, UK: Cambridge University Press, 2004.

Guha, Ramachandra. *Gandhi: The Years That Changed the World*. Gurgaon: Penguin Random House India, 2018.

——. *Gandhi Before India*. Gurgaon: Penguin Random House India, 2013.

Hasan, Mushirul, ed. *Towards Freedom: 1939* (Part 2). New Delhi: Oxford University Press, 2008.

Hyndman, H.M. *The Emancipation of India*. London: The Twentieth Century Press Ltd, 1911.

Ismail, Sir Mirza. *My Public Life*. London: George Allen & Unwin Ltd, 1954.

Jinnah, Muhammad Ali. *Some Recent Speeches and Writings of Mr Jinnah*. Lahore: Sh. Muhammed Ashraf, 1942.

Joglekar, J.D. *Veer Savarkar: Father of Hindu Nationalism*. Lulu, 2006. First published in Marathi in 1983.

Karandikar, Shivram Laxman. *Swatantryaveer Savarkar Charitra*. Pune: Varda Prakashan, 2011. First published 1943.

Keer, Dhananjay. *Dr Babasaheb Ambedkar: Life and Mission*. Mumbai: Popular Prakashan, Mumbai, 1990.

——. *Veer Savarkar*. Mumbai: Popular Prakashan, 1966.

Khaparde, G.S. *Source Material for a History of the Freedom Movement: Correspondence and Diary of Shrimant G.S. Khaparde*, Vol. 7. Mumbai: Government of Maharashtra, 1934.

Leaming, Thomas. *A Philadelphia Lawyer in the London Courts*. New York: Henry Holt, 1911.

Lelyveld, Joseph. *Great Soul: Mahatma Gandhi and His Struggle with India*. Noida: HarperCollins India, 2015.

Maclean, Kama. *A Revolutionary History of Interwar India: Violence, Image, Voice and Text*. Gurgaon: Penguin Random House India, 2015.

Madhok, Balraj. *Portrait of a Martyr*. Mumbai: Jaico Publishing House, 1973.

Majumdar, R.C. *History of the Freedom Movement in India*. Vols 1–3. Calcutta: Firma K.L. Mukhopadhyay, 1971.

Malgonkar, Manohar. *The Men Who Killed Gandhi*. New Delhi: Roli Books, 2008.

Mathur, L.P. *History of the Andaman and Nicobar Islands (1756-1966)*. Delhi: Sterling Publishers, 1968.

Mehta, Asoka, and Achyut Patwardhan. *The Communal Triangle in India*. Allahabad: Kitabistan, 1942.

Mookerjee, S.P. *A Phase of the Indian Struggle*. Kolkata: Monojendra N. Bhowmick, 1942.

Nehru, Jawaharlal. *Selected Works of Jawaharlal Nehru*, Vols 3, 5, 15 (Part 1), 39. Delhi: BR Publishing Corporation, 1988.

Nichols, Beverley. *Verdict on India*. London: Johathan Cape, 1944.

Ohsawa, J.G. *Two Great Indians in Japan*, Vol. 1. Kolkata: Kusa Publications, 1954.

Padmanabhan, R.A. *V.V.S. Aiyar*. Delhi: National Book Trust India, 1980.

Pande, B.N., ed. *A Centenary History of the Indian National Congress*, Vol. 3. New Delhi: Academic Foundation, 1985.

Patel, Sardar Vallabhbhai. *Sardar Patel's Correspondence, 1945–1950*, Vol. 6. Edited by Durga Das. Ahmedabad: Navjivan Press, 1973.

Payne, Robert. *The Life and Death of Mahatma Gandhi*. Delhi: Rupa Publications, 1997.

Phadke, Y.D. *Shodh Savarkarancha*. 3rd ed. Pune: Srividya Prakashan, 2017. First published 1984.

Raghavan, G.N.S. *Aruna Asaf Ali: The Compassionate Radical*. New Delhi: National Book Trust, 1999.

Raghavan, Srinath. *India's War: The Making of Modern South Asia 1939–1945*. Gurgaon: Penguin Random House India, 2016.

Rath, Radhanath, and Sabitri Prasanna Chatterjee, eds. *Rash Behari Basu: His Struggle for India's Independence*. Kolkata: Biplabi Mahanayak Rash Behari Basu Smarak Samity, 1959.

Read, Anthony, and David Fischer. *The Proudest Day: India's Long Road to Independence*. Pimlico, 1998.

Reid, Walter. *Keeping the Jewel in the Crown: The British Betrayal of India*. Gurgaon: Penguin Random House India, 2016.

Rejali, Darius. *Torture and Democracy*. Princeton, New Jersey: Princeton University Press, 2009, accessed on Google Books.

'Report of the Proceedings of the International Socialist Congress at Copenhagen, 1910'. Chicago: HG Adair, n.d.

Savarkar, V.D. *Aitihasik Nivedaney*. Kolhapur: Riya Publications, 2012.

——. *An Echo from Andamans: Letters from Barrister Savarkar to His Brother Dr (N) Savarkar*. Vishwanath Vinayak Kelkar, 1924.

——. *Bhasha Shuddhi*. Kolhapur: Riya Publications, 2012.

——. *Gandhi Gondhal*. Savarkar Smarak (accessed on the Smarak website www.savarkarsmarak.com)

——. *Garmagaram Chivda*. Kolhapur: Riya Publications, 2012.

——. *Hindu Rashtra Darshan*. Savarkar Smarak (accessed on the Smarak website www.savarkarsmarak.com).

——. *Hindutva*. Mumbai: Swatantryaveer Savarkar Rashtriya Smarak, 1999. First published in 1923.

——. *Historic Statements*. Kolhapur: Riya Publications, 2012.

——. *Krantighosh*. Kolhapur: Riya Publications, 2013.

——. *Ksha-Kirney*. Kolhapur: Riya Publications, 2013.

——. *Londonchi Batmipatre* (Newsletters from London). Kolhapur: Riya Publications, 2013.

——. *Majhi Janmathep*. Mumbai: Parchure Prakashan Mandir, 2011. First published 1927.

——. *Majhya Athvani* (My Reminiscences). Accessed on savarkarsmarak.com.

——. *My Transportation for Life*. Accessed on savarkarsmarak.com.

——. *Samagra Savarkar Sahitya*, Vols 1–8. Mumbai: Swatantryaveer Savarkar Smarak.

——. *Shatruchya Shibirat* (Inside the Enemy Camp). Accessed on savarkarsmarak.com.

——. *Six Glorious Epochs of History*. Mumbai: Bal Savarkar, 1971.

——. *Tejaswi Taare*. Kolhapur: Riya Publications, 2013.

——. *Vidnyan-nishta Nibandh*. Mumbai: Savarkar Smarak, 1992.

——. *Vividh Lekh*. Kolhapur: Riya Publications, 2013.

——. *Whirlwind Propaganda: V.D. Savarkar's Statements and Messages*. Edited and published by A.S. Bhide, Mumbai, 1941.

'Sedition Committee Report, 1918'. Kolkata: Superintendent, Government Printing (India).

Sethna, Khorshed Adi. *Madam Bhikaiji Rustom Cama*. Delhi: Publications Division, Information and Broadcasting Ministry, Government of India, 1987.

Sharma, M.S.M. *Peeps into Pakistan*. Patna: Pustak Bhandar, 1954.

Shewalkar, Ram, ed. *Lokmanya Tilakanche Nibandha*. Delhi: National Book Trust, 2004.

Sitaramayya, Pattabhi. *History of the Indian National Congress*, Vol. 3. Mumbai: Padma Publications, 1947.

Source Material for a History of the Freedom Movement in India, Vol. 2 (1885–1920). Mumbai: Government of Bombay, 1958.

Sydenham, Lord. *My Working Life*. London: John Murray, 1927.

Talwalkar, Govind. *Naoroji Te Nehru*. Mumbai: Majestic Prakashan, 1969.

Tendulkar, D.G. *Abdul Ghaffar Khan: Faith Is a Battle*. Mumbai: Popular Prakashan, n.d.

——. *Mahatma*, Vol. 2. Mumbai: Vithalbhai K. Jhaveri and D.G. Tendulkar, 1951.

Treanor, Tom. *One Damn Thing After Another*. New York: Doubleday, 1944.

Tunzelmann, Alex Fon. *Indian Summer*. Henry Holt and Company, 2007.

Wilson, Jon. *India Conquered: Britain's Raj and the Chaos of Empire*. London: Simon & Schuster, 2016.

Wolpert, Stanley. *Jinnah of Pakistan*. New Delhi: Oxford University Press, 2006.

Yashpal. *Sinhavalokan*, Vol. 2. Lucknow: Viplav Karyalay, 1952.

Index

Index

Acknowledgements

Thanks, first and foremost, to Chiki Sarkar of Juggernaut Books for her enthusiasm for this book and for bringing it to readers. My editor, Parth Mehrotra, is a quiet young man who knows his mind; when he speaks, it is to make superb and accurate observations. This book has benefited massively from his interventions. Gurcharan Das, Bibek Debroy and Sudheendra Kulkarni, all generously offered their comments, and I am hugely indebted to them. To Kulkarni, a person of great erudition and someone largely responsible for the fact that I can write at all, I am especially thankful for suggesting key points that helped to further illumine Savarkar's personality and those of his contemporaries such as Tilak, Gandhi, Ambedkar and Jinnah, even where he had views completely different from mine.

I am truly grateful to Lata Mangeshkar, who knew Savarkar extremely well personally, for having granted me an interview in which she recollected her and her family's interactions with him, and to Hemant Kenkre and Rachna Shah for the help they immediately and large-heartedly extended when I most needed it. Naren Parchure of Parchure Prakashan, a prestigious publishing house in Maharashtra, sent across a photocopy of a long-out-of-print Marathi book that I was looking for frantically, within hours of me calling him up; and after my friend the writer Ambarish Mishra generously alerted me to a key text, Monika Gajendragadkar of Mouj Prakashan, a publishing house whose works are a touchstone of literary quality in Marathi, helped me find it immediately. My friend the actor Kartika Rane and her mother, Asharaje Rane, helped me to access information about Bhaurao Chiplunkar, a key figure in Savarkar's life, at extremely short notice. It is such kindnesses really that make any endeavour possible.

To the staff at the Maharashtra State Archives in Mumbai who secured for me so many files more than a hundred years old, a big thank you. Savarkar's grand-nephew Ranjit Savarkar pointed me in the right direction when I was looking for certain materials, and his associates at the Swatantryaveer Savarkar Smarak in Mumbai were patient in offering assistance and access to Savarkar's works and correspondence. My gratitude and appreciation for them.

The time I took working on this book while holding a full-time job rightfully belonged to my dearest wife, Swapna, and our wonderful son, Vikrant. I could have done nothing without their affection and unstinting support. This book is for them. My parents Jyotsna and Jagdish Purandare and my brother Kunal have been by my side always, to show the path, to course-correct whenever necessary, and to keep morale high. My heartfelt thanks to them, as ever.

A Note on the Author

Vaibhav Purandare is a senior editor with the *Times of India*, and author of the critically acclaimed *Sachin Tendulkar: A Definitive Biography* and *Bal Thackeray & the Rise of the Shiv Sena*.

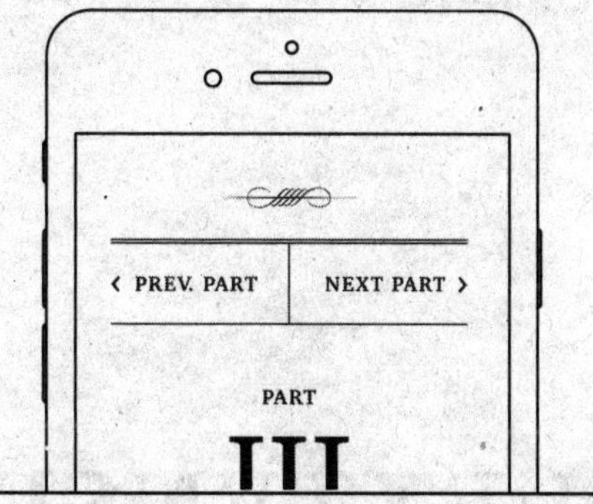

Beautiful Typography

The quality of print transferred to your mobile. Forget ugly PDFs.

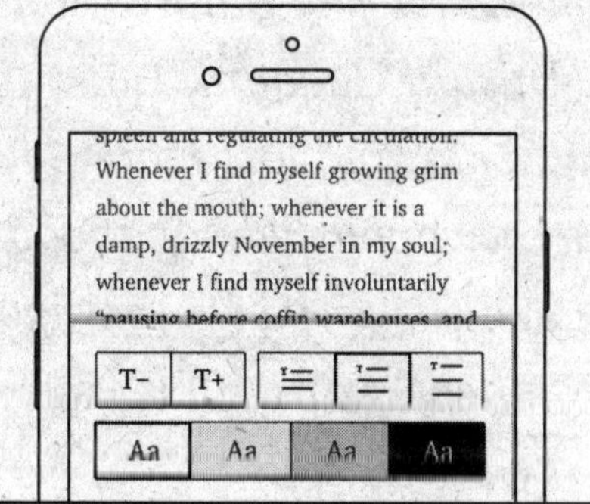

Customizable Reading

Read in the font size, spacing and background of your liking.

juggernaut.in

AN EXTENSIVE LIBRARY

Including fresh, new, original Juggernaut books from the likes of Sunny Leone, Praveen Swami, Husain Haqqani, Umera Ahmed, Rujuta Diwekar and lots more. Plus, books from partner publishers and loads of free classics. Whichever genre you like, there's a book waiting for you.

juggernaut.in

We're changing the reading experience from passive to active.

juggernaut.in

Ask authors questions

Get all your answers from the horse's mouth. Juggernaut authors actually reply to every question they can.

Rate and review

Let everyone know of your favourite reads or critique the finer points of a book – you will be heard in a community of like-minded readers.

Gift books to friends

For a book-lover, there's no nicer gift than a book personally picked. You can even do it anonymously if you like.

Enjoy new book formats

Discover serials released in parts over time, picture books including comics, and story-bundles at discounted rates. And coming soon, audiobooks.

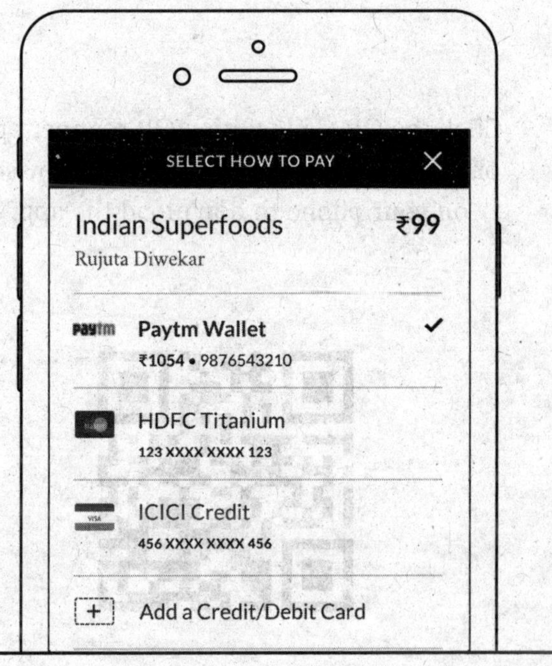

Paytm Wallet, Cards & Apple Payments

On Android, just add a Paytm Wallet once and buy any book with one tap. On iOS, pay with one tap with your iTunes-linked debit/credit card.

Click the QR Code with a QR scanner app
or type the link into the Internet browser
on your phone to download the app.